THE FUNDAMENTAL TECHNIQUES OF CLASSIC BREAD BAKING

Published in 2011 by Stewart, Tabori & Chang
An imprint of ABRAMS

Library of Congress Cataloging-in-Publication Data

The fundamental techniques of classic bread baking / by the French Culinary
Institute ; photographs by Matthew Septimus.
   p. cm.
 ISBN 978-1-58479-934-4 (alk. paper)
 1. Bread. I. French Culinary Institute (New York, N.Y.)
 TX769.F86 2011
 641.8'15—dc22
                              2010048673

Editor: Natalie Kaire
Project Manager: Kate Norment
Designer: Liam Flanagan
Production Manager: Anet Sirna-Bruder

The text of this book was composed in Trade Gothic and Granjon.

Printed and bound in China
10 9 8 7 6 5 4 3 2

Stewart, Tabori & Chang books are available at special discounts when purchased in quantity for premiums and promotions as well as fundraising or educational use. Special editions can also be created to specification. For details, contact specialsales@abramsbooks.com or the address below.

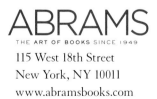

THE ART OF BOOKS SINCE 1949
115 West 18th Street
New York, NY 10011
www.abramsbooks.com

THE FUNDAMENTAL TECHNIQUES OF CLASSIC BREAD BAKING

THE FRENCH CULINARY INSTITUTE

Judith Choate *with*

The Master Bread Bakers and Chefs of

The French Culinary Institute

Photographs by Matthew Septimus

Stewart, Tabori & Chang *New York*

Contents

Sessions

Foreword

Bread is mystical. Bread is life. So says Chef Alain Sailhac, the sage dean of The French Culinary Institute. Through these and other culinary metaphors, Chef Alain has taught me many things about life. Perhaps the most poignant is his own story about food deprivation during World War II. It is how he came to view bread as the giver of life, and the breaking of bread as a mystical experience.

When Chef was eight years old, the war had been raging for years. There was little food for the natives in his hometown of Millau in southwest France, as most of the food went to the German army. Alain, his mother, and his five siblings were lucky to be sent that summer to work on a farm. He said it was as though they had been sent back in time two centuries. There was no electricity on the farm and the food was primitive, but at least there was food. Once a week the local farmers would go to the village where a baker would bake rounds of sourdough bread. Each farm would get one very large loaf (to illustrate just how large, Chef Alain rounds his arms as if hugging a tree when telling this part of his story). This single loaf was meant to feed everyone at the farm for an entire week. There were many workers with their children at the farm, and at meal times they would all sit at a long wooden table. The cooking fire would crackle as they all waited for their meager ration of soup and some cheese, but the bread was the star of the meal. The farmer, wearing a large, floppy black hat, would sit at the head of the table and bless the round of bread with his knife; the workers would bless themselves. The farmer would then peer into the eyes of those around the table and stake his knife into the edge of the bread, starting at the farthest quadrant, and slowly inch his knife back to cut off a small piece. Then, one by one, he would look intently at the eater, then at the bread, and pass it as if it were a communion host. This drama was not lost on an eight-year-old boy, and today our bread program at The French Culinary Institute instills a similarly sacramental regard for bread.

Industrial American bread coming off conveyor belts, wrapped in plastic and filled with additives, created a different and even sadder drama. Not only did these loaves lack nutritional value, they also lacked taste; some were no more appealing than cardboard. Bread had become a convenience on which to slap some meat or slather peanut butter. The art of commercial handmade breads had almost disappeared in the United States, but the back-to-the-land revolution of the 1970s—during which young, educated Americans backpacked in Europe and came home with a taste for real, fire-baked bread—helped revive an interest in different types of flours, salts, and aged starters, as well as techniques such as stone grinding. The artisanal bread movement was born.

In the formation of a novice chef, developing a taste for honest bread is essential. The artisanal approach is the foundation of the bread program at The French Culinary Institute. Our courses range from the classic French, regional Italian, and dense European loaves, to gluten-free breads. Our faculty is exceptional. They are passionate and inspiring bakers. Today we have thousands of graduates who have gone on to work in the finest bakeries and compete with great success in highly regarded competitions around the world. Many are entrepreneurs who own their own shops. Others are chefs who make specialty breads in their own restaurants.

Best of all, good bread has become easier and easier to find. Let me divulge a little secret on where to find the best baguettes: here at The French Culinary Institute. We at The French Culinary Institute enjoy our famous baguette every day in our restaurant L'Ecole. Chef Alain is duly proud of it, for it is handmade, well-proofed, and revered as only a mystical food could be.

Dorothy Cann Hamilton
Founder and Chief Executive Officer
The French Culinary Institute

A Brief History of Bread

One of the simplest of crafts, bread making is the seed from which all other baking has sprung. Beginning with the development of primitive grains in the Middle East some ten thousand years ago, man conjured up a mix of grain and water to create a nourishing food, but the invention of bread as we know it has been attributed to the ancient Egyptians. Remnants of bread-making tools—grinding stones, baking ovens, agricultural implements used for growing grains— have been found in tombs, and depictions of bread making are shown in great detail in the art preserved there. Further proof is seen in archaeological documentation of their mastering the art of fermentation for use in both baking and brewing. Egyptians continued to advance bread baking through the invention of clay ovens that could produce a risen loaf, rather than the usual flat one produced in the ashes of a spent fire or on a baking stone.

Throughout history, cultural beliefs influenced how a society baked its bread. Conversely, knowing how a civilization regards its bread can impart deeper understanding of its culture. From earliest time, grains and the primitive breads made from them were symbols of fertility and resurrection. The Hebrews thought that fermentation was a form of corruption and was, as such, impure, so only unleavened breads, much like today's matzoh, were deemed worthy of honoring God. Ancient Greeks had the extreme opposite opinion, and worshipped the source of leavened bread as a goddess. The priestesses of the goddess Demeter presided over the harvest festivals of the autumnal equinox during which Demeter and her daughter, Persephone, were honored with a nine-day Celebration of the Bread. Roman culture followed suit, but called their goddess Ceres. The Essenes, a dissident Jewish sect who settled in Palestine, heralded the arrival of a Messiah who was a bread god.

During the Middle Ages, as agriculture began to flourish, the division between growers and bakers was intensified as the price and weight of a finished loaf was dependent upon the regulated price of grain. When the price was raised and the weight lowered, the fury of the populace was directed toward the baker, not the grower. In addition, during this period of time, when most communities grew within a walled city built around a castle, millers and bakers were often regarded as too untrustworthy to give an honest count; grain theft, short weights, and excessive prices were commonplace. And, since bread was such an integral part of the daily diet, those found committing such offences were severely punished. Perhaps because of this mistrust, bakers became the first craftsmen to form structured guilds with defined roles for the apprentice, journeyman, and master. The guilds also worked to help stabilize prices and develop a uniform system of weights and measures. Guild members were required to swear an oath to the prescribed bread ordinance to "always bake sufficient bread." And it was during this period that the term "baker's dozen" came into being, as an honest baker would often give that extra piece so that he might never be known as a thief.

In France, during this time when social classes were carefully defined and programmed, there were breads prepared for each of the higher ranks: *pain de cour, pain de pape, pain de chevalier, pain d'éuyer, pain de paire, pain de valet*, and so forth. For the lowly masses there was only one bread: a large, round (*boule*) loaf called *pain de boulanger*. And, should serfs decide to mill grain and make bread in their huts, the feudal lord would fine them heavily or kill them, as he was considered the sole owner of the mill and bake house.

The development of bread at the end of the Middle Ages varied widely depending on the location. For example, Italy became a congregation of city-states and breads varied from state to state, Germany remained a group of warring feudal castles so its bread stayed quite basic, and France was unified by a predominant city ruled by an ironfisted court with breads being created to please the royals. As the Renaissance spread throughout Europe, the French court envisioned France as the inheritor of the Greco-Roman civilization that had taken wheat to the grand art of bread baking and, as such, would produce, to quote the first-century Roman poet Juvenal, "a delicate loaf . . . white as snow, and kneaded of the finest flour."

In France, from the thirteenth century on, every stage of the bread-baking process was regulated by the government. The type, price, and quality of flour and other ingredients as well as the weight, quality, and price of the finished loaf were carefully monitored. Bakers had formed their own guild with defined rules: To become a master baker, an applicant had to receive a certificate of his skill by producing a "masterpiece" and was required to pay dues to the guild. Once declared a master baker, the baker commanded journeymen (*valets*) who, in turn, ruled the apprentices (*geindres*).

By the fourteenth century, Parisian bakers produced more than thirty different types of bread, each one differing in shape or containing different ingredients from the next. Among them were *pain de brode*, *pain balle*, *pain de couleurs*, *pain coquille*, *pain de magne*, *pain rousset*, *pain de Chailly*, and an exceptionally fine bread called *pain de Gonesse*. Each of these represented an evolution in the art of bread making.

The first printed recipe for bread can be found in an early French cookbook entitled *Les délices de la campagne*, published in 1654. Written by Nicolas de Bonnefons, a valet to Louis XIV, the book contains two recipes for *pain de Gonesse*, one using only fine white flour and adding fresh beer yeast, and one using white and brown flour leavened by the sourdough process. A primitive brioche recipe can also be found in this seminal book.

By the seventeenth century, the most striking change seen in French bread making is the use of beer yeast (*levure*) as a leavening agent in place of the natural fermentation created by a sourdough starter. It is assumed that this occurred as bakers sought a way to use the whitest flour to create a soft, fluffy loaf of bread that would appeal to the discerning royal court. This was only the beginning of the ongoing quest to make an even lighter, finer bread with a crisp crust and a fine crumb.

After a revolution brought on, in part, by the scarcity of bread and a long period of bad harvests, inflation, and war, the Paris Commune forbade the sale of any bread other than *bis*, a whole wheat bread which came to be called *pain d'égalité*, or equality bread. Each worker and head of the family received a free 1½ pounds per day, while others were given 1 pound. By the beginning of the nineteenth century this same equality bread had become *pain de blanc*, a fine white loaf that was good enough for both the rich and the poor.

As the nineteenth century continued, major revolutions occurred in almost every aspect of the technical production of wheat and grain. Increasing knowledge about crop rotation and genetic management radically changed the way grain was grown, harvested, and processed. The invention of harvesting machinery and the development of transportation systems to move grain to mills created unprecedented growth as well. Milling advanced due to the invention of iron rollers (the Hungarian system), which provided an alternative to the commonly used stone roller. And, more than any other development, the changes in methods of leavening dough sped up the manufacture of bread. This industrialization, while it made bread easier and cheaper to produce, also created bread that was lacking in flavor, texture, and nourishment.

Although France had a long history of fine bread making and had led the world in the creation of extraordinary loaves, by the 1960s the art of bread making had almost died as artisanal bread culture was supplanted by industrial bread making. Most of the shapes developed over the centuries remained, but the intense flavor, fine crumb, crisp crust, and admirable shelf life had disappeared.

At this point, there were very few traditional bread bakers left and the much-loved classic baguette was fast becoming an endangered species. However, in Paris, the bakery Poilâne stood fast. The bakery was established by Pierre Poilâne in 1932, and the Poilâne baguette became the standard by which all other loaves were judged. Poilâne was steadfast and stubborn and never veered from his ideal of what constituted a classic French bread. His sons, Lionel and Max, carried forth their father's ideals and by the 1970s, were leaders in the force to restore France's wide variety of artisanal breads—sourdough, whole grain, and regional.

Although the United States did not have the same long history of bread making as France, it did have a dedicated force of home bakers who kept nourishing loaves on the table. However, more so than any other country, the United States eagerly embraced modern bread-making technology and mechanization, and by the mid-twentieth century, traditional bread baking was a lost art. Commercial bakeries turned out airy, tasteless, vitamin- and mineral-enriched white bread as home bakers, many of them now working women, abandoned the tradition of baking enough loaves to provide a family with toast and sandwiches for a week. Neighborhood bakeries became distant memories. A few nationally known dieticians and health gurus promoted whole grain breads, but theirs was a cry in the wilderness. Bread had gone from being the staff of life to being an inexpensive filler at mealtime.

However, shortly after the Poilânes began the regeneration of the art of bread making in France, young American bakers began their own revolution. Many of them spent time working with the Poilânes or in the few remaining small, regional bakeries in France, gaining the knowledge they needed to restore the art in their own country. In the 1970s, bakers like Michael London of Rock Hill Bake House in New York State, whose sourdough bread became renowned, began helping others establish artisanal bread bakeries throughout the United States.

By the early 1990s, the expansion of small, artisanal bakeries in the United States had led to the creation of the Bread Baker's Guild of America, whose mission is to shape the knowledge and skills of the artisan baking community through education. They have defined their community as follows:

"An Artisan is a worker in a skilled trade that involves making things by hand; a skilled worker or craftsperson. Artisan Bakers utilize knowledge of traditional methodologies, a mastery of hand skills, and an appreciation for the best quality raw materials and ingredients, to produce goods that meet the highest possible standards of taste, appearance, aroma, and texture. The Artisan Baking Community is a community of professional bakers, farmers, millers, suppliers, educators, students, home bakers, technical experts, and bakery owners and managers who work together to support the principle and the practice of producing the highest quality baked goods. Our members are a funky, iconoclastic, independent, creative, and colorful group who value and promote baking education and thrive on the lively exchange of ideas."

It was with the encouragement and assistance of many of these fine artisanal bakers that The French Culinary Institute initiated its acclaimed bread-baking program. The program, taught by a distinguished gathering of professional bread bakers from around the world, has grown to include classes not only for professional bakers, but also for interested home cooks. *The Fundamental Techniques of Classic Bread Baking* is both a compilation of the work of history's bakers and the culmination of the revival of artisanal bread baking in America.

This book contains formulas for the wide variety of recipes executed in the bread-baking classrooms of The French Culinary Institute at The International Culinary Center in New York City. We believe that it will serve not only as a reference in the bakery, but also as a guide for professionals, amateur chefs, and home cooks desiring a total immersion in the art of bread baking. It moves the reawakening of the curious and committed baker into the twenty-first century. At The French Culinary Institute we know that the breadth and scope of contemporary bread making in America offers the baker new possibilities for creative expression in the bread kitchen while still paying homage to the past.

Session 1

Introduction to the Professional Bread Kitchen: Basic Principles and Terms

When moving from the home kitchen into the professional bakery, it becomes necessary for the baker to rethink the habits of a lifetime. Bread baking cannot make the leap from chore to art without many principles, rules, and terms becoming second nature. Before learning basic bread-baking skills and techniques, the fledgling baker must, without thinking, be able to step into the kitchen with a complete understanding of the classic bread-baking terms, the rules guiding personal and workspace hygiene, and the standards of professional bread baking. When contemplating bread making as a profession, it is important to realize from the outset that a professional baker's life is a disciplined one guided by a set of unwavering standards. If you follow these standards and guidelines, the rewards will be greater efficiency, ease of preparation, and enjoyment of performing the tasks at hand.

Instruction to work in the professional bakery must teach the baker not only to follow a recipe with precision, but also to execute that recipe with the speed and organization expected in a commercial atmosphere. Unlike general cooking, where a cook can usually adjust a recipe to personal taste, it is not so easy to reconfigure a recipe for bread. Because it is as much a science as it is an art, working with bread dough requires that ingredients always be measured accurately so that they conform to a calibrated formula. This means that the baker must understand fully the interaction of ingredients as well as how a mix of ingredients reacts to temperature, blending, fermentation, and storing. Only then can a baker test the limits of his or her imagination and create exciting breads with a stamp of originality that has evolved from a clear understanding of the fundamentals.

The Baker's Regulation Dress Uniform

Professional chefs and bakers all over the world dress alike. Starting at the top with a toque or chef's hat (a tall, often disposable, paper, pleated, or plain hat), the dress code remains standard no matter the type of kitchen. The complete uniform is always a double-breasted white jacket, a neckerchief tied neatly around the neck to absorb perspiration, a white apron tied to the front with a thick, absorbent towel for grasping hot pans tucked into the ties, and black-and-white houndstooth cotton or cotton-polyester blend pants or, for many bakers, sparkling white trousers. The one difference between a chef's and a baker's uniform is the shoes; a chef will wear highly polished black shoes while a baker's will be white so that they don't show a constant dusting of flour.

With the more relaxed climate of recent years, some bakers who work in their own kitchens can be found in brightly colored pants and extravagantly embroidered jackets, and wearing clogs or other utilitarian shoes. Even home bakers are now wearing an informal version of these uniforms, probably as much for their convenience as for the feeling of professionalism that they impart.

Principles of Cleanliness

Before any work can begin in a culinary school bakery, students must learn proper standards of cleanliness. Likewise, in a professional bakery, excellent health and external cleanliness of the staff are prerequisites for the maintenance of a hygienic, disease-free environment. In addition to personal cleanliness, all materials and equipment, as well as the workspace itself, must be antiseptic. When organizing your ingredients, the work surface on which you lay your *mise en place* (this French term defines the organization of all the necessary ingredients required to put the recipe together up to the point of its final preparation) should be absolutely pristine. To the novice, these rules may seem unnecessary or extreme; **however, variance from these principles can result in extremely serious, even disastrous, results to the health of others**. Adherence to the following principles will help ensure that this does not occur:

○ General daily hygiene must be practiced; bathing, shaving, and tooth brushing are mandatory.

○ Hair must be clean, well groomed, and covered with an immaculate hat. If hair is long, it should be pulled back and kept covered.

○ Nails should be trimmed, clean, and polish-free.

○ All jewelry should be removed before entering the bakery to avoid mishaps of loss or entanglement with utensils or machinery.

○ Perfumes, colognes, and aftershave lotions are not permitted.

○ Hands must be washed upon entering the bakery kitchen and after touching raw ingredients, telephones, money, soiled linens, eggs in or out of the shell, fresh produce, and soiled equipment or utensils, as well as after using chemicals or cleaners, picking up anything from the floor, performing personal actions such as using the lavatory, coughing, sneezing, smoking, eating, or drinking, or at any time necessary when working to ensure that the hands are always immaculate.

○ Proper hand-washing technique includes generously soaping; vigorously rubbing for at least 20 seconds to cover the backs of the hands, wrists, between the fingers, and under the nails; rinsing under warm

(100°F–200°F / 40°C–95°C) running water; and drying with a paper towel and using the towel to turn off the water and open any doors necessary to exit the washroom.

○ Do not enter the bakery kitchen if you have a skin or respiratory infection, intestinal problem, or rash of unknown origin, as these may well cause the spread of disease.

○ If working in a school or professional environment, clean uniforms should be issued and impeccably maintained. In a home kitchen, clothes should be clean and covered with a clean apron or smock. Street clothes should never be worn.

○ Wear inexpensive and easily disposable rubber gloves when working with products that spoil easily or are known to readily transmit bacteria. These include eggs, meats, or dairy products.

○ Never use a kitchen towel, wipe cloth, or side towel when performing personal actions.

○ Never taste anything with your fingers.

○ Never smoke, drink alcoholic beverages, or use controlled substances in the kitchen.

○ Cover your face with an easily disposable paper towel or tissue when you sneeze or cough, and discard it immediately. If you have to use a cloth, place it in a resealable plastic bag and remove it from the kitchen immediately. Wash your hands immediately. If the cough or sneeze seems to be an indication of the onset of an upper respiratory infection, ask to be excused from kitchen duties.

o Never sit on worktables or preparation areas.

o In the event of an accidental cut or burn, make immediate use of a first-aid kit or, if necessary, call for emergency assistance.

Principles of First Aid

Burns, abrasions, and cuts are part and parcel of work in all kitchens. These occupational hazards must be dealt with promptly and knowledgeably to prevent further injury and to maintain a sanitary workplace.

Follow these simple kitchen safety rules and you will avoid many accidents:

o Keep a well-maintained fire extinguisher within arm's reach at all times.

o Immediately clean spills from floors and worktables. If a mop or other cleanup tool is not within reach, spread salt over floor spills to absorb moisture and prevent falls.

o Always use guards and other safety devices provided for small equipment.

o Never attempt to remove food from a machine that is in motion, and always unplug electrical appliances before unloading, disassembling, or cleaning.

o Do not touch or handle electrical equipment, switches, or outlets with wet hands or if standing in water.

o Make sure that the kitchen is well ventilated.

o Check that pilot lights are lit and relight when necessary.

o Do not attempt to lift heavy objects without assistance, and when obliged to lift heavy objects, bend your knees and lift using your legs.

Burns

Burns are often the most serious kitchen accidents, so it is extremely important to know how to treat them. Burns are classified as follows:

First-degree burn: A burn caused by quick contact with a moderately hot surface or liquid, resulting in inflammation and reddening of the skin. First-degree burns are painful, but not serious. Cover the burn with a bandage but **do not put any burn cream on the area**.

Second-degree burn: A very painful burn, most often associated with scalding, that forms a blister on a

localized area. Do not pop or attempt to open the blister. Cover the burn with antiseptic or antibacterial cream and sterile gauze.

Third-degree burn: An extremely serious burn that destroys all layers of the skin. The damaged skin appears white but may well be charred. These burns are most often the result of contact with hot (400°F / 205°C) cooking oil or fat. Keep the victim warm to prevent shock. **Immediately call emergency medical assistance or, if necessary, transport the victim to the nearest medical facility.** Do not undress the victim unless the clothes are saturated with a liquid that is still burning. Do not touch the burn or attempt to treat it yourself beyond using cold running water to cleanse it. In an educational or professional setting, make certain that all necessary medical insurance and liability forms are completed and that all insurance and liability information is made available to the victim.

There are precautions you can take that will greatly reduce the likelihood of kitchen burns, such as using a side towel to handle hot cookware and utensils, and warning your coworkers when you are moving hot pots, pans, and utensils, especially when they are not in use but remain hot. It is particularly important to alert dishwashers and other cleanup personnel who handle soiled cookware and utensils. At home, these warnings should be directed to others present, especially young children and the elderly.

Cuts

The seriousness of a cut is determined by its depth and location on the body. Obviously, a paper cut on the finger is treated quite differently from a knife slice that severs a vein or artery. Whenever possible, hold a cut under cold running water for at least one minute to cleanse the area. Then, using a clean towel, apply pressure to stop the flow of blood. If possible, elevate the injured area above the victim's heart to slow the blood flow. If the cut does not stop bleeding after a few minutes, is very deep, or bleeds profusely, it may require medical attention and stitches. Immediately call emergency medical assistance or transport the victim to the nearest medical facility while continuing to apply pressure to the cut. Manageable hand cuts or those that have stopped bleeding should be covered with an antibiotic ointment, a clean bandage, and, for a cut on the finger, a rubber finger cover. This is to protect the cut from infection as well as to prevent the spread of bacteria from the wound to any food being prepared, as uncovered wounds are a ready source of food contamination.

Kitchen cuts can be avoided if a few basic precautions are taken.

- Learn good knife skills. Hold your knife properly, keeping the fingertips of the hand opposite your knife curled under when slicing and dicing.

- Always carry a knife properly—at your side, point down, with the sharp edge to the back.

- Warn coworkers when moving about the kitchen with an unsheathed knife.

- Avoid cutting with the knife point moving toward you.

- Pay keen attention when using a knife.

- Keep knives sharp. A dull knife is more difficult to control; it takes more pressure to make a cut and affords more opportunity for slippage.

- Keep cutting boards stationary by placing a damp kitchen towel or a layer of damp paper towel underneath.

- Never try to catch a falling roll of plastic film or aluminum foil; the cutting edge is extremely sharp.

- Always use the hand guard when slicing on a mandoline, as the blades are razor sharp.

Principles of Sanitation

Preventing food-borne illness is the obligation of every foodservice professional and is essential to the success of any food-related business. State and local boards of health set rigid standards for foodservice establishments, offer mandatory safety courses for foodservice professionals, and routinely inspect all types of establishments to ensure that their standards are being met; however, it remains the responsibility of the establishment to enforce these standards in the work environment. In the home kitchen, it is the responsibility of the cook to create impeccably clean conditions.

There are numerous principles that must be observed in the purchase, storage, preparation, and service of food to prevent contamination from the three most common contaminant sources: biological, chemical, and physical.

Biological Contamination

Bacteria, the primary biological contaminant, is the cause of most food-borne illnesses. Bacteria are single-celled microscopic organisms that are present everywhere and on everyone. They multiply by splitting in two, and under optimal conditions, a single bacterial cell can multiply into 281 billion cells in three days.

Some bacteria are beneficial, such as those needed to produce certain cheeses and cultured milk products, beer, and wine. While it is presently thought that most bacteria are benign, those that are harmful can be deadly.

Undesirable bacteria can cause food spoilage, which can usually be identified by the presence of an unusual odor, a sticky or slimy surface, discoloration, or mold. Bacteria that are also disease agents are known as pathogens. The presence of pathogens may not always alter a food's odor, taste, or appearance, and this makes them particularly difficult to detect. To lessen the risk of contamination, purchase food from reliable sources and practice good hygiene along with sanitary handling and proper storage.

Factors That Influence Bacterial Growth

Type of food: Almost all foods, except those that are dry or preserved by sugar or salt, can become hosts for bacteria. High-protein foods such as eggs and dairy products are very active supporters of speedy bacterial expansion.

Potentially hazardous foods (PHF): These are foods that support the rapid growth of bacteria. A partial list of PHF items includes raw or undercooked meat, especially bacon; dairy products, such as cut cheeses and sour cream; fresh shelled eggs; unrefrigerated fresh garlic in oil; raw seeds or sprouts; soy products; and any sauces containing PHF ingredients.

pH level: Acidity and alkalinity are measured by a pH factor that spans from 1 (strongly acidic) to 14 (strongly alkaline), with pure water measuring 7 (neutral) on the pH scale. Almost all bacteria thrive in a neutral or midlevel pH environment.

Temperature: Bacteria grow best in temperatures ranging from 41°F (5°C) to 135°F (57.2°C). This range is referred to as the **food danger zone**, as it is in this zone that food finds a favorable climate for bacterial growth. Bacteria need time to adjust to their host environment, however, before they begin to grow and multiply. This gives a cook a brief period during which it is acceptable to leave food at room temperature as preparation is commencing.

Oxygen: Most bacteria are aerobic, which means that they need oxygen to grow. However, some of the deadliest bacteria, such as those that cause botulism, are anaerobic and able to grow without access to air.

Moisture: All bacteria require liquid to absorb nourishment; therefore moist, damp foods such as cream-based salads make the perfect host.

There are two categories of diseases caused by pathogens: **intoxications** and **infections**. Intoxications are the result of poisons or toxins that enter the system after they have been produced in food as a result of bacterial growth rather than from the bacteria themselves. Infections are caused by bacteria or other organisms that enter and attack the human body.

Bacteria have no means of locomotion; they must be carried from one place to another. Travel may be initiated by unwashed hands, coughs, sneezes, other foods, unsanitary equipment or utensils, or environmental factors such as air, water, insects, and rodents. Only sterilization will eliminate bacteria, so it is extremely important to understand a few simple rules that will help prevent bacterial contamination in the kitchen.

Rule 1   **Keep bacteria from spreading.** Do not touch anything that may contain disease-producing bacteria. Protect food from bacteria in the air by keeping it covered at all times.

Rule 2   **Prevent bacterial growth.** Keep food at temperatures that are out of the food danger zone.

Rule 3   **Kill bacteria.** Heat food to a temperature of 170°F (80°C) or hotter for thirty seconds. Wash equipment and utensils with hot water and detergent and rinse well, or sanitize.

Chemical Contamination

Chemical poisoning can result from defective, improperly used, or poorly maintained equipment. Such poisons might include antimony from chipped enamelware, lead found in containers or soldering material, or cadmium found in electroplating. Chemical contamination can also result from commercial cleaning compounds, silver polish, and insecticides.

To prevent chemical contamination, thoroughly wash containers and equipment and rinse in extremely hot water; store food separately from cleaning products and other chemical-based materials; and label all containers.

Physical Contamination

Physical contamination, the adulteration of food by a foreign object such as broken glass, hair, metal shavings, paint chips, insects, or stones, can be avoided by following the basic safety and sanitation guidelines provided in this chapter. However, if physical contamination does occur, immediately discard all affected raw and prepared foods.

Temperature

Temperature control is critical for safe food handling. Most bacteria, including those that cause milk to go sour, grow best in warm temperatures, that is, those between 41°F (5°C) and 135°F (57.2°C). Pathogenic bacteria favor slightly warmer temperatures in the 70°F (20°C) to 125°F (50°C) range. Temperatures of 170°F (80°C) or hotter will kill most non-spore-forming bacteria and all pathogenic organisms. Although low temperatures (32°F / 0°C) will not kill bacteria, they will hamper or slow growth so food can be preserved through refrigeration or freezing.

A food thermometer should always be used whenever an exact temperature reading is required. Never use a hands-on method to determine whether food is hot or cold enough.

Storage

In a bakery, all products should be dated and labeled before storing them in a manner that prevents contamination from exterior sources and prohibits growth of any bacteria already in the product. Once stored, all foodstuffs should be rotated according to the first in, first out (**FIFO**) system. Following are basic guidelines for safe storage.

Dry Storage

○ Dry storage pertains to those foods that do not support bacterial growth because they do not contain moisture or because they have been packaged by the manufacturer to have a long shelf life. This includes flour, sugar, salt, leavening agents, cereals, grains, oil and shortening, and canned and bottled foods.

○ Dry storage containers should be closed tightly to protect from insect and rodent infestation, as well as to prevent contamination from dust or other airborne particles.

○ Dry food should be stored in a cool, dry place that is raised off the floor, away from the wall, and not under a sewage line.

Refrigerated Storage

○ Items that do not fall into the category of dry goods are considered perishable and should be refrigerated to protect them from spoilage and contamination.

○ Refrigeration may be done with the use of a walk-in refrigerator, reach-in refrigerator, refrigerated showcase, refrigerated counter, or refrigerated table.

○ Refrigerators must be equipped with a calibrated thermometer.

○ Interior walls and shelves of the refrigerator should be immaculate.

○ Refrigerated foods should be properly labeled and wrapped or stored in a nonreactive, nonabsorbent container to avoid contamination.

○ Raw and cooked foods should be stored in separate areas inside the refrigerator.

○ Do not allow any unsanitary surface, such as the outside of a container, to touch any food.

○ Most perishable foods keep best at a temperature of 38°F (3°C).

○ Air must be able to circulate around all sides of a refrigerated item; therefore, do not overcrowd a refrigerator, and keep products off the refrigerator floor.

○ Keep refrigerator doors closed except when placing food into or removing food from the interior.

Freezer Storage

○ Food items to be frozen must be tightly wrapped first in plastic film then in aluminum foil or a re-sealable freezer bag, or sealed in Cryovac packaging to prevent freezer burn.

○ Stored items should be labeled and dated.

○ Frozen products must be kept at 0°F (-20°C) or colder until ready to use.

○ Freezers must be equipped with an external thermometer so that the freezer temperature can be read without opening the door or entering the freezer box.

○ Frozen products must be stored so that cold air is allowed to circulate on all sides. This means that food should not be stored directly on the freezer floor.

○ Thaw frozen products in the refrigerator or under cool, running water. Never thaw foods at room temperature because, at some point, this method will place the thawing product in the danger zone for optimal bacterial growth.

Equipment and Utensils

A well-stocked professional bakery is built around a formal arrangement of heavy-duty ovens, ranges, refrigerators, freezers, dishwashers, workstations, and cleanup areas. Cookware and other equipment should be made of exceptionally strong elements that can withstand long and hard use. Any well-supplied home kitchen will have much of the same equipment, with less emphasis on quantity but the same insistence on quality to ensure that equipment and utensils purchased for the kitchen will offer many years of use.

Cookware

As you work in the kitchen, always use the appropriate name for each pot and pan. It is extremely important to learn the correct names because often the head baker or another baker will call out for a piece of equipment that must be delivered as quickly as possible. If the name is not on the tip of the tongue, time will be wasted while the desired piece of equipment is located. The assortment of pans in a professional bakery will include some or all of the following items, many of which come in a variety of sizes:

Baguette trough pan: Long, narrow pan used exclusively in setting and baking baguettes.

Black steel pan: Heavy-gauge steel baking pan whose thickness and dark color promote even baking and browning. Types of black steel pans most commonly available are American sheet pans, French sheet pans (slightly smaller than American), large loaf pans, and round disks called *tourtiers* that are used for baking tarts.

Brioche à tête mold: This round, fluted pan with flaring sides is used to bake a classic brioche.

Disposable paper loaf pan: A decorative paper pan, available in a variety of shapes, in which bread may be baked and sold.

Loaf pan: A rectangular pan used for baking bread or cake.

Muffin pan: A multi-welled pan used for making individual muffins or small breads.

Pain de mie pan or **Pullman pan:** A long, lidded mold used to make rectangular loaves of bread. Loaf pans are available in stainless steel, black steel, disposable aluminum, ceramic or red clay, and glass.

Loaf pans, disposable paper loaf pans, and *kugelhopf* mold

Baguette trough pan, *couche*, and cutting boards

Sheet pan: A rectangular aluminum or stainless steel pan with shallow sides. Most common sizes are full-size sheet pans (18 inches by 26 inches) and half-size sheet pans (18 inches by 12 inches). They are used both for baking and holding breads. For a home oven, a recipe that requires a full-size sheet pan can be baked in two jelly roll pans, which normally measure 17¼ inches by 11½ inches by 1 inch.

Miscellaneous Tools and Utensils

All kitchens, whether professional or home kitchens, are equipped with an assortment of tools and utensils. As with pans and other equipment, when used as directed, the highest-quality tools will last the longest. These are some of the tools that might be found in a professional bakery:

Bagel board: A flat, sheet pan–sized board of plywood-like material about ⅜-inch thick that is used for proofing bagels. It can also be used for proofing rolls and breads.

Baking stone or tile: A heavy, unglazed clay round or square used to radiate a flow of indirect heat to baking breads. Commercially made stones are available for this purpose, but large, unglazed pottery tiles can also be used.

Bench brush: A soft-bristled brush similar to a whisk broom that is used to brush excess flour off of dough and worktables.

Bench knife: An almost rectangular, slightly flexible metal blade with a sturdy handle used to clean work surfaces as well as to divide and lift portions of dough. Alo known as a dough scraper or bench scraper (see *Scrapers*).

Bread knife: A knife that can be anywhere from 6 to 10 inches long with a serrated blade made specifically for cutting breads or other products with a crisp or firm exterior and a soft interior. Bread knives can be straight or offset.

Cooling rack: See *Wire rack*.

***Couche*:** A linen cloth that, when folded between loaves, helps artisanal bread loaves keep their shape during the final rising. A *couche* is especially useful for loaves that are too large for a *banneton* (see *Rising basket*).

Cutting board: Made of hardwood, such as maple, or plastic, such as polypropylene, cutting boards provide a safe cutting surface for dividing dough and protect the knife edge from damage. Cutting boards should be soaked periodically in a disinfecting solution of bleach

Pastry brushes, rolling pin, and bench brushes

Rising baskets and plastic rising tubs

Measuring cups and spoons

and water. A worn board should be discarded, as small food particles may become trapped in the uneven cutting surface, making it unsanitary.

***Kugelhopf* mold:** A tube pan with decorative fluting that is used to bake the Alsatian sweet bread *kugelhopf.*

***Lame*:** An extremely sharp, curved blade used to score the top of a bread loaf prior to baking. It often also has a razor attached to it.

Laser thermometer: An analog or digital thermometer with a laser component that uses an infrared beam to read surface temperature. Mixtures should be stirred lightly as the temperature is taken to get the most accurate reading. The laser thermometer is helpful for measuring the temperature of tempered chocolate.

Measuring cups: Measuring cups usually range in size from ¼ cup to 4 cups and can be made of metal, plastic, or glass. Single-measure metal or plastic cups are generally used for dry measurement, while multiple-measure glass cups are used for liquid.

Measuring spoons: Available in metal and plastic, measuring spoons come in sets that range from ¼ teaspoon to 1 tablespoon. In the pastry kitchen, measuring spoons are used to measure small amounts that would not register on a scale.

Oven mitt: Extremely thickly padded mitt used to protect hands and arms when handling hot pans and racks, and when placing breads into and taking them out of ovens.

Parchment paper: A thin paper, also known as pan-liner paper, treated with chemicals to make it nonstick. It is available in rolls and sheets.

Pastry brush: A small brush used to apply egg wash or to brush off excess flour. A separate brush should always be used for egg washes to avoid cross-contamination.

Peel: A wooden or aluminum tool, also known as a baker's peel or transfer peel, that has a short handle and a large, flat front piece that is used to slide breads into and remove them from the oven.

Pizza wheel: A sharp metal disk with a handle or encased in a plastic cover that is used to cut baked pizza. It is also a useful tool for cutting raw dough into pieces.

Plastic film: Also called plastic wrap, plastic film is used to cover fermenting dough and to wrap perishable food for storage in the refrigerator or freezer.

Plastic rising bucket or tub: Large, plastic container in which dough is placed to ferment and rise.

Oven mitts, peels, and cooling rack

Sheet pan, silpat liner, parchment paper, and plastic film

Wooden spoon, whisks, spatula, and scrapers

Rising basket: A shallow, woven basket used to hold an artisanal bread dough's shape during the final rise. Unlined willow baskets are known as *brotformen* and coarse muslin-lined ones are known as *bannetons*. These baskets not only determine the final shape of a loaf, but also leave a pattern on the crust when dusted with flour.

Rolling pin: A wooden, metal, marble, or glass cylinder used for rolling out dough. A French pin, which has no handles, is the most common in the bakery kitchen; however, a weightier pin with ball-bearing handles makes rolling large or heavy doughs easier.

Rolling rack: Also known as a speed rack or bun pan rack, a rolling rack is a cart with slots to hold sheet pans loaded with bread or rolls to be proofed. For proofing, the entire rack is generally enclosed with a custom-fitted plastic cover that can be closed with a zipper or Velcro to keep the dough at the proper temperature. The rack can be rolled around the kitchen with ease to be placed where needed at any time.

Ruler: A simple tool to insure accurate measurement of dough amounts as well as to create straight lines when necessary.

Scale: A scale is essential in bread making. Three types are commonly used in a bakery kitchen: dial scales, digital scales, and balance scales. Scales are available in a variety of maximum weights that can measure accurately all types of ingredients. All scales are marked to indicate the maximum weight allowed and the divisions provided on the dial face; for example, 2 kg x 5 g means a maximum of 2 kilograms in divisions of 5 grams. Many bakers prefer digital scales, as they are easy to use and often have a tare button, which allows the user to weigh an item, tare the scale (which takes the displayed weight back to zero), and weigh another item right on top of the first. The tare feature also allows the user to measure ingredients into a container—the scale is tared with the empty container so that the container's weight will not have to be taken into account. A balance scale requires the user to put weights on one side of the scale and add the ingredient to be weighed on the other until the scale is balanced, indicating that the desired weight has been achieved.

Scrapers: There are a several different styles of scraping utensils. A metal bench scraper, also called a bench knife, is used to clean off a work surface or divide dough. A plastic bowl scraper is used to remove dough from a mixing bowl as well as to fold in ingredients.

Sieve: A round, flat, or cone-shaped metal utensil with a mesh or perforated bottom, and usually a handle. Also known as a strainer, it is used to strain liquids or liquid-based mixtures or to sift dry ingredients.

23

Whisks, pastry brushes, and sieve

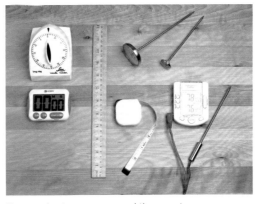

Timers, ruler, tape measure, and thermometers

Table mixer

Silpat liner: This reusable, nonstick silicone mat can be used in place of parchment paper in baking. Silpat liners are made of woven fiberglass that has been injected with food-grade silicone. The liners come in two sizes: 12 inches by 16 inches for half-sheet pans and 16 inches by 24 inches for full-sheet pans. Each liner lasts for about 2,000 bakings and should be washed with soap and water both before and after using. After using, cool the Silpat on a flat surface before storing. Do not cut a Silpat to fit your pan, use it as a cutting board, or wash it with abrasive cleansers, all of which will render it unusable.

Spatula: A wood, plastic, or metal tool with a long handle and a rubber head that is used to scrape the interior of a mixing bowl or stir or lift a dough.

Stem thermometer: This common kitchen thermometer, provided to all students upon entering The French Culinary Institute, measures temperature through a metal stem just past a dimple located about 2 inches from the tip. The dimple must be placed in the middle of the food item to get an accurate temperature reading. To calibrate a stem thermometer, place the probe end in ice water for 3 minutes, stirring occasionally. Carefully adjust the nut under the reading dial if necessary so that the thermometer reads 32°F (0°C). This type of thermometer should not be used for oven readings, as it will melt.

Table mixer: An electric, variable-speed stand mixer used to mix, beat, blend, and knead small amounts of batter and dough. The stainless steel bowl is inserted into a moveable stand and then locked into place. Then, the specific attachment is installed. The three most commonly used attachments are the paddle, the dough hook, and the whisk. The paddle is a flat, fan-shaped piece of metal that is used to mix stiff items such as firm batters or doughs. The dough hook is a question mark–shaped attachment used solely to knead bread doughs. The whisk is balloon-shaped and is made of thin wires that are quite fragile and easily broken when used on mixtures that are too firm. It is recommended only for incorporating air into liquids such as heavy cream or egg whites.

Tape measure: A flexible tool used to measure rolled or formed dough.

Timer: An analog or digital device used to time fermenting or baking.

Whisk: A tool, usually metal, comprising several turned wires and used to incorporate air into an ingredient or mix of ingredients. Whisks are available in various sizes and weights and may also be made of bamboo.

Wire rack: A metal mesh or wire rack, also known as a cooling or dipping rack, used for cooling or glazing baked

items. A wire rack speeds cooling as it allows air to circulate around the entire item and, with bread, will ensure a crisp crust. When used during glazing, the mesh allows the glaze to drip off the item rather than pool around it. Racks are available in a variety of sizes, some of which are intended to fit inside full-size or half-size sheet pans.

Wooden spoon: A nonreactive stirring utensil, available in many sizes and shapes.

Zester: This small hand tool is used to cut decorative strings of citrus peel.

Zesting plane: Also known by the brand name Microplane, this kitchen tool, modeled after a tool originally designed for woodworking, is used to remove the zest quickly and cleanly from citrus fruits. The small pieces of zest that result are used to add flavor to a recipe, whereas the longer strips made by a zester (see above) are used to decorate food.

Stoves, Ranges, and Ovens

There are many different types of stoves, ranges, and ovens available. While some can accommodate many different uses, others are best suited to specific types of cooking or baking.

Burners may be placed in a range top with an oven (or ovens) either below or above, or they may be placed alone into a stovetop that is fitted into a specific setting. The burner types available are:

Open burner (gas): An open flame that provides direct heat and responds quickly to changes in temperature setting.

Flat-top burner (gas or electric): A thick steel plate over the heat source that offers even, indirect heat. A flat-top burner requires flat-bottomed cookware and time to adjust to changes in temperature setting.

Ring-top burner (gas): Concentric rings and plates that can be removed to expose the flame so that indirect heat can be converted to direct heat. These burners typically have a higher BTU (British thermal unit, a universal measure for heat energy) than a regular open burner. Ring-top burners are particularly well suited to stir-frying.

Some types of available ovens are:

Conventional oven (gas or electric): The indirect heat source is located on the bottom. An adjustable shelf can be placed at the desired level for proper cooking or baking.

Deck oven (gas or electric): A type of conventional oven in which the food is set directly on the oven floor. Deck ovens take a minimum of 20 minutes to preheat to temperature. Most bakeries are equipped with multi-level deck ovens made especially for bread baking, but single-level deck ovens are also available.

Convection oven (gas or electric): In a convection oven, a fan blows hot air through the oven, allowing food to heat evenly and brown more efficiently than in a conventional oven, making it a popular choice for pastry and other baked goods. Convection ovens take a minimum of 15 minutes to preheat to temperature. If a recipe is written with a temperature designated for a conventional oven, the temperature in a convection oven should be reduced by 10 percent.

Masonry oven: These ovens, used for artisanal bread baking, are lined with composite stone, ceramic, or clay, and hold and radiate heat more than conventional ovens.

Steam-injection oven: Steam-injection ovens automatically introduce steam, replacing the old method of hand spritzing the baking loaves. The added moisture helps create the crisp crust on artisanal breads.

Refrigerators and Freezers

All kitchens require some type of refrigeration. The following are some of the available types of refrigerators and freezers:

Walk-in unit: A large, box-shaped unit with a door large enough to allow a person to enter without bending. Walk-in units may be for cold storage or freezing and are generally outfitted with storage shelves. A compressor, often located outside the box, cools it.

Reach-in unit: A single- or multiple-unit commercial refrigerator or freezer that is simply a larger version of a home unit. Reach-ins come in various sizes and are equipped with adjustable shelving.

Retarder/proofer with rolling racks

Spiral mixer

Miscellaneous Large Equipment

Hobart mixer: A large, permanently placed electric mixer that comes in sizes ranging from 20 quarts to 100 quarts or more. The Hobart is similar to the smaller table mixer in that it has the same types of attachments, but it is substantially larger and has a stronger motor that enables it to handle large batches. The other major difference between the two is that the Hobart has gears and only three possible speeds. In order to change gears, the mixer must be brought to a complete stop before moving to another speed. Hobart mixers also have a number of safety devices that table mixers do not. The wire screen on the front of the Hobart bowl must be in place, or the mixer will not run. The bowl must be fully raised as well. There is also a timer on the machine that, when set, will operate the machine for a specified period.

Retarder/proofer: An enclosed, programmable box that is used to control the fermenting of yeast-based doughs by creating the ideal humidity and temperature conditions for a dough to ferment.

Sheeter: Used in commercial bakeshops where large amounts of dough are rolled, this machine is composed of two stainless steel rollers that can be adjusted to produce any thickness of dough. Conveyor belts to the left and right of the rollers pass the dough back and forth through the rollers, with the gap being lessened each time, until the desired thickness is achieved. Sheeters are most useful when making large batches of laminated doughs, such as for croissants.

Spiral mixer: This mixer, also known as a bread dough mixer or flour mixer, is a very expensive, high-powered, specialized mixer that has two speeds and is designed to mix bread dough efficiently with a minimum of oxidation.

Session 2

Ingredients and Their Functions

In bread baking, as with all other culinary techniques, each ingredient has a particular, defined function in creating the desired finished product. However, because most artisanal breads are composed of just four basic ingredients—flour, yeast, salt, and water—ingredient quality is exceedingly important. And, since flour is the primary ingredient in all bread, its quality and type will determine the defining character of the baked loaf. In addition to these four basic ingredients, we will also take a look at sugar and some dairy products, such as butter and milk, that are, from time to time, used in creating enriched bread doughs.

Flour

Flour provides the structure and framework for all bakery products, and is the single most important ingredient in bread making. Flour is produced when grasses, seeds, nuts, or vegetables are finely ground. The ground matter is then processed through some type of sieve to generate a fine, sometimes almost powdery substance. The use of the term *flour* is always based on the presence of starches or complex carbohydrates in the final product. Whether creating something sweet or savory, flour, as one of the primary structural elements used in baking, is the key ingredient to create volume, crust color, crumb color, grain, texture, and taste.

Grains were first milled about 75,000 years ago by rubbing or pounding them between two rough stones. This process was the first step in making them more digestible, because it removed the rough, outer layer. Milling was followed in about 6000 B.C. by the development of sieving, which separated the finer flour from the coarser fragments by pushing the milled grain through a fine, woven grass sieve. Later, milling was greatly improved by the development of hand-powered stone mills that consisted of two large stones placed one on top of the other. Grain was placed between the stones and milled by rubbing the movable top stone over the stationary bottom stone. By about 100 B.C., the Romans had developed a water-powered mill that sped the making of finer flours. Modern mills are powered by electricity, but essentially follow these same principles.

Beyond being a basic building block for breads and pastries, flour has other important responsibilities. It provides nutrients, creates texture, produces the desired appearance, generates flavor, and serves as an agent for the incorporation of liquid, through binding and absorption. Although we are most familiar with wheat flours, there are a number of different flours available. Since the type of flour used will have an impact on the desired result, it is essential for the baker to be familiar with the properties of all flours.

When attempting to understand how the proteins in a flour act, it is helpful to think of them as strands of wool. In their original state, they are very loose and have neither elasticity nor strength. If working with actual wool, when water is added to it and then it is pressed or worked, the mixture will turn into felt—a strong, dense fabric. To bring this analogy back to flour, imagine that the strands of wool are two proteins called **glutenin** and **gliaden**. Just as with actual wool, these proteins absorb large amounts of water and, when kneaded or mixed, begin to combine and gain strength. The resulting mix is called **gluten**. As the flour and water are worked further, the proteins begin to connect and form large sheets of gluten. The structure becomes elastic and strong, which enables it to trap gases and air that will leaven the product (increase the volume and lighten the texture) or, conversely, if over-mixed, will toughen a dough and make it difficult to work.

When flour is milled, it is tested and classified according to its ratio of gluten-forming proteins to starches. The protein content of a flour affects the strength of the dough. In wheat flour, the protein content is determined by the type of wheat used, where and when it was grown, as well as what parts of the wheat kernel were used. Therefore, the type of flour used will determine how much gluten can be developed in the dough.

The amount of water or other liquid in a recipe will also affect the mixing style used to create the dough. The temperature of the water has an effect on fermentation and the dough temperature at the end of the mix. Fats also play an important role in the creation of a dough, as they coat the glutenin and gliaden strands, preventing them from bonding with one another or with the liquid. Recipes using a greater amount of fat will generally be softer and more tender because the fat shortens the gluten strands. For the artisanal bread baker, it is particularly important to remember that gluten develops over time. That is, if you combine flour and water and give them enough time, a dough will be created. This concept is seen very clearly in the practice of making no-knead bread.

Flour Terminology

Amylase: A group of enzymes found in almost all flours that speeds the conversion of starches into sugars.

Gliaden: One of two proteins, the other being glutenin, found in wheat flour that, when combined with water, forms gluten.

Gluten: A protein network that is responsible for the structure of bread.

Glutenin: One of two proteins, the other being gliaden, found in wheat flour that, when combined with water, forms gluten.

Pentosan: A sugar found in abundance in rye flour.

Wheat Flour

Wheat is one of the world's largest cereal grass crops, second only to rice. The first grains to be cultivated were einkorn and emmer, both types of wheat, but centuries of evolution and genetic manipulation have created about thirty thousand types. Throughout the world, common wheat, durum, einkorn, emmer, and spelt are the major types still cultivated. The countries of the European Union produce the largest amount of wheat, while the United States is the world's fourth largest cultivator. In the U.S. today, wheat is classified as hard or soft with almost all wheat breads using one of six types: hard red winter, hard red spring, soft red winter, hard white, soft white, and durum. Hard wheat has a higher protein content and is lower in starch, ideal conditions for gluten to develop.

Soft wheat is higher in starch and has a lower protein content that, aided by the presence of the enzyme alpha-amylase (starch-digesting enzymes), yields a more tender dough.

Wheat's popularity for use as a flour is based on its ability to develop gluten when mixed with water or other liquids. This gluten development provides the elasticity which, when worked, will retain gas bubbles that create the familiar, spongelike texture of breads and pastries.

Wheat berries, the whole kernels of wheat, are composed of three distinct parts: **bran**, **germ**, and **endosperm**. The bran is the hard, protective cover. The germ is the embryo from which a new plant grows. The endosperm is the food source for the germ. Whole wheat flour is created when all three parts are ground together. White (wheat) flours are created solely from the endosperm. Both the bran and germ are rich in vitamins and are used as additives or as animal feed.

Parts of a Wheat Kernel

Bran: This outer shell of the wheat kernel comprises about 15 percent of the kernel's weight. Bran is high in protein, celluloses (fiber), and minerals, but it is brittle and must be tempered through a process called conditioning so that it will not shatter during the milling process. Bran is always removed from white flour during processing though the use of friction, as its sharp edges will impact gluten formation.

Germ: This embryonic wheat part inside the kernel comprises about 2 percent of the kernel's weight. Germ is high in protein, lipids, minerals, and sugars. To create different types of flour, the germ is removed from the kernel and processed separately from the bran and endosperm.

Endosperm: This large, inner component of the kernel just beneath the bran layer and surrounding the germ comprises about 83 percent of the kernel's weight. Endosperm is composed of starch granules that are entangled in a matrix of gluten-forming proteins, so it needs to be softened during the milling process so that it may easily be reduced to small particles.

Both the milling and refining of wheat flours are carried out with various objectives; in addition, flours are frequently treated, either chemically or by other means, to improve their inherent properties and nutritional value. During milling, for instance, different "streams" of flour—varying in their starch-to-protein ratios—might be removed for another use. To further illustrate this process, if you begin with 100 pounds of grain, after milling you will be left with 72 pounds of straight flour. This straight flour is referred to as having a 72 percent extraction rate. The remaining 28 pounds is the bran and the germ, which can, if desired, be added back to the straight flour in designated amounts to create whole wheat flour. Because European wheat is traditionally lower in protein content (softer) than American wheat and contains more bran and germ, most European flours have a 75 to 78 percent extraction rate.

The protein content of flour is what generally determines its use. Flour that has a high percentage of protein is called "hard" and one with a lesser amount, "soft." In the United States, wheat flours are divided into categories based on their protein density. Starting from the hardest and moving to the softest, they are bread flour, all-purpose flour, and finally cake or pastry flour.

Milling is a long, multistep process. Once it is delivered to the flour mill, wheat is cleaned and tested and may then be blended with other varieties of wheat to create the desired flour type. The wheat is then tempered by

INGREDIENTS AND THEIR FUNCTIONS

How Flour Is Milled: A Simplified Diagram

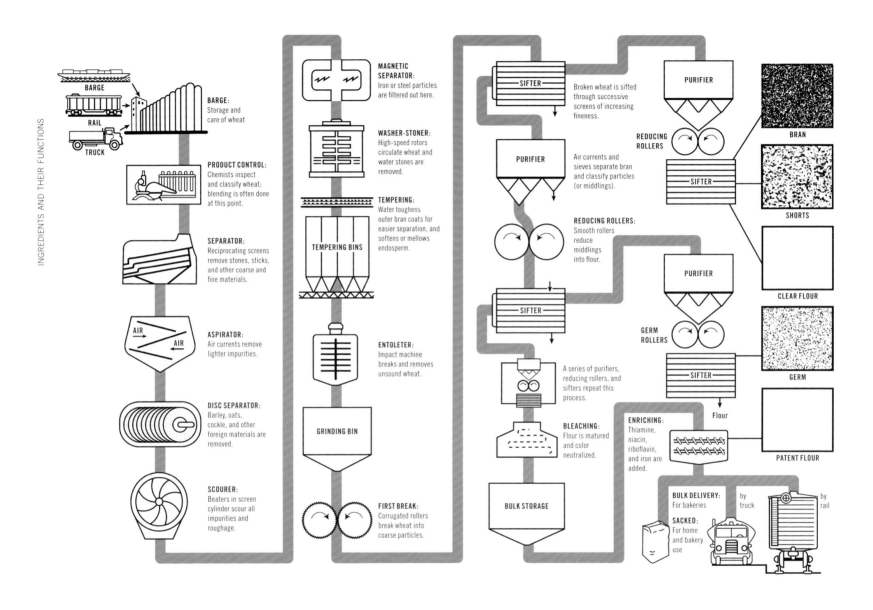

adding water for ten to twenty hours. Tempering, or conditioning, toughens the bran and softens the endosperm, which makes for more efficient milling. After tempering, wheat is rolled or crushed, sifted, and purified. The rolling (or crushing) and sifting may be done up to twelve times and, after each time, the flour is purified by forcing air through it to push the larger pieces to the top for easy separation.

After milling, flour must go through a number of other steps before it is ready for commercial use. To make the flour behave consistently in baking, it must be oxidized or matured. This is done either naturally, by exposing the flour to air for two to three months, or chemically, by adding potassium bromate, which quickly ages the flour with no effect on the color. Chemical maturation is used only in commercial flour processing in the United States, where speed is of the essence. Some flours are also bleached with chlorine dioxide. In artisanal bread baking, unbleached, unbromated flour is preferred.

Once mature, the flour is enriched by the addition of certain nutrients that were lost during the milling process. Vitamins B_1 (thiamine), B_2 (riboflavin), B_3 (niacin), B_9 (folic acid), D, and minerals, such as iron and calcium, are added. Mold inhibitors may be also be added, and a miller may add malted wheat or barley flour for better fermentation.

Components of Flour

Carbohydrates: These are made up of the starch, dextrins, pentosans (polysaccharide sugars that bind substantially in water), cellulose, and sugars contained in the milled flour. Almost all of the pentosans and cellulose are removed during the milling process. The starch granules that have been altered during milling are the most valuable source in the development of yeast-based bread doughs, as they help, when impacted by the amylase enzymes, to produce the sugars necessary to feed the yeast during the fermentation process.

Proteins: The protein content in flour comes from gliaden and glutenin, usually present in equal amounts. They, in turn, come from the protein contained in the endosperm. In bread making, gliaden assists in creating the volume required, while glutenin offers strength and elasticity to the dough. The protein content of a dough determines how much water the flour will be able to absorb; the higher the protein content, the greater the hydration potential. The protein content of a flour depends both on the genetic qualities of the wheat and the environment in which it was grown and milled.

Gluten: Gluten is formed when flour is mixed with water and kneaded. Both the gliaden and glutenin proteins unite with the water and then commingle to form sheets of flexible gluten. Gluten is the component that traps gases and air that cause the dough to rise. The yeast feeds on the sugars and produces carbon dioxide and alcohol. The carbon dioxide enlarges the air bubbles in the dough and the alcohol converts to gas and makes the air bubbles even larger. Gluten also holds on to the starch granules, allowing them to bend around the air bubbles. Then, as the bread bakes, the gluten proteins begin to cook, releasing water into the starch granules, firming the proteins, and providing the desired crumb.

Enzymes: Flour contains small amounts of two natural enzymes—amylases and diastases—that help break down the starch granules into the simple sugars required to nourish the yeast. They also improve the Maillard reaction (see page 53) as well as add sweetness. If a flour is deficient in either of these enzymes (which will cause a sticky, flaccid dough), additional enzymes may be added during the milling process.

Lipids: Evident only in small amounts, lipids appear to help gluten-forming proteins hold onto carbon dioxide formed during fermentation. They also increase flexibility and rise in doughs and help retain freshness in baked breads.

Minerals: Derived from the soil in which the wheat was grown, the presence of these inorganic substances, also known as the ash content of flour, causes gluten to be more malleable.

Wheat Flour Components

Protein

○ Makes up 6 to 18 percent of the kernel

○ Glutenin and gliadin are the gluten-forming proteins in wheat; glutenin gives dough its elastic properties, gliadin gives dough its extensible quality.

Starch

○ Makes up about 60 percent of the kernel

○ Found in the endosperm

Two types of starch:

Undamaged

○ Doesn't absorb much water until it is heated to 130°F (55°C)

○ Gelatinizes between 130°F (55°C) and 145°F (65°C). This helps form the crumb of the loaf.

Damaged

○ Broken during milling

○ Makes up 5 to 10 percent of flour weight

○ Absorbs water at room temperature

○ Can be converted by the enzyme alpha-amylase into sugar, which provides food for the yeast

Fiber

○ Absorbs ten times its weight in water

○ Accounts for 10 percent of the flour weight

○ Concentrated in the outer layers of the kernel (the bran)

Fat

○ Accounts for about 2 percent of the flour weight for whole wheat flour, less than 1 percent for white flour

○ Affects the shelf life of flour. Whole grain flours, because of their increased fat content, go rancid faster than white flours.

Minerals

○ Amount in flour is called ash content

○ Majority are located in the outer layers of the kernel

○ Makes up 2 percent of the flour weight for whole wheat flour, between .53 and .60 percent for white flour

○ Higher ash content results in lower loaf volume

Water

○ Makes up about 14 percent of the flour weight

Enzymes

○ These are proteins that are also biocatalysts, meaning they increase the rate of a reaction without undergoing permanent changes to themselves. The rate of reaction is dependent on temperature. At room temperature the rate is slow, at mild heat the rate generally increases, and at high heat the enzymes are deactivated.

○ During fermentation, alpha-amylase breaks down damaged starch into sugar, making food more readily available for the yeast; if there is too much alpha-amylase, the dough will be sticky, with little oven spring.

○ During the early part of the bake, amylases can break down the gelatinized starch before becoming deactivated. In small amounts, this helps crumb formation, but too much breakdown results in a less stable, sticky crumb.

Types of Wheat Flour

When choosing a flour, a bread baker will look at not only the protein content but also the protein quality. In addition, the bread baker looks at ash content and the flour's ability to form gluten. A hard flour will form an excellent-quality, elastic gluten that will produce an equally excellent baked bread. At the other extreme, a soft flour will produce a flabby dough that will produce a flat, wet baked bread. The harder flour, with the higher proportion of protein, is generally desired for superb bread making.

The following descriptions will help in choosing the appropriate flour for any task:

All-purpose flour: A blend of various grades of flours combined to make a medium-protein (10 to 12 percent) flour that can be used in artisanal bread making as well as for almost any other type of baking. Available bleached or unbleached, it was originally created primarily for use in the home kitchen; professional bakers often use a specific flour (bread, cake, or pastry, for example) to better control the protein content of the dough. All-purpose flour tends to vary widely from mill to mill. Most recipes calling for all-purpose flour should be mixed sparingly, as gluten development is usually not desired. Self-rising all-purpose flour, to which baking powder and salt have been added, is also available.

Whole wheat flour: An unbleached flour in which the whole grain has been used, making a flour that is substantially higher in nutrients, fiber, and fat than white flour. Available as soft whole wheat flour with a low protein content (about 11 percent) and hard red winter whole wheat flour with a protein content of approximately 13 percent. Whole wheat flour may be milled finely or coarsely, although finely milled is more readily available.

Bread flour: A strong white flour with a high protein content (12 to 13 percent) that makes it especially well suited for yeast-risen doughs. Bread flour may be milled from red or white wheat, hard winter wheat or spring wheat. It may be bleached or unbleached, and bromated or unbromated. Bread flour, primarily used to create yeast breads and yeast dough–based pastries such as croissants (*viennoiserie*), tends to be slightly granular with a yellowish color. It is often used in combination with lower-protein flours in bread-making recipes and can also be used in this way when making pastry doughs, such as puff pastry (*pâte feuilletée*), which rely on the gluten structure in the dough to trap steam and enable the dough to rise.

High-gluten flour: This flour, at 13 to 15 percent protein content, is used to increase the protein content of weaker flours. It is milled from red spring northern wheat. It may also be added to some bread recipes that require high gluten development, such as for bagels and pretzels. The addition of gluten flour to a bread dough can shorten the kneading time, require the addition of more liquid, and create a tighter crumb in the finished product.

Patent durum flour: An unbleached, high-protein flour (about 12 percent) milled from hard winter wheat. It is very fine, pale yellow, and used in some artisanal bread doughs.

Cake flour: This is a very low-protein flour (6 to 8 percent) that is used to create quick breads, cakes, cookies, and certain pastry doughs. It is often blended with higher-protein flours to reduce the strength of a dough. Cake flour is white and, when squeezed in the palm of your hand, will remain in a clump when your fingers are released. Doughs or batters using cake flour should be mixed gently to discourage gluten development. In fact, in some recipes the flour is delicately folded into the batter to avoid this development.

Pastry flour: A medium-low-protein flour, falling between all-purpose and cake flour at about 8 percent protein content. It is well suited to creating pastry and tart doughs and cookies. Like cake flour, pastry flour is often used in quick breads in which low gluten development is desirable to maintain a fine crumb in the finished product.

Graham flour: This is a whole wheat flour in which the endosperm is very finely ground and the bran and germ are left fairly coarse. It is an American flour invented by Dr. Sylvester Graham, who also created the graham cracker, for which the flour is still primarily used today, though it can also be used to add texture and nutrition in any cracker making.

Vital wheat gluten: A high-protein product (about 40 percent) from which the starch has been removed during the washing process. It is used to introduce protein in doughs created with grains that lack in gluten-forming capabilities.

Wheat bran: Bran that has been removed from the wheat kernel during milling. It contains all of the cellulose that ordinarily provides the fiber in flour and is mainly used in health and quick breads.

Wheat germ: The germ that has been removed from the wheat kernel during milling and is then toasted. It is mainly used in health and quick breads.

Semolina flour: Milled from high-gluten, high-protein durum wheat, semolina flour is used primarily for making pasta and noodles, but is also used in some Italian breads as well as in pizza dough. The flour granules are so hard that they will cut the gluten strands as the gluten develops. Semolina flour is occasionally called for in Italian and Middle Eastern cakes and some cookies. It is also used to make flatbreads.

Instant flour: Exceedingly fine granular flour that is used primarily in the home kitchen as a thickener for sauces and gravies because it can quickly absorb liquids without clumping. It has a very low protein content and is used by some pastry chefs to make quick puff pastry (*pâte feuilletée rapide*).

Other Flours

Although we are most familiar with wheat flour, flour can be made from many, many different foods. Legumes such as soybeans and acorns, ancient grains such as teff and amaranth, and potatoes and other tubers are but a few ingredients used to make flour around the world. In contemporary bread making, many of these once-unfamiliar grains and seeds (particularly amaranth, millet, and quinoa) are now used to add depth of flavor and nutrition to breads made with wheat flour.

One of the most important non-wheat flours in artisanal bread making is rye flour, a low-gluten flour ground from rye, a cereal grass substantially hardier than wheat, that thrives in a cold, wet climate. Since it does not form gluten like wheat flour (it does contain gluten-forming proteins, but not in sufficient quantities) and contains less starch and strengthening protein than wheat, it is usually mixed with a high-protein flour. On the other hand, rye flour contains more soluble sugar, more water-binding semi-liquid substances, more starch-digesting enzymes (alpha-amylases), more minerals, bran, and fiber than wheat flour. Due to its low gluten content, a rye-based dough will retain less gas than one made primarily of wheat, so it should be mixed and handled gently to preserve any intrinsic air in the dough. Rye dough also ferments faster than wheat dough and therefore has a lower fermentation tolerance, meaning it cannot support as long a fermentation period. The enzyme content of rye flour can impact its baking if it is not properly managed. Available in a variety of styles (light, medium, and dark, as well as coarse pumpernickel), rye flour easily absorbs moisture, so breads made with a high proportion of rye flour generally have a long shelf life.

Special Considerations for Rye Flour

Rye flour has a higher enzymatic activity than wheat flour and is much more susceptible to crumb breakdown during baking because it contains more of the enzyme alpha-amylase than wheat flour, which can result in a sticky dough with little oven spring.

During the early part of the bake, amylases break down the gelatinized starch and convert it to sugar before becoming deactivated by the heat; this breakdown is called starch attack, which in small amounts helps crumb formation. Rye starch gelatinizes at a lower temperature than wheat, which can lead to too much breakdown and a wet or gummy crumb. In extreme cases, the crumb could become liquefied and cause the interior of the loaf to collapse.

The way to limit alpha-amylase activity in rye breads is to use a sourdough starter. The acidity of the starter inhibits the activity of the enzymes, thereby preventing too much starch attack and yielding a more perfect crumb.

Following are some of the other flours that are used in the American bread kitchen.

Barley flour: Made from either malted or unmalted barley, barley flour is often used in gluten-free breads. Malted barley flour has a higher nutritional value than unmalted because it is milled with the hull of the grain intact.

Buckwheat flour: Made from the kernels or seeds of an herb native to Russia, buckwheat flour has a strong flavor. While it is sometimes used to make pancakes and some breads in the United States, it is more commonly used in Eastern European breads as well as in the traditional Russian *blini* that accompany caviar, and in Japanese soba noodles.

Cornmeal and corn flour: Cornmeal, consisting of dried corn kernels ground into fine, medium, or coarse textures, is used for breads, griddle cakes, a few desserts, and in bread coatings for deep-fried items. Cornmeal that has been bleached with lye is called masa harina and is used to make traditional Mexican dishes such as tortillas and tamales. Corn flour is finely ground cornmeal that is used in baking and for bread coating. In the United Kingdom, corn flour is the term used for the ingredient referred to in the United States as cornstarch.

Nut flours: Almost any nut can be ground into flour, but it is the oilier ones, such as almonds, macadamia, and hazelnuts, that are most often used. They can be used alone or in combination with wheat flour to produce cakes and pastries. Many nut-based flours are used to make traditional cakes throughout Central Europe. Occasionally, they are also used to make quick breads and gluten-free products.

Oat flour: The fine powder from ground whole oats has a high nutritional value and does not contain gluten. It is used to add nutrients, texture, and a nutlike flavor to wheat breads, as well to create gluten-free products.

Potato flour: Also known as potato starch, this flour is ground from cooked, dried potatoes. It is gluten-free and consists mostly of starch with a little protein. Though it is rarely used in bread making, it is sometimes used to create a moist crumb in baked goods or to thicken soups, stews, gravies, and sauces.

Rice flour: This extrafine, almost powdery flour ground from white rice is used for some baked goods and edible papers. It consists mainly of starch and is gluten-free. Whole grain brown rice flour and glutinous rice flour are also available, the latter of which is used mainly in Japanese cooking as a thickener or to make *mochi*, a traditional rice cake prepared for the Japanese New Year.

Soy flour: Although it can be used to create breads for people with wheat protein allergies, soy flour, in commercial bread making, is generally used in very small amounts in combination with wheat flours to improve crumb, give excellent toasting quality, increase nutritional value, and prolong shelf life. Soy flour is approximately 50 percent protein and contains more fat than most other flours. Commercial bakeries that use soy flour tend to use the low-fat variety; full-fat soy flour is used mainly in sweet goods where it can comprise up to 12 percent of the total flour weight. Enzyme-active soy flour is soy flour that has not been heat-treated as much as other soy flours thereby retaining some of its enzymes, specifically lipoxygenase. Lipoxygenases function as bleaching agents on the carotenoid pigments of flour to produce a whiter crumb color; they may also improve dough strength and mixing tolerance. The Food and Drug Administration (FDA) sets a maximum usage level for enzyme-active soy flour at .5 percent of the total flour weight.

Spelt flour: An ancient cereal grain with a high protein content that can be used in place of wheat flours in breads made for people with wheat protein allergies. It is highly digestible and has a fragrant aroma and mild taste.

Teff flour: Made from the grain of the ancient cereal grass teff, this highly nutritional flour is used to make flat breads, such as *injera*, a major component of Ethiopian cuisine.

Triticale: A hybrid grain, produced by crossbreeding wheat and rye, triticale is used only in combination with wheat flour, as it is high in protein but does not have the ability to create good gluten structure. It is usually only found in dense health breads.

compressed fresh yeast

instant dry yeast

active dry yeast

Yeast and Other Leaveners

Leavening, the main function of yeast, occurs when yeast produces carbon dioxide (CO_2). Alcohol, acids, and energy (heat), the other by-products of yeast fermentation, biochemically condition the flour by mellowing and softening the protein and contribute to the flavor of the finished product. The average (fresh) yeast content of most bread doughs is 2 to 5 percent based on flour weight. In the bakery, yeast is principally controlled through the regulation of times and temperatures, but food supply, water, and the pH of the dough will also affect the rate of yeast activity. Understanding what influences yeast activity gives the baker added control over the fermentation process.

Yeast is a living organism—a microscopic fungus—and as such is considered a biological leavener. There are always wild yeasts in the atmosphere, in soil, and on plants, and they can be captured and cultivated for commercial use. Although they have made the fermentation process in bread making more reliable, commercial yeasts still require the proper conditions to do their work.

The visible result of fermentation, the rising of a product, is caused by the production of carbon dioxide by yeast, a natural process of organic leavening. There are many types of yeast, but the yeast most commonly used in baking (and brewing) is *Saccharomyces cerevisiae*.

Yeast requires food, moisture, oxygen, and a warm temperature to do its job and dough provides the best of all possible worlds for fermentation to occur. When mixed into a dough, yeast devours sugars and damaged starches and converts them into alcohol and carbon dioxide. This takes some time to occur. The dough must also have a well-developed gluten structure for the gases to remain trapped inside; the sheets of gluten retain these gases and have enough elasticity to grow and stretch once placed in the oven. The fermentation process also aids in production of the distinctive flavor and aroma of so many yeasted products.

The speed of fermentation is affected by temperature and the availability of food and water. Generally, yeast lives and continues to ferment in a temperature ranging from 40°F (5°C) to 130°F (55°C) but is at its most active at about 75°F (25°C). Fermentation activity will slow on either side of 75°F (25°C). Yeast will begin to die when the temperature rises above 138°F (58°C) or goes below freezing (32°F / 0°C). As well, a wet dough will ferment more quickly than a dry dough. These factors will impact the amount of time required for the yeast to properly ferment.

There are two types of commercially available organic leaveners—baker's yeast and brewer's yeast—but we are concerned only with those used in bread baking.

Organic Leaveners

There are four types of baker's yeast: active dry yeast; compressed fresh yeast; instant dry yeast; and *levains* (starters), created from captured wild yeast spores.

Active dry yeast (ADY) is composed of tiny, dehydrated granules that are alive but dormant because of lack of moisture (moisture content is 5 to 7 percent). When mixed with warm (105°F–115°F / 42°C–47°C) liquid, the yeast will activate. Active dry yeast is available as regular or quick-rise, with the latter taking about half as long to do its leavening work. Each type can, however, be used interchangeably with an adjustment to the amount of yeast used. Both types should be stored in a cool, dry place and can be refrigerated; however the yeast should be brought to room temperature (68°F–77°F / 20°C–25°C) before using. Although the general recommendation for substituting active dry yeast for fresh yeast in a formula is one part dry to two parts fresh, it is always best to check the manufacturer's package directions. Active dry yeast must be rehydrated in four times its weight of 105°F–115°F (42°C–47°C) water. To test whether active dry yeast is viable, dissolve it in warm water with a pinch of sugar and set it aside in a warm spot for 10 minutes. If the mixture begins to foam and swell, the yeast can still do its leavening job.

Compressed fresh yeast is a perishable product that must be refrigerated and, if properly stored, has a shelf life of up to four weeks. It has a moisture content of 70 percent, produces the most carbon dioxide per cell out of all the types of yeast mentioned here, and requires no hydration time. It should not be frozen. It is very easy to scale and can be added directly to a dough mix. Although the general recommendation for substituting fresh yeast for active dry yeast in a formula is two parts fresh to one part dry, it is always best to check the manufacturer's package directions. To test whether fresh yeast is viable, follow the same instructions as for active dry yeast above.

Instant dry yeast (IDY), like active dry yeast, has a low moisture content (5 to 7 percent) but instant dry yeast has a coating of ascorbic acid, developed by European bakers, which cuts production time. It needs no initial proofing and is mixed directly into the dry ingredients. The word instant simply means that the yeast can be added to the dough immediately without the usual hydration step needed for active dry yeast. Instant dry yeast cannot be mixed directly with ice cold liquids or into very cold doughs. It can be substituted for fresh yeast by using 40 percent of the amount of fresh yeast called for in a formula. Because of its stable shelf life (up to 2 years when properly stored), instant dry yeast is the yeast most frequently used by artisanal bread bakers. When marketing instant dry yeast to the home baker, a manufacturer might give it a different name, such as rapid-rise, quick-rise, fast-rise, and so forth.

Levains (also called starters) are simply cultivated, captured wild yeast spores. To create a *levain*, flour and water are mixed together and left to rest for a substantial period of time. Yeast spores collect on the mixture and begin to multiply. The starter is fed and watered regularly to cultivate the yeast and prevent the spores from dying. Once a large amount of starter has been created, a measured amount can be mixed into a dough to provide leavening while the remainder of the starter continues to be fed and watered for future use. Some starters are very, very old and have been handed down from generation to generation. It is this naturally fermented mix that produces breads with a very distinct, but desirable sour taste and aroma.

Yeast Equivalents

Any yeast will work in any dough. Using the following ratios will allow you to substitute one type for another.

The prescribed ratio is: 100% fresh yeast = 50% active dry yeast = 40% instant dry yeast.

In weight that translates to: 1 ounce fresh yeast = .5 ounces active dry yeast = .4 ounces instant dry yeast.

Other Leavening Agents

Leavening in bread and pastry making occurs with any of three elements: air, steam, and carbon dioxide. These can be produced mechanically, chemically, or biologically; used alone or in combination; and each will expand substantially when heated. Air trapped in a dough or batter will expand to several times its size when heated. Liquid in a mix will turn to steam when heated and, when it does, expand to eleven hundred times its original volume. Carbon dioxide is formed when a chemical agent, such as baking powder, creates gases during baking, which in turn cause a dough to rise. Other ingredients (usually some combination of flour, sugar, and eggs) incorporated into the mixture solidify when baked and become a mass that will retain its expanded form once removed from the heat source.

Mechanical Leavening

Mechanical leavening results when air is physically incorporated into a mixture and allowed to rise, or when steam in a mixture expands under heated conditions. When butter and sugar are mixed together during creaming, the sugar cuts into the butter and causes it to trap air. When egg foams are beaten, the protein in the eggs causes the air to be trapped, which is why they must be treated delicately to ensure that the foam retains the trapped air. Laminated doughs, such as puff pastry, are another example of a dough made using mechanical leavening, but instead of using trapped air from rising or creaming, pockets created by butter collect steam from the water in the dough. The steam begins to push the layers apart, creating the desired airy, flaky pastry.

Chemical Leavening

Chemical agents, such as baking soda and baking powder, cause a chemical reaction that produces gases during baking that will cause a dough to rise. Baking soda and baking powder both produce carbon dioxide, but they cannot be used interchangeably, as soda is four times stronger than powder and requires an acidic batter in which to work its magic. Used to make quick breads, muffins, biscuits, crackers, cakes, and cookies, chemical agents produce carbon dioxide when they react with added acids, liquids, and heat. This reaction gives the baked product a light, airy, tightly grained network. When using chemical leaveners, great care must be taken not to overdevelop the gluten in a mixture. Overworking will not only affect the ability of the dough to rise, but will also toughen the finished product and result in uneven or flat tops and tunnels in quick breads or muffins.

Baking soda: Also known as sodium bicarbonate, baking soda is a naturally occurring element found in all living matter. It is extracted from a mineral called trona, but it can also be manufactured. When mixed with an acid, baking soda releases carbon dioxide and leaves a small amount of salt. Gas is released immediately on contact, therefore batter should not be left to sit for any length of time, as the texture of the finished product will be radically affected. Some of the acids used with baking soda are buttermilk, citrus juices, sour cream, yogurt, molasses, chocolate, honey, or cream of tartar. If baking soda is not mixed with the appropriate amount of acid, the finished product will have an unpleasant, almost soapy taste.

Baking powder: There are three types of baking powder: single-acting (also called fast-acting), slow-acting, and double-acting. Single-acting is made from an acid that will quickly dissolve and produce gases when placed in cold water. Slow-acting will not react until heated. Double-acting has both elements so that some leavening (about one-third) occurs during mixing and the remainder during baking. The latter allows a mixed dough or batter to be stored for several days with no loss of leavening power. Once opened, baking powder has a shelf life of up to six months. To test its viability, add 1 teaspoon to a cup of water. If it fizzes, it is still active.

Salt

Although there are hundreds of different salts, there is only one salt used in baking—sodium chloride. Necessary for good health (though overuse is detrimental), sodium chloride is primarily used in baking and cooking to improve flavor and prevent spoilage. Salt can be mined from the earth or taken from a body of water; the former method requires that the salt be dissolved in water and the brine evaporated, the latter requires that salty water be allowed to evaporate via sunlight or artificial means, leaving behind usable salt crystals. The method used to process the brine will determine the size, shape, and, occasionally, the taste of the final crystals.

Because it retards yeast activity, salt is essential to bread making. If it is added to the flour in the early phase of mixing, more time will be required for adequate fermentation. Conversely, if it is added during a later phase, the effect on fermentation will be lessened.

Indirectly, salt contributes to crust color as a result of its ability to retard fermentation. By slowing the rate at which amylase converts starch to sugar, it slows the rate at which sugar is consumed by the yeast; therefore, there are more residual sugars available at the time of baking which, in turn, will serve to brown the exterior of the loaf.

Without salt, bread dough is slack and sticky and lacking in volume. Salt strengthens the gluten, making it firmer and more tolerant of pulling and stretching. This, in turn, makes kneading more difficult. Today, most artisanal bread makers add salt early in the mix to slow down oxidation of the dough. The normal level of salt in most breads ranges from 1.75 to 2 percent based on flour weight; however, some enriched products contain more, as do breads with added ingredients, such as fruit and nuts.

In addition, salt provides and enhances the flavor of the finished product. Breads containing less than 1.5 percent salt usually taste bland, and those with levels above 2.5 percent taste too salty.

Among the types of salt available to the baker are:

Table salt: There are three types of table salt—granular, flaky, and dendritic—all of which are produced through the use of vacuum evaporators. Granular table salt is the most familiar; it is fine grained and usually contains both iodine and anti-caking agents. The flaky variety is similar to granular salt but is compacted, resulting in large flakes that can be used as a topping on bagels, breads, and crackers. Dendritic salt has the addition of sodium ferrocyanide, which changes the shape of the crystals, making them dissolve almost instantly when combined with a liquid.

Sea salt: Also known as mined salt, sea salt crystals are flatter than those of table salt and have irregular edges. Sea salt can vary in color from pale cream to black, with some even taking on a pink, green, or yellow hue depending on the minerals present. Sea salt can have a strong mineral flavor and, since it is usually created through a long, natural evaporation process, it is often quite expensive. The large-grained salt is generally used as a topping on breads or rolls or as a garnish for cooked foods. In The French Culinary Institute bread kitchens, only fine-grained sea salt is used.

Kosher salt: This is a coarse-grained salt that has been created for use in "koshering" meat following the strict rabbinical rules of the Jewish faith. Since kosher salt is not processed using one specific processing method, each brand can be quite different when it comes to texture and solubility.

Water

The primary function of water in bread making is hydration. Without water, the proteins in the flour cannot form gluten. In addition, water plays a role in yeast functionality, enzymatic activity, and starch gelatinization. The amount of water in a formula determines the consistency of the dough (stiff or soft, extensible or elastic) and the quality of the finished product. Water is also the means by which the temperature of the final dough is controlled.

Although water is a substance that has many qualities, in bread making there are only three qualities that will have an impact on dough formation: alkalinity, hardness, and chlorination.

Alkalinity: Natural water varies greatly in its alkalinity depending upon its source. Even when water comes from a municipal treatment plant, its alkalinity can vary from one moment to the next. Alkalinity and acidity are measured on the pH (from the French *pouvoir hydrogène*, meaning power of hydrogen) scale, the standard that rates alkalinity based on the concentration of hydrogen ions in a substance, with 0 suggesting strong acidity and a strong concentration of hydrogen ions and 14 for strong alkalinity.

Hardness: Water that has a low mineral salt content is called soft and water that has a high mineral salt content is called hard. Excessively hard water will produce a dough with very little rise but excellent color when baked. Soft water will produce a dough that ferments quickly, but will also inhibit color and texture during baking. When working with hard water, increasing fermentation time will produce a better result. When using soft water, adding salt to the dough can help strengthen the gluten structure.

Chlorination: Tap water often has chlorine added to prevent the formation of undesirable microbes. Chlorination does not affect the work of commercial yeasts, but has a negative effect on *levains* (starters). This is because chlorine destroys the friendly bacteria that assist the wild yeast. Chlorine is a gas, so letting the water rest uncovered in the refrigerator for 24 hours will allow the gas to dissipate, making it safe for use in starters.

Mineral Yeast Food

Mineral yeast food (MYF) is used in commercial bread baking to condition water for optimal fermentation. Since the amount and type of conditioners added to water supplies vary from one area to another, the baker must choose the appropriate mineral yeast food for their particular water supply so that the yeast will have the optimal environment for growth. Normal MYF usage levels are from 0.75 percent, based on flour weight. Mineral yeast food is not used in artisanal bread making.

Eggs

Since some rich, yeast-based doughs require the use of eggs, the following will provide the information a baker needs to ensure that egg safety is always observed. An egg is composed of an outer shell made of a calcium compound, such as calcium carbonate. The shell color does not affect the thickness of the shell or the quality, flavor, nutritive value, or cooking characteristics of the egg, but is determined by the breed of chicken or other bird that produced it. Brown eggs come from reddish-brown hens such as Rhode Island Reds, Plymouth Rocks, and New Hampshires (obviously all New England favorites). White eggs are produced by Leghorns, America's most common breed of chicken. Rare breeds such as Araucanas lay eggs in an array of pastel blue and green shades. No matter the color, if the eggs are handled in the same manner, the taste and nutrition will be equal.

The most common eggs used today come from chickens, although turkey, goose, duck, and quail eggs are also sold.

Eggs are considered by many to be one of the most versatile and nutritious foods available. One large egg contributes approximately 6.5 grams of protein (or about 13 percent of the average adult's minimum daily requirement), as well as substantial amounts of iron, choline, thiamine, phosphorus, and the vitamins A, B_{12}, D, and E. The yolk contains most of the fat, cholesterol, vitamins, and half of the protein while the white, also knows as the albumen, is composed almost entirely of water and proteins called albumins. It also contains niacin, riboflavin, and minerals.

Parts of an Egg

Following are the various parts of an egg and their functions:

Shell: The egg's outer shell accounts for 9 to 12 percent of its total weight and is the egg's first line of defense against bacterial contamination. A protective coating called the cuticle, or bloom, covers the surface of the shell and serves to preserve freshness and prevent microbial contamination of the contents by blocking the pores in the shell. The strength of the shell is greatly influenced by the vitamins and minerals in the hen's diet—the higher the consumption of calcium, phosphorus, manganese, and vitamin D, the stronger the shell. There are as many as eight thousand almost infinitesimal pores covering the shell of a typical chicken egg. These pores permit air to enter the egg and allow moisture and carbon dioxide to escape.

Air cell: The pocket of air found at the larger end of the egg. It is easily observed at the flattened end of a peeled, hard-boiled egg. When first laid, the egg is quite warm. As it cools, the contents contract and the air cell is formed as the inner shell membrane separates from the outer membrane. As the egg ages, the air cell increases in size as air enters, replacing the original moisture and carbon dioxide that exit through the pores of the shell as time passes. The size of the air cell is one method used to determine the grade of an egg.

Shell membranes: Immediately inside the shell, two membranes—inner and outer—surround the albumen (white) to provide a protective barrier against bacterial penetration. The air cell forms between these two membranes.

Albumen: The albumen, the white part of the egg surrounding the yolk, is made up of four concentric layers. They are, listed from the yolk outward, the chalaziferous layer, the thick albumen, the internal thin albumen, and the external thin albumen. The external thin albumen, located nearest to the shell, encloses the other layers of albumen. In a high-quality egg, the thick layers stand higher and spread less than the thin layers when the egg is broken, while in lower-grade eggs the thick layers become indistinguishable from the thinnest layer. As the egg ages, the albumen tends to thin, as the egg protein changes in character over time. Together, the albumen layers account for about 67 percent of an egg's liquid weight as well as half of its protein content and a good portion of its niacin, riboflavin, choline, magnesium, potassium, sodium, and sulfur. Albumen is actually more opalescent than pure white. Its cloudy appearance is linked to the carbon dioxide contained in the white. As an egg ages, carbon dioxide escapes, making the albumen of older eggs clearer and more transparent than those of fresh eggs. When vigorously beaten by hand or machine, albumen foams and can increase to six to eight times its original volume.

Chalazae: These thick, twisted, ropelike strands of egg white attached to two sides of the yolk serve to hold the yolk in place at the center of the thick albumen. If the chalazae are readily observed upon cracking open a raw egg, it is a sign of freshness. Although sometimes rather strange looking, chalazae are not the beginnings of an embryo and do not interfere in the baking, cooking, or beating process.

Vitelline membrane: A transparent, paper-thin seal that covers the egg yolk and keeps it intact. It is weakest at the germinal disc and tends to become more fragile as the egg ages.

Germinal disc: This is the entrance of the latebra, a channel leading to the center of the yolk. It is a barely noticeable slight depression on the surface of the yolk through which the sperm enter when an egg is fertilized.

Yolk (vitelline): The interior yellow globe that accounts for about 33 percent of the egg's total liquid weight and includes all the fat and half the protein, as well as the higher proportion of vitamins and minerals (except niacin and riboflavin) such as phosphorus, manganese, iron, copper, iodine, and calcium. The yolk contains all the egg's vitamins A, D, and E, and is one of the few foods with vitamin D. The color of the yolk will vary depending upon the type of feed given to the hen, but whether the yolk is pale or deep yellow is not indicative of its nutritive value. The yolk is responsible for the emulsifying and enrichment properties of the egg. The yolk carries 59 calories, which is 90 percent of the calories in a whole egg.

Determining the Freshness of an Egg

Is a farm-fresh, just-laid egg the freshest you can buy? There is some debate on this issue, as so many other factors help determine the freshness of an egg: the temperature at which it has been held, the storage humidity, and the handling process to name a few. Proper handling translates to prompt gathering, washing, and oiling within a few hours of the egg's being laid. Most commercially produced eggs are handled with extreme care from laying to market and reach the marketplace within a few days of leaving the laying house. So, if handled properly by the producer, the market, and the buyer, even a commercially produced egg should be farm fresh when it reaches the table.

An egg deteriorates very rapidly at room temperature, as the warmth allows moisture and carbon dioxide to escape through the pores in the shell. This, in turn, causes the air cell to expand and the albumen to thin. The ideal storage temperature is one that does not go above 40°F (5°C) with a relative humidity of 70 to 80 percent. Consequently, a freshly laid egg held at room temperature for one day will age as much as a properly refrigerated egg will age in a week.

As an egg ages, the albumen becomes thinner and the yolk becomes flatter. These changes do not have any significant effect on the nutritional quality or the functional cooking properties of the egg. As a general rule of thumb when purchasing and storing eggs, choose a reputable market with high volume and rapid turnover, where eggs are kept in cartons in a refrigerated case. Before buying, open the carton and check for dirt and cracked shells and, of course, do not purchase eggs that are in anything less than pristine condition. If an egg is damaged after purchasing and leaks into the carton, discard it and wash and dry the remaining eggs before refrigerating. Do not remove eggs from the storage carton, as it helps preserve their freshness and prevent moisture loss as well as the absorption of odors from other foods stored alongside them.

Do not rely on old wives' tales to determine the freshness of an egg. For instance, freshness cannot be judged by placing an egg in salt water to determine if it sinks or floats. A carefully controlled brine test is sometimes used in the commercial marketplace to judge the thickness of an egg's shell for hatching purposes, but it has no application for determining the freshness of an egg. Freshness and high quality in eggs will produce, in turn, the finest baked goods.

Grading, Sizing, and Packaging of Eggs

In the grading process, eggs are judged on both their interior and exterior quality and are sorted according to weight. Grade and size are not related to each other. In descending order of quality, standard grades are AA, A, and B. There is no difference in nutritive value among the different grades.

Several factors influence the size of an egg, including the breed of chicken, the age and weight of the laying bird, and the environmental conditions in which the hen was raised. Obviously, a healthy, drug-free, well-adjusted bird raised in a natural setting will produce more and better-quality eggs than one raised in less-than-desirable conditions. And, in general, the older the hen, the larger the egg.

Egg sizes are based on their minimum weight per dozen, as follows:

Jumbo: 30 ounces per dozen; 56 pounds per standard 30-dozen case

Medium: 21 ounces per dozen; 39½ pounds per standard 30-dozen case

Extra Large: 27 ounces per dozen; 50½ pounds per standard 30-dozen case

Small: 18 ounces per dozen; 34 pounds per standard 30-dozen case

Large: 24 ounces per dozen; 45 pounds per standard 30-dozen case

Peewee: 15 ounces per dozen; 28 pounds per standard 30-dozen case

The most commonly available sizes are extra large, large, and medium.

For commercial distribution, eggs are packed in flats. There are 30 eggs in one flat and 12 flats in one case to equal 30 dozen eggs; there are 6 flats in a half-case to equal 15 dozen eggs.

Egg Safety

Although very, very few eggs carry internal bacterial infection at the beginning of their production cycles, through improper handling or cooking eggs can become contaminated. Most often, the bacteria *Salmonella enteritidis*, which can cause severe gastrointestinal illness, are found to be the culprit. As well as being contracted through improper handling or cooking, these virulent bacteria can survive and grow in hens and subsequently be transmitted to the egg. This occurs very rarely—about 1 in 20,000 eggs—but it indicates that all eggs should be handled properly. The yolk of the egg is generally the point of infection, with the white almost never becoming infected. The bacteria rarely cause fatalities in healthy adults but can cause extremely serious health complications in infants and small children, pregnant women, the infirm, those with compromised immune systems, and the elderly.

Because of the virulence of the salmonella bacteria, kitchen sanitation is of the utmost importance when using eggs. Following are a few guidelines to minimize the occurrence of salmonella and other bacterial infections:

○ Eggs, raw or cooked, should always be refrigerated as quickly as possible and should only be left unrefrigerated for as short a period as is sensible to just bring them to room temperature before using, usually no more than an hour.

○ Hands, utensils, work surfaces, and pots and pans should be washed in very hot, soapy water after coming into contact with eggs.

○ Raw eggs should not be served to infants and small children, pregnant women, the infirm, those with compromised immune systems, or the elderly.

○ Before adding eggs to doughs or other ingredients, they should be checked for purity by breaking them, one at a time, into a small bowl.

Sugar

Sugar, also known as sucrose, is the water-soluble substance obtained by processing sugarcane, sugar beets, and sorghum. Although the most commonly used sugar comes from cane and beets, it is also available in other forms, such as glucose or dextrose (corn or grape sugar), fructose or levulose, maltose (malt sugar), and lactose (milk sugar); it is also found in maple sap. Not only does sugar add sweetness to products, but it can preserve foods, caramelize the surfaces of cooked or baked foods, delay coagulation in egg-based mixtures, and add stability to, strengthen, and tenderize doughs and other mixes. Sugar also aids in the retention of moisture, which prolongs a product's shelf life.

Because of its diverse functions, sugar is used in a great number of food preparations. Although sugar is available in many forms, and high fructose corn syrup (HFCS) is the most common sweetener used in large-scale commercial baking, we will mainly focus on the functions of the type of sugar most commonly used in the home kitchen. It should be noted that there are also many types of granulated sugar, but most of them are available for use only in the commercial processing of foods and baked goods or by professional bakers. These sugars differ in crystal size, with each type of crystal providing unique functional characteristics to aid in a variety of commercial uses. The amount of sugar used in bread making varies greatly, from 0 to 12 percent based on flour weight, and the percentage can go higher in products such as hamburger buns and sweet doughs such as panettone and *kugelhopf*.

light brown sugar

granulated sugar

pearl sugar

Demerara sugar

confectioners' sugar

dark brown sugar

White Sugar

White sugar is sucrose that has been highly refined through a purifying process using phosphoric acid or any number of filtration strategies to achieve pure white crystals. These crystals are the commonly used granulated sugar. In a bread bakery, generally only regular granulated sugar is used, but occasionally other types are used in the decoration of sweet breads.

Regular sugar, fine sugar, extra-fine sugar: Regular sugar is the granulated sugar found in 1-, 5-, and 10-pound bags on the supermarket shelf and in almost every kitchen's sugar bowl. It is the most common sugar for everyday use and is the white sugar called for in most home-baking recipes. In commercial food processing or baking, this same granulated sugar is called fine or extrafine sugar. It is ideal for bulk handling because its fine crystals are not susceptible to caking.

Confectioners' or powdered sugar (also often called 10x): This is simply granulated sugar that has been ground into a powder, sifted, and lightened with about 3 percent cornstarch to prevent caking. Confectioners' sugar is often sifted before being used for glazing breads and cakes or for icings. It is called icing sugar in the United Kingdom and *sucre glace* in France.

Glazing sugar: This extremely fine confectioners' sugar (most often 12x) may have maltodextrin added for stabilization and absorption of moisture. It is used to assist in the retention of a high gloss on glazed products over an extended period of time.

Coarse sugar: Coarse sugar is usually processed from the purest sugar liquor and has larger crystals than regular sugar. It is highly resistant to color change or inversion (the natural breakdown of sucrose to fructose and glucose) at high temperatures. It is also known as crystal sugar and is used to decorate sweet breads and other baked goods.

Sanding sugar: This coarse-grained sugar is used primarily to decorate baked goods. The large crystals reflect light beautifully and create a sparkling appearance.

Brown Sugar

Brown sugar is granulated white sugar that has been combined with molasses to achieve a rich, dark flavor and light texture. It is most commonly marketed as light or dark. Brown sugar is also available in both dry granular and liquid forms. Its rich flavor adds depth to any product.

Brown sugar (light or dark): Because it contains more moisture than granulated sugar, brown sugar tends to clump and harden when exposed to air. Light brown sugar has a more delicate molasses flavor; dark brown has a deeper brown color and a stronger molasses flavor.

Muscovado or Barbados sugar: A British specialty, this unrefined sugar is a very dark brown and has a strong molasses flavor that comes from the sugar cane juice from which it is made. Also known as

moist sugar, its coarse crystals are stickier than American brown sugars.

Free-flowing brown sugar: Less moist than regular brown sugar, this finely powdered specialty sugar is produced by a co-crystallization process, which prevents it from clumping and allows it to be poured like granulated sugar.

Turbinado sugar: A less refined granulated white sugar that holds a small amount of molasses both inside and on the surface of the individual crystal. It is coarser than granulated sugar, light brown in color, and carries a delicate molasses flavor.

Demerara sugar: This specialty raw cane sugar is very popular in the United Kingdom. Native to the Demerara region of Guyana, it is light brown in color with large, slightly sticky, golden crystals. It is most commonly used to sweeten drinks or cereals.

The Roles of Sugar in Bread Baking

Although sugar has been an important commodity worldwide for centuries, its chemical and biochemical properties have only been explored over the past 150 years. Up to this point, cooks could only guess why sweetened, preserved fruits, jams, and jellies did not spoil or why cakes were moist and light of crumb when sugar and fat were creamed together. Guessing, however, does not work in a bakery, be it home or professional. Since sugar is an integral part of some bread recipes, it is extremely important to know the role it plays.

The following list is a brief introduction to sugar's functions beyond those of sweetener and flavor-enhancer:

- Incorporates air into fat in the creaming process of a batter or dough

- Nourishes yeast to speed its growth in a mix, or in large percentages, it inhibits yeast activity

- Acts as a tenderizer by absorbing liquid and arresting the development of flour gluten.

- Collaborates with the protein and starch molecules during cooking and baking

- Keeps starch gelatinization in check

- Caramelizes the surface of cooked or baked goods and imparts a golden color and an inviting aroma

Although myriad sweeteners can be used in various types of bread baking, most bread recipes that call for sugar do so because of its ability to enhance the product's sweetness profile, flavor, color, and texture; to add tenderness and evenness of grain; or to help retain moisture and extend its period of freshness. In addition, when used in combination with yeast, sugar will assist in fermentation.

Gluten Development

Flour proteins are surrounded by water (hydrated) during the mixing of doughs and batters, thereby forming gluten strands. Gases that are formed during leavening are trapped by the thousands of small, balloonlike pockets that gluten forms. These gluten strands are highly elastic and allow the mixture to stretch as the trapped gases expand. When too much gluten develops, the mixture becomes tough. Sugar performs the extremely important role of tenderizing agent during the mixing process by attracting liquid, which in turn slows gluten development.

During mixing, sugar challenges the gluten-forming proteins for the liquid in the mix. When the amount of sugar called for in a specific recipe is used in correct proportion to the other ingredients, however, the gluten will be kept at its maximum elasticity, which in turn keeps the yeast-formed gases within the interior grid of the dough. Because the gases are trapped, the mixture will rise and expand. By preventing gluten development, sugar also allows the final baked product to achieve the correct texture, a tender crumb, and expanded volume and height. When a recipe calls for a large percentage of sugar, the sugar is usually added later in the mixing process so it will not interfere with gluten development.

Fermentation

Sugar provides an instant, usable source of nourishment for yeast that increases its effectiveness as a leavening agent. Given the correct temperature and moisture conditions, yeast cells break down the sugar, releasing carbon dioxide gas at a greater rate than would occur if only the carbohydrates in flour were available to feed the yeast. Thus, the dough will rise quickly and consistently.

Creaming

When mixing sugar and solid fat together, the sugar crystals are distributed throughout the fat molecules. As mixing incorporates the sugar into the fat, air becomes trapped on the sugar crystals' irregular surfaces and creates small air cells throughout the mixture. During baking, the tiny air cells expand as they are filled with carbon dioxide, resulting in a light, airy finished product. The creaming process is never used in yeast-raised products.

Egg Protein Coagulation

Egg proteins coagulate to form bonds with each other as the temperature rises during baking. When a bread dough is lacking in fat, the sugar molecules will scatter throughout the egg proteins and slow down their coagulation during baking. By surrounding the egg proteins and interfering with their ability to form bonds, sugar increases the temperature at which egg proteins coagulate. As a result, a rich bread dough contains both eggs and fat to allow it to set, or form its desirable, solid, screenlike texture at a temperature that doesn't cause the crust to brown too quickly.

Gelatinization

The heat used during baking causes the flour starches to absorb liquid and swell. This process is called gelatinization. Sugar slows gelatinization by sparring with the starch for the liquid. This delay allows the sugar to tenderize the finished product and, in the case of cakes, results in excellent texture and the desired volume. It is unclear if this same effect occurs when making breads, but it is assumed that sugar's influence on gelatinization is similar in breads with a high sugar content, resulting in a tender texture and fine crumb.

Caramelization

Melted granulated sugar oxidizes, turns amber colored, and exudes an inviting aroma and flavor when it reaches about 347°F (175°C). This breakdown of sugar is known as caramelization. In bread doughs containing sugar, this degree of heat will lead to surface caramelization, giving the bread a golden brown crust, a barrier that allows the finished loaf to retain moisture. Caramelization can take place on the stovetop, in the oven, or on the grill, as all types of heat are capable of producing the surface browning that results in an inviting odor, a beautiful golden color, a wonderful flavor, and a slightly crispy exterior.

Maillard Reaction

The Maillard reaction is a heat-induced chemical reaction that occurs between sugar and amino acids which are found in proteins. In baked goods, the sugar reacts with proteins in the heat of the oven to contribute their golden-brown exterior. The greater the sugar content of a mix, the deeper the resulting brown color. In addition, the crisp exterior helps the bread retain its moisture. The Maillard reaction also contributes to the wonderful, inviting aromas that emanate from baking breads, cakes, and cookies.

Dairy Products

In bread baking, milk and butter are the most frequently used dairy products. Among other roles, the fat in milk and cream offers richness, creaminess, and deep flavor, while acidic products such as buttermilk contribute depth of flavor as well as help activate the leavening in some breads. The sugars (lactose) in dairy products feed the yeast in doughs and assist in browning during baking as well. Depending on how they are used, butter and other shortenings, such as vegetable shortening or vegetable oils, act as lubricants for the cell expansion of the dough and contribute to a finer crumb structure, smoother texture, and greater volume in the baked product.

Milk

Although there are many different types of animal milk available, cow's milk is, by far, the most popular and readily available. Goat and sheep milk are sometimes available in specialty and health food stores; they are rarely seen in supermarkets. The milk of llamas, reindeer, camels, and water buffalo is widely used in other parts of the world for both drinking and cheese making. No matter which animal it comes from, milk is high in nutrients and contains protein, calcium, phosphorus, vitamins A and D, lactose (milk sugar), and riboflavin. It is also high in sodium. Unless purchased directly from a farm, almost all milk sold commercially has been pasteurized to destroy the microorganisms that can cause disease and speed spoilage. To ensure a uniform liquidity, most commercial milk products have also been homogenized, or emulsified, to prevent the fats from separating from the liquid.

Cow's milk is available in a number of forms.

Raw milk: Generally available only through licensed raw milk distributors in health food stores or directly from a dairy, raw milk is, pure and simple, milk that goes directly from the cow through a rapid cooling system, which lowers the temperature to 36°F to 38°F (2°C–3°C), and is then bottled. There is no pasteurization or homogenization or addition of vitamins or minerals. Because it has not been pasteurized, it is not recommended for use in the commercial kitchen.

Whole milk: Containing about 3½ percent butterfat by weight, whole milk is the most full-flavored milk product. Because it is produced commercially, whole milk will have been pasteurized and will have vitamins A and D added to it, but otherwise this is milk just as it comes from the cow.

Lowfat milk: As its name indicates, this is milk from which almost all of the fat has been removed. Generally, it is sold as 2 percent butterfat by weight, meaning 98 percent of the fat has been removed, or 1 percent butterfat by weight, indicating that 99 percent of the fat has been removed.

Nonfat or skim milk: These are milks that contain less than ½ percent butterfat by weight. Since nonfat milk is usually quite pale and liquidy, it is sometimes fortified with protein to add body, richness, and flavor.

Buttermilk: This is, technically, the liquid remaining when cream has been churned into butter. However, commercial buttermilk is in fact pasteurized skim milk that has been thickened and altered with a bacterial culture to replicate traditional buttermilk. The bacterial culture transforms the milk sugar into lactic acid to simulate the slightly sour flavor of natural buttermilk. Cultured buttermilk tends to be thicker with a more pronounced tartness; natural buttermilk has a slightly thinner consis-

tency and are a milder sour flavor. Buttermilk's acidity hinders bacterial growth, which in turn adds to its ability to withstand prolonged refrigeration. Buttermilk is also available in a dry, powdered form.

Ultra-pasteurized milk: This is milk that has been rapidly brought to 300°F (149°C) and then vacuum packed to allow for long-term storage without refrigeration. Although the heat destroys any microorganisms that would precipitate spoilage, it also gives the milk a rather flat, cooked taste. Once the vacuum seal is broken on ultra-pasteurized milk, it must be refrigerated and handled the same as any other milk.

Milk By-products and Replacements

In commercial bread making, milk solids and milk replacements such as soy/whey blends and sweet whey are the most frequently used milk by-products.

Milk solids (whole or nonfat): Packaged, highly nutritious milk solids are milk with all (or almost all) of its moisture removed and are used extensively in commercial bread making. Nonfat dry milk (NFDM) contains 36 percent protein and 51 percent carbohydrates (in the form of lactose) and minerals (such as calcium). Milk solids are used both for their nutritional content and their ability to heighten crust color. This is due, to a great extent, to the browning reaction of the protein and to the caramelization of the lactose that has not been fermented by yeast. The proteins and calcium also have a strengthening effect on the gluten. Using milk solids also seems to have a buffering effect on pH. This buffering effect helps retard fermentation; however, milk solid levels of less than 3 percent in a formula will have little effect on the final flavor of the baked bread. Milk solids for yeast doughs must be high heat treated to denature the serum protein, which exerts a weakening effect on the gluten in the dough. In breads, the use of milk solids will range from 0 to 8.2 percent. Whole milk solids must be refrigerated; nonfat dry milk is shelf stable. Recently, the popularity of nonfat dry milk has decreased due to an increase in cost,

and it has been replaced by soy/whey blends, milk substitutes, and sweet whey, with an average usage of about 2 percent in any given formula.

Soy/whey blends: These milk replacers are comprised of a blend of soy flour (because of its protein content) and whey (because of its sugar content). This combination offers many milklike characteristics in both the dough and the finished product. Soy/whey blends are substantially cheaper than nonfat dry milk and can replace nonfat dry milk pound for pound. Used in both retail and large-scale wholesale bakeries, soy/whey blends average 1 to 4 percent of any given formula.

Whey: Water solubles remaining after processing milk for cheese making are called whey. Dried at the dairy source, the resulting whey powder is easily handled in the bakery. Composed of about 11 percent protein and 74 percent sugar, powdered sweet whey heightens the crust color in baked products. It is often used as a replacement for nonfat dry milk, but absorption and fermentation are affected by whey's low protein content—only about one-third that of nonfat dry milk—so adjustments should be made accordingly. The use of whey also impacts the taste of the finished product, so it is generally used only when necessary to lower ingredient cost. Average usage in a formula ranges from 1 to 4 percent in commercially made breads and buns.

Cream

Left to its own devices, milk straight from the cow will separate into layers—a bottom layer of almost fat-free liquid and a top layer of almost solid milk fat–rich cream. Cream is no more than the rich, fatty part of whole milk. Since straight-from-the-cow cream is rarely available, we are most familiar with commercially prepared creams that have been separated from the milk by centrifugal force. There are a number of different types of cream on the market.

Heavy (or heavy whipping) cream: This is the richest, highest-quality commercial cream, with 36 to 40 percent milk fat. As heavy cream will double in volume when whipped, it is used primarily to make whipped cream. Unlike the more widely available ultra-pasteurized whipping cream, heavy cream is generally found only in fine grocery or specialty food stores or dairies.

Ultra-pasteurized cream: Also called whipping cream, this is cream that has been quickly heated to 300°F (149°C) to increase its shelf life by destroying any microorganisms that would create spoilage. It is not as clean-flavored nor does it whip as easily as heavy cream.

Light whipping cream: A less rich, lower-fat cream, light whipping cream has only 30 to 36 percent milk fat. It may also have added emulsifiers and stabilizers to assist in its whipping capabilities.

Light (table or coffee) cream: Somewhat lighter than light whipping cream, light cream most frequently contains about 20 percent milk fat, although it can have up to 30 percent. It is, as its alternative names indicate, most often used to lighten and cool hot beverages.

Half-and-half: Just as its name indicates, this is a mixture of equal parts whole milk and cream with 10 to 12 percent milk fat, though a nonfat variety is also available. It is most often used in beverages and cannot be whipped.

Butter

Most butter used in America today comes from cow's milk, although it can be made from the milk of almost any milk-producing animal. In other parts of the world, butter is made from the milk of horses, goats, sheep, and camels. Traditionally, butter was created by churning cream by hand in a butter churn to solidify the milk fat to a spreadable consistency. In contemporary commercial butter making, the process remains almost the same, but all of the elements of it have been mechanized.

Commercially produced butter is, by governmental dictate, no less than 82.5 percent butterfat and no more than 16 percent water. It may or may not have added salt, color, and vitamins and minerals. Today's specialty food markets now feature many artisanal or imported butters that replicate the old-fashioned hand-churned texture and flavor. These very high-fat (85 percent or more) butters are often referred to as European style and are substantially more expensive than the supermarket varieties. In bread baking, butter not only offers wonderful flavor to rich doughs, but also emits enticing aromas when heated.

Unsalted (or sweet) butter is pure, unflavored butter that is made from pasteurized fresh cream. It is almost always the butter of choice in making rich doughs and sweet breads. Salted butter is butter to which either fine salt or brine has been added during the churning process. The addition of salt not only flavors the butter, but also acts as a preservative. It can be used in baking if the recipe also contains salt, but to do so, decrease the amount of salt in the recipe by 1 teaspoon of salt per stick of salted butter.

All butter is highly perishable and must be kept refrigerated, though it can be frozen for longer storage. There are other butters made from nuts and cheeses, but they cannot be substituted for dairy butter.

Cheese and Other Cultured Dairy Products

Cheeses are categorized in two very broad groupings: fresh and ripened. Within each group there are a multitude of subdivisions that classify a specific cheese by texture, terroir (place of origin), mechanics of its manufacture, and ripening process, among other delineations. In addition, a classification may be altered by the aging process because a young, unripened cheese is entirely different from the same cheese that is fully matured.

Almost all cheese is created by allowing milk (usually from cows, sheep, or goats) to thicken until it separates into whey (liquid) and curds (semi-solids). Often rennin, an enzyme that coagulates milk, or other enzymes or special bacteria are added to speed the thickening. Once separated, the liquid is drained and the curds are either allowed to drain completely or pressed into a shape, depending on the type of cheese being made. At this point, the cheese may be consumed as unripened or fresh cheese. Some familiar fresh cheeses are cottage cheese, cream cheese, farmers cheese, and ricotta.

In making a ripened or aged cheese, the curds are treated by heat, bacteria, marinating, soaking, or other processes that result in curing. The specific requirements of some aged cheeses also call for the addition of herbs, spices, salt, or dyes, as well as coating with other ingredients such as ash, herbs, or leaves. Once cured, cheese must be ripened (usually uncovered) in temperature- and humidity-controlled storage that will guarantee the appropriate conditions for the desired texture and flavor of cheese that is being produced. Ripened cheeses are then classified according to their texture.

The most commonly used cheeses in artisanal bread making are Parmigiano-Reggiano, Pecorino Romano, or dry Monterey Jack; the Italian *pasta filata* (spun paste) cheeses mozzarella and provolone; and the soft whey cheese ricotta, all of which can be used for flavoring or, as is the case with the harder cheeses, for dusting rustic breads and pizzas.

Other Ingredients

In addition to flour, yeast, salt, water, eggs, sugar, and dairy products, bread made by artisanal bread bakers may also include added vitamins and minerals, malt, and mold inhibitors.

Enrichments

During milling, wheat loses some of its vitamins and minerals. These may be replaced or supplemented by the miller or the baker. In the United States, the Food and Drug Administration has set guidelines for supplementation levels of enrichments that can be added to bread to ensure proper nutrition. The following vitamins and minerals may be supplemented up to the amounts specified:

Iron at 12.5 milligrams per pound of bread
Riboflavin at 1.1 milligrams per pound of bread
Niacin at 15.0 milligrams per pound of bread

Thiamine at 1.8 milligrams per pound of bread
Calcium at 600 milligrams per pound of bread

Malt

Malt is produced by germinating barley, wheat, or another cereal grain, stopping its growth, and then extracting the enzymes (amylases and proteases) produced during the germination process. In bread making, the amylases are the most important because of their ability to break down starches into sugars, which, in turn, can be used as food by the yeast cells. Today, most flours are malted at the mill, but the baker can still add malt in either syrup or powder form. The syrup has about 60 percent maltose sugars and is used at a level of 1 to 2 percent in a formula; the powder, which is used in much smaller quantities than the syrup, has no sugars.

Malt is classified as diastatic or non-diastatic. **Diastatic malt** has active amylase enzymes that will convert damaged starch into fermentable sugar and is used to provide additional food for the yeast, improve dough handling, boost crust and crumb color, and lengthen the shelf life of the bread. Excess diastatic malt will result in a gummy crumb and weaker side walls in the finished product. **Non-diastatic malt** has been heat-treated to denature the enzymes. It is an amber-colored syrup containing about 60 percent maltose sugars. The sugars aid in the fermentation of dough, contribute to a richer flavor and crust, and heighten the color of the finished product.

Mold Inhibitors

These compounds either kill or slow the growth of common bread molds and bacteria. The most commonly used mold inhibitors and directions for usage are as follows:

Calcium and sodium propionate: add to bread dough at a level of .1 to .35 percent

Potassium sorbate: spray the bread dough with a solution of one part potassium sorbate to 9 parts water

Vinegar: add 100 or 200 grain vinegar to bread dough at a level of .5 to 1 percent

Raisin juice concentrate or crushed raisins: based on individual recipe requirements

Sourdough: based on individual recipe requirements

It is essential that the novice baker learn the following techniques and terms, as they will be used over and over throughout this book, as well as in any professional bakery.

Amylase: A natural enzyme that speeds the transformation of starch into sugar; used in some French bakeries in a product called *levit* as a food for yeast.

Ash content: The mineral content of any flour, usually around .5 to .6 percent. The higher the ash content, the grayer the crumb will be.

Aspect: The final, overall look, texture, aroma, and crumb of a baked loaf of bread.

Autolyse: This is the resting period after the first stage of mixing flour and water together at low speed. The dough is allowed to rest for a designated period of time, usually no more than 30 minutes. This allows the flour to hydrate to its maximum, the gluten to develop, and the enzymes to organize the gluten structure as the dough rests. No other ingredients are added during this preliminary stage; yeast would acidify the dough and salt would tighten it. Although it is an additional step in the process, it reduces mixing times, improves the handling ability of the dough, and boosts the quality of the finished product by reducing oxidation of the carotenoid pigments in the flour.

Bench rest: The period, usually from 5 to 20 minutes, whereby scaled, shaped pieces of dough are set aside to rest and allow the gluten to relax before further shaping is attempted. Because the relaxed gluten is not re-sistant, benching allows smaller pieces to be stretched and formed into more defined finished shapes.

Biga: A pre-ferment used in making Italian breads. With a hydration of 50 to 100 percent, a biga is usually denser than a French poolish or a sourdough. It creates a bread that has an open crumb with a slightly nutty flavor.

Bloom: This describes the overall external look of a baked loaf of bread, including its color and the completion of properly opened slashes or cuts.

Boulanger: French for baker of bread, it also means to shape dough into a *boule* or round loaf. This is the word from which the French word for bakery, *boulangerie*, was derived.

Boulangerie: French for bakery or bake shop.

Build: To create a *levain* large enough to be used in the final dough; synonymous with the term *elaborate*.

Chef: Another term used to describe a wild yeast starter. It is also known as the mother culture or simply as "mother."

Couche: A sheet of natural, untreated fabric, often linen, used to hold and separate loaves while they are rising.

A piece of clean white cotton duck or a plain white linen kitchen towel can also be used for this purpose.

Coups de lame (knife cuts): Incisions made on the surface of the bread dough just before it is placed in the oven.

Crumb: The interior texture of a baked bread, which includes its hole structure, the gelatinization of the starch, and the flavor.

Desired dough temperature: Since yeast activity is affected by even the smallest change in temperature, when dough does not ferment at the proper rate, both the final product and the production schedule will be adversely impacted. Desired dough temperature (DDT) is the ideal temperature at which bread dough should ferment. A dough that is too cool will ferment too slowly while a dough that is too warm will ferment too quickly; neither one is desirable. Because it is virtually impossible for a baker to control the temperature of the kitchen, the ingredients, or the friction (heat) caused by the electric mixer, water is used to adjust the dough to the desired temperature. Therefore, it is essential for a baker to understand the formula to find the correct water temperature for any dough. The formula is as follows:

Number of known temperatures x DDT = Total Temperature Factor (TTF)

TTF – known temperatures = water temperature

Three temperatures can be taken using a thermometer—flour, room, and pre-ferment. Unfortunately, the friction factor can be learned only through experience.

Here is an example: When making a baguette with a pre-ferment, the number of known temperatures is four: flour, room, pre-ferment, and friction. If the desired dough temperature is 75°F (25°C), then the first part of the equation is:

Number of known temperatures x DDT = TTF or 4 x 75 = 300

Imagine that this baguette is being made during the hottest part of the summer. Consequently, the flour is quite warm (80°F / 27°C) as is the kitchen (82°F / 28°C). The pre-ferment was refrigerated and is 45°F (7°C). The friction temperature is 26°F (-3°C). So, the second part of the equation is:

TTF – known temperatures = water temperature
300 – 80 – 82 – 45 – 26 = 67

The water temperature should be 67°F (19°C)

Direct method: A method in which dough is made in one step with no pre-ferment. All ingredients, including the yeast, are added at one time and mixed together until the dough has reached the desired state of readiness. Dough made using this method is called straight dough.

Dock: Occasionally used to describe the process of scoring the top of a loaf ready to be baked, but usually used to describe pricking holes in a pastry dough to prevent bubbling.

Folding dough

Double hydration: A process whereby the flour and other ingredients are first mixed with just enough water to bring the dough into the bounds of usual hydration (between 65 and 75 percent). Once the gluten in the dough has been cultivated, the remaining water is drizzled in and kneading is continued until the second addition of water is completely incorporated. This is also known as the *doppio impasto* method or, in French, as *bassinage*.

Ears: The result of scoring the top of a loaf, which, when baked, produces lifted pieces of crisp crust that resemble ears and give an inviting appearance to the surface.

Elaborate: To turn a starter into a dough; synonymous with build.

Elasticity: A dough's ability to be stretched and formed into specific shapes.

Enriched dough: A bread dough, often referred to as a rich dough, that contains enhancements such as eggs, butter, sugar, or cream.

Extensibility: A dough's ability to expand during fermentation as well as to be stretched and hold its shape without springing back or ripping.

Fermentation: The organic chemical activity whereby yeast changes sugar to carbon dioxide. Fermentation, also known as the first rise or primary or bulk fermentation, is the stage when the dough is still dealt with in one piece before being divided and shaped. It is also during this first stage that most of the desired flavor will develop and, of course, that the dough's appearance will change dramatically as it rises. Low temperature creates a long, slow fermentation and a complex bread, while a high temperature will cause quick

Proofing

fermentation and, frequently, an unpleasant odor and flavor. It is, in fact, the baker's ability to elicit proper fermentation that translates to exemplary breads.

Fermentation tolerance: A dough's ability to withstand variations of timing and temperature during fermentation.

Fold: To turn a dough onto itself in order to strengthen its gluten structure, even out its temperature, redistribute the yeast to give it access to new food (sugars), and aid in slowing down fermentation by releasing carbon dioxide from the dough. In home bread baking, this is also known as a turn or a punch.

Gelatinization: The term used to describe the full hydration of bread dough starches. At an internal temperature of 180°F to 185°F (82°C–85°C), a dough will be considered gelatinized.

Hearth: A type of oven in which bread can be baked, usually called a deck oven in a commercial bakery.

Hydration: The process whereby water is absorbed by the other ingredients. This also refers to the percentage of liquid in a dough, for example, a hydration of 70 percent.

Indirect method: A method in which dough is made in stages, beginning with a pre-ferment, rather than in a single phase.

Intermediate starter: A pre-ferment, usually a *levain*, that is used to add more-intense flavor and defined structure to a bread dough.

Kneading: The method by which all yeast-based doughs are mixed, either by hand or machine, to turn a basic

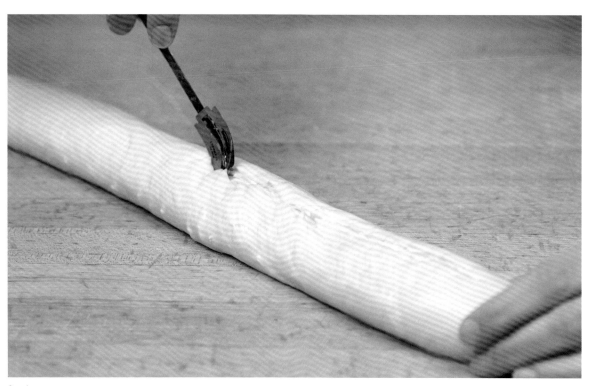
Scoring

mix into a soft, pliable mass of dough. For the most part, all kneading done in commercial bakeries is done by machine and, at home, the process can be replicated to a degree using a heavy-duty electric stand mixer fitted with the dough hook. Commercial mixers designed especially for bread making knead dough in a way that mimics hand-kneading and, as such, do not overheat or overwork the dough or significantly tear the gluten. To test for proper gluten development in a dough, perform a windowpane test (see page 64).

Levain: A traditional French leavening or pre-ferment that is made using a sourdough starter, flour, and water. It is used to produce breads with excellent texture, fine aroma, and superb shelf life.

Old dough: A small amount of dough, also called *pâte vieille* or *pâte fermentée*, reserved from a previous batch and used to add leavening and intense flavor to a new batch.

Poolish: A traditional French pre-ferment, more wet than firm, that is made with baker's yeast, flour, and water. Poolish was first used in the mid-1800s by Polish bakers (for whom the French named it) and was brought to France in the early twentieth century.

Pre-ferment: A preparation made from a portion of the dough's ingredients that is allowed to ferment in advance and then added to the final dough (see pages 71–76).

Proofing: The final rise of the shaped bread dough, also known as the second rise. During this rise, the crumb and final texture of the bread is set. A skilled baker will have learned to determine the necessary adjustments to time and temperature during proofing to create the desired finished loaf.

Refresh: To add flour and water to a starter to keep it alive.

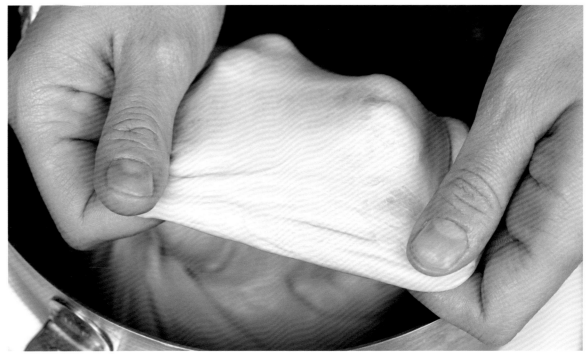

Windowpane test ("pulling a window")

Retarding: Slowing down fermentation, usually under refrigeration, thereby allowing the dough to be kept for a longer period of time, up to 18 hours, before baking.

Scaling: Dividing the dough into pieces of a specific weight to produce the particular size and shape of loaf desired. Scaling is always required in bakeries to determine the exact weight of a finished loaf or roll.

Scoring: Cutting or slashing a design in the top of a shaped piece of dough to control its expansion during baking and to create a defined look to the finished loaf. Scoring is done with a razor blade, a curved blade called a *lame*, or even a small, serrated knife, just prior to the bread being placed in the oven. The cuts or slashes should just graze the surface of the loaf (usually about ¼ inch deep) and should be done in a quick, smooth movement at about a 45-degree angle. The baked bread will then have an open cut called a *grigne*. Not all breads are scored, particularly those that are enriched with butter and eggs.

Sourdough: A dough, usually made with a *levain*, that results in a bread with an intense, slightly sour taste.

Sponge: Any one of a number of different pre-ferments used to enhance the flavor, leavening ability, and gluten structure of a dough.

Starter: A small piece of pre-ferment (or a sponge) used to leaven a batch of dough.

Straight dough: See *Direct method*.

Windowpane test: The test, also called pulling a window, is used to determine the gluten development in a bread dough. If the dough can be stretched to an almost translucent film, it has been sufficiently kneaded. If not, the dough must be kneaded longer and the windowpane test must be redone.

Baguette and *Bâtard* Scoring

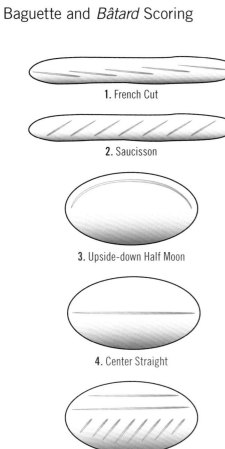

1. French Cut

2. Saucisson

3. Upside-down Half Moon

4. Center Straight

5. Modified Leaf Cut

6. Straight Saucisson

7. "S" Cut

8. Double French Cut

9. Triple French Cut

10. Leaf with Center Cut

11. Leaf Cut

12. Diamond Crosshatch

13. Diagonal Saucisson A

14. Diagonal Saucisson B

Round Scoring

1. Single Straight

6. Center Windowpane

2. Cross

7. Saucisson

3. Windowpane

8. Diamond Crosshatch

4. Leaf Cut

9. Spiral

5. Half Moon

10. Crosshatch

Mixing Styles

Mixing is generally divided into several stages or phases. The first phase is the **incorporation phase**, during which the ingredients are combined to form a homogenous mass. This is done on a low speed (first speed on a spiral mixer) to prevent any ingredient from being ejected from the mixing bowl as well as to allow the proteins in the flour to begin to absorb water, or hydrate, as the moisture is gradually distributed throughout the dough. During the incorporation phase, the baker should assess whether the dough has the proper consistency.

The next phase in mixing is the **kneading or development phase**. This is generally done on medium speed (second speed on a spiral mixer), and it is during this phase that the dough forms its gluten network. As the dough is kneaded, the gluten-forming proteins in the flour gradually align and the dough becomes stronger. This gluten structure allows the dough to expand as it rises, trapping the gas given off by the yeast fermentation. Without proper gluten development, the baked bread will be heavy and flat. During the kneading phase, the baker should assess whether the dough has developed a sufficient gluten structure.

In between the incorporation and kneading phases, there is often a rest period called **autolyse**. The flour and water are first mixed and then allowed to rest—autolyse—for 15 to 30 minutes (or occasionally longer) to allow the proteins to absorb the water and begin forming the gluten network without oxidizing the dough. Salt and yeast are added after the rest period and then the dough is mixed further. This technique decreases the time it takes to develop the gluten structure, which means less mixing is required, resulting in **less oxidation; better volume, color, taste, and aroma; and better crumb structure**. The disadvantage is that it takes additional time and planning and, for a dough that requires many added ingredients (such as butter, sugar, nuts, or fruits), the flavor benefits will not be as apparent. For these types of dough, we do not recommend an autolyse.

There are three different methods of mixing doughs, and each one must be fully understood and carefully chosen to create the correct finished product.

Mixing Styles at a Glance

Style	Technique	Dough	Product
Short (also known as traditional)	Little gluten development Sometimes done on first speed only Very little oxidation Often used in conjunction with a series of folds	Wet dough (averages 74 percent hydration or greater) Long bulk fermentation times (little yeast)	Creamy crumb color Open cell structure Less volume Excellent flavor **Ciabatta, miche, rustic baguettes**
Intensive	Full gluten development A lot of oxidation	Stiff dough (averages 62 percent hydration or less) "No-time" dough or short bulk fermentation time (a lot of yeast)	White crumb color Tight, fine crumb structure Greater volume Poor flavor **White pan loaves, bagels, pretzels, commercial breads**
Improved	Moderate gluten development Minimum oxidation Typically used in conjunction with one fold Often includes autolyse	Medium-hydration dough (65 to 72 percent hydration) Medium bulk fermentation time (typically 1½ to 2 hours)	Creamy crumb color Open cell structure Good volume Good flavor **Baguettes, levain breads**

Short mix: Used for *ciabatta*, *miche*, and rustic baguettes, among others, the short or traditional mix is sometimes done on the lowest speed (first speed on a commercial mixer). It offers little gluten develop-ment, very little oxidation, and is frequently used in conjunction with a series of folds. Doughs mixed in a short-mix style require long bulk fermentation times, high hydration, and little yeast, and they produce a wet dough averaging 74 percent hydration or greater. The end product has a creamy crumb color, an open cell structure, excellent flavor, and typically less volume than other breads.

Intensive mix: Used for white pan loaves, bagels, pretzels, and commercial breads, the intensive mix offers full gluten development and greater oxidation than the short mix. Doughs mixed in an intensive-mix style require short bulk fermentation, lots of yeast, and low hydration, so they can be considered "no-time" doughs. Intensive mix produces a stiff dough averaging 62 percent hydration or less. The end product has

a white crumb color, a tight or fine crumb, and greater volume than other breads, but imparts a poor flavor.

Improved mix: Used for baguettes and *levain* breads, the improved-mix technique often includes autolyse and offers moderate gluten development, minimum oxidation, and is most often used with only one fold. Doughs mixed in an improved-mix style require medium bulk fermentation. Improved mix produces a medium-hydration dough averaging 65 to 72 percent hydration. The end product has a creamy crumb color, an open cell structure, and good volume and flavor.

Shaping Styles

There are five basic styles for shaping bread dough: round, log, *bâtard*, baguette, and pan loaf. Regardless of which style is desired, a pre-shape is always done prior to the final shaping. And even if both the pre-shape and final shape are of the same style, the dough must be reshaped as directed before proofing and baking. During both pre-shaping and final shaping, the dough should be placed on a lightly floured surface; too much flour will impact both the crust and texture of the baked loaf. Before creating the final shape, the dough is always turned seam side up using a bench scraper before any actual shaping is done.

When using a *couche*-covered board, the *couche* is folded so that a double layer of cloth serves as a divider between each loaf. The *couche* layers also help hold the shape of the loaves as they proof.

Round

Log

Round: Form a scaled portion of dough into a rough ball. Place the dough on a lightly floured surface and, with the palm of your hand, push lightly to degas slightly. Then pull the two top corner pieces toward you into the center of the now slightly flattened ball. Flip the ball over and tighten it by cupping your hands together gently around the top of the dough and carefully pulling the ball toward you, working quickly and easily until you have a nice round shape that stands up well. Using a scraper, turn the round seam side down to bench rest. After it is done resting, turn the dough seam side up and repeat this same process for the final shape.

Log: Form a scaled portion of dough into an almost rectangular shape. Place the dough on a lightly floured surface with the shorter end facing you and, with the palm of your hand, push lightly to degas slightly. Pull

the bottom short side to the center, making a seam, then fold the whole piece over itself to form a neat rectangle. Flip the rectangle over and tighten it slightly by cupping your hands together around the top of the dough and gently pulling the dough toward you, working quickly and easily until you have a neat, fat, almost oval shape that stands up well. Using a scraper, turn the oval seam side down to bench rest. After it is done resting, turn the dough seam side up and repeat this same process for the final shape.

Bâtard: Form a scaled portion of dough into a rough ball. Place the dough on a lightly floured surface and, with the palm of your hand, push lightly to degas slightly. Then pull the two top corner pieces toward you into the center of the now slightly flattened ball. Flip the ball over and tighten it by cupping your hands together gently around the top of the dough and carefully pulling the ball toward you, working quickly and easily until you have a nice round shape that stands up well. Using a scraper, turn the dough seam side up to bench rest. After it is done resting, when you are ready to create the final shape, place the dough on a lightly floured surface and, with the palm of your hand, push lightly to degas slightly. Flatten the dough into a rectangle, then fold the top third into the center, making a seam. Fold the dough again to bring it to the bottom edge, sealing the seam with the heel of your hand. Take the top two corners and fold them into the center by about 1 inch. If you are right handed (or reverse if you are left handed), place your left thumb on the center seam and fold the dough over your thumb, using your fingers to push the dough up and over your thumb, moving down the length of the dough. Use the heel of your hand to seal the dough closed at the seam that is at the bottom edge. Then fold the top over to the bottom edge and lightly seal the seam closed with the heel of your hand. Tighten the loaf slightly by cupping your hands together around the top of the dough and gently pulling the dough toward you, working quickly and easily until you have a fat log shape with tapered ends that stands up well.

Bâtard

Baguette: Form a scaled portion of dough into an almost rectangular shape. Place the dough on a lightly floured surface with the shorter end facing you and, with the palm of your hand, push lightly to degas slightly. Pull the top short side into the center, making a seam, then fold the whole piece over itself to form a neat rectangle. Flip the rectangle over and tighten it slightly by cupping your hands together around the top of the dough and gently pulling the dough toward you, working quickly and easily until you have a neat, fat, almost oval shape that stands up well. Set the oval seam side down to bench rest. After it is done resting, using a bench scraper, lift the dough on the long side and turn so that the long side is facing you and push lightly to degas slightly. Fold the top third down into the center and seal the seam with the heel of your hand. Turn the dough around and repeat the process. There should now be a little groove where the seam has formed. If you are right handed (or reverse

Baguette

if you are left handed), place your left thumb on the center seam and fold the dough over your thumb, using your fingers to push the dough up and over your thumb, moving down the length of the dough. Use the heel of your hand to seal the dough closed at the seam. Repeat this process twice, with the final fold being exactly in half. Place your hands one on top of the other and using just a little pressure, begin rolling the dough from the center out (a 350-gram / 12½-ounce piece of dough should roll out to about 23 inches long). To achieve the tapered ends needed for a baguette, apply more pressure at both ends while rolling. This same process is used to make the strands for Challah (see pages 225–27), Sourdough Bagels (see pages 247–48), and Pretzels (see pages 251–52).

Pan loaf: Form a scaled portion of dough into a rough ball. Place the dough on a lightly floured surface and, with the palm of your hand, push lightly to degas slightly. Then pull the two top corner pieces toward you into the center of the now slightly flattened ball. Flip the ball over and tighten it by cupping your hands together gently around the top of the dough and carefully pulling the ball toward you, working quickly and easily until you have a nice round shape that stands up well. Set the round seam side down to bench rest. After it is done resting, when you are ready to create the final shape, using a scraper, turn the dough seam side up onto a lightly floured surface. Gently stretch both ends of the dough to form a rectangle and push lightly to degas. Working from the bottom up with the long side facing you, fold the bottom to the center and seal the seam with the heel of your hand. Then fold the top into the center and seal. If you are right handed (or reverse if you are left handed), place your left thumb on the center seam and fold the dough over your thumb, using your fingers to push the dough up and over your thumb, moving down the length of the dough. Use the heel of your hand to seal the dough closed at the seam that is at the bottom edge. Then fold the top over to the bottom edge and lightly seal the seam closed with the heel of your hand. Using a scraper, transfer the dough, seam side down, to a prepared loaf pan.

Pan loaf

Proofing

With the exception of enriched doughs, such as *Pain Brioche* (pages 115–17), *Kugelhopf* (pages 241–43), and Challah (pages 225–27), there will not be an enormous increase in volume during the final proofing of most bread doughs. This is contrary to what home bakers often use as a measurement—let rise until doubled in volume—and makes it difficult to explain the point at which the dough is sufficiently risen. At The French Culinary Institute, bakers are taught to press gently on the dough with a fingertip to make a little indentation, then to watch how fast the dough springs back to its original position. If it quickly pops back, the dough is not ready to be baked; if it gradually (over a few seconds) returns, then it is ready to go into the oven. If the dough does not spring back at all, it is overproofed and should go into the oven as quickly as possible.

Enriched doughs may almost double in volume during proofing and, when gently pressed, they will be light and springy and yield with just a little resistance. You should sense a great amount of carbon dioxide at work in enriched doughs; most lean doughs will show minimal volume change, if any at all, during the final proof.

Baking

One of the most important elements in baking fine artisanal breads is steam. It is used to moisten the surface of the dough just as the bread enters the hot oven so that the bread can expand fully as it bakes. Steam is effective only during the first 2 to 3 minutes of the bake, so the oven must be filled with steam the moment the bread is placed in the oven. One of the difficulties that home bakers face when attempting to make artisanal breads is the lack of an oven that produces steam. We have devised a method for creating steam in a home oven that we feel does a good job of replicating the work of the excellent commercial bread ovens used at The French Culinary Institute.

To create an excellent steam source in a home gas oven, place a large heavy-duty pan directly on the bottom of the oven—not on a rack—1 hour before you are ready to bake. A cast-iron or heavy-duty stainless steel roasting pan is an excellent choice, although stainless steel will warp in high heat so it is a good idea to have a pan dedicated to this use. The steam pan can be heated at the same time the baking stones or tiles are being heated. A second before the bread is to be placed into the oven, place 1 cup of ice into the blazing hot pan. As the steam rises, place the bread in the oven and quickly close the door. The melting cup of ice should generate an adequate amount of steam to moisten the dough. This cannot be done in an electric oven!

The use of baking stones or tiles will offer a close facsimile to an artisanal bread or masonry oven. They can be purchased from kitchen supply stores or you can simply use unglazed ceramic tiles. For optimal baking power, stones or tiles should always be preheated for about an hour in a very hot oven before being used. Since the stones hold heat, they should be used even when bread is baked in pans.

At The French Culinary Institute, we prepare our baguettes using *couche*; for ease of preparation in the home kitchen, we recommend the use of baguette pans. These are usually made of steel and can hold a single loaf or up to three loaves. They are available from bakery and kitchen supply stores.

Session 5

Pre-ferments

A pre-ferment is a preparation made from a portion of the dough's ingredients that is allowed to ferment in advance and is then added to the final dough. The water used to make a pre-ferment is generally cool, that is, about 70°F (20°C). However, no two pre-ferments are alike. Some are loose and runny, some stiff, some salty, some unsalted, some made with commercial yeast, others from natural wild yeasts, and some are simply a small percentage of a mixed bread dough. Because pre-ferments vary dramatically, they can present quite a challenge for the baker, who otherwise requires such precision in all things.

For instance, the flour portion in a pre-ferment can be anywhere from 5 to 75 percent (or higher) of the total flour in a formula. The amount of flour in a pre-ferment will affect both the process and the finished product. The flour can also be fermented by a commercial yeast or a natural (sourdough) starter; both will have an impact on the flavor of the finished product. The pre-ferment can be made anywhere from 10 minutes (in the case of a quick sponge for a sweet dough) to 18 hours in advance.

With all of these variables, why do we bother to use pre-ferments at all? Although pre-ferments require both an extra step in the entire baking process and the space in which to store them, they play an extremely important role. Because of the development of acidity during the fermentation process, a pre-ferment strengthens the gluten structure of the dough and increases the shelf life of the finished product. Since pre-ferments produce organic acids and esters, they offer a finished bread with a superior taste, an inviting flavor, an enticing wheaty aroma, and improved volume and crumb structure. In addition, pre-ferments allow the baker the benefit of long fermentation times without a significant increase in production time, which in a commercial bakery results in cost savings in both labor and time.

When using a pre-ferment, the baker has to use his expertise to judge when the pre-ferment has done its job completely. The dough must have risen (usually to about double its original size) and be slightly fallen in the center, except in the case of a poolish, in which a properly fermented dough will be covered with a multitude of small air bubbles. In either case, the dough should be invitingly aromatic with a slight sweet-sour smell and taste. If the dough is heavy and flat, the pre-ferment has not yet worked, which might be due to inadequate time or too cold a temperature. When you begin with an ineffective, underdeveloped pre-ferment, the baked bread will be dense and lacking in flavor, aroma, and crumb. However, a seasoned baker can often add additional yeast and increase the bulk fermentation time to achieve the desired result.

To ensure proper development of the finished product, there are a number of things to keep in mind when using pre-ferments:

- The more flour you pre-ferment, the shorter the final process will be.

- In a dough that uses a large amount of pre-ferment, the yeast will have eaten most of the available sugar, therefore the crust will often not brown properly. In many commercial kitchens, a small amount (0.5 to 1 percent) of diastatic malt is added to the final dough to aid in the browning process.

- Dough requiring a large amount of pre-ferment, especially a stiff pre-ferment or *levain*, will sometimes become overly elastic. This is the result of excess acidity and the tightening effect it has on gluten structure.

- Whole grain flours will ferment faster than white flour. When using whole grain flour, it is advisable to add a small amount (0.1 percent) of salt to the pre-ferment to impede the yeast activity.

- When a dough uses a high proportion of rye flour, rye flour should be added to the pre-ferment to ensure proper crumb texture in the finished product. In many cases, almost all of the rye flour will be used in the pre-ferment.

- When a dough is comprised of both whole grain and white flour, it is preferable to pre-ferment the whole grain flour, as doing so results in a better flavor and gluten structure.

- If mixing a dough without an autolyse, that is, mixing "straight," the pre-ferment should go into the mix at the beginning of the process.

- When using an autolyse in the mixing process, the pre-ferment should be added to the mix after the autolyse, so that fermentation does not begin too rapidly. However, there are some cases in which the pre-ferment is required for hydration and must be added before the autolyse. This requirement is always noted in a recipe.

- It is possible to use more than one type of pre-ferment in the same dough. Some breads may have as many as four or five pre-ferments. The use of multiple pre-ferments is found more commonly in competition baking rather than in commercial production, where it would be both time- and space-consuming as well as cumbersome to manage.

Initial pre-ferment mix

Six hours into pre-ferment

Twelve hours into pre-ferment

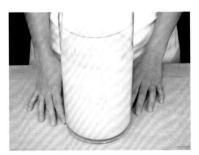

Over-fermented pre-ferment

Guide to Pre-ferments

Type	Association	Leavening	Hydration	Average Length
Poolish	Poland/France	Yeast	100%	12–16 hours
Pâte fermentée	France	Yeast	60%–75%	24 hours
Levain	France	Sourdough	50%–125%	14–16 hours
Biga	Italy	Yeast	50%–100%	12–16 hours
Rye sour	Germany	Sourdough	50%–100%	12–16 hours
Sponge	England/USA	Yeast	50%–85%	.25–16 hours

Types of Pre-ferments

At The French Culinary Institute, we categorize pre-ferments into two types: those made from commercial yeast and those made with a natural (sourdough) starter.

Pre-ferments from Commercial Yeast

The terms used in this category are commonly used in commercial baking worldwide.

Poolish: Developed in Poland in the 1840s and later adapted for use by the French and Viennese, a poolish uses equal parts water and flour (that is 100 percent flour and 100 percent water) and no salt. It can be fermented for as little as 4 hours or for long as 18 hours, depending on the amount of yeast (a small amount of yeast requires a longer period of fermentation than a large amount). Poolish is now used worldwide.

Pâte Fermentée: Also known as pre-fermented dough or "old dough," *pâte fermentée* is a piece of dough that has been allowed to ferment for at least 3 hours and is then added to the next batch of dough to create the desired flavor and texture. Because it comes from a finished dough, a *pâte fermentée* is a complete dough of flour, water, salt, and yeast.

Biga: For Italian bakers, the term *biga* is often used generically to mean pre-ferment. Almost all traditional biga pre-ferments have a hydration of 50 to 55 percent and a long (18-hour), cold (60°F / 15°C) fermentation. A biga does not contain salt.

Sponge: The term *sponge* has two meanings: a pre-ferment that has a hydration of less than 100 percent, and a pre-ferment that is used in a sweet dough. No matter the meaning, a sponge does not use salt.

Quick sponge: A type of pre-ferment that is used in doughs containing a lot of sugar. It is used to activate the yeast before the sugar is introduced, and has a short fermentation, typically about 30 minutes.

Natural or Sourdough Pre-ferments

Although they are technically not generated by the same method, the words *sourdough* and *levain* are often used interchangeably throughout the world of commercial baking. In France, the word *levain* is used to describe a natural culture that is made from white flour and water, while in Germany the word *sauerteig* (sourdough) is used to describe a natural culture composed of rye flour and water. Both are the result of naturally occurring yeasts and bacteria that are able to flavor and leaven breads.

A natural pre-ferment is a simple combination of flour and water that has been fed consistently with additional food and water, during which it develops a family of microorganisms that multiply as they ferment. While the bulk of a natural pre-ferment is used to leaven the current dough, a small amount of this uncontaminated starter is always held back to feed a new batch of pre-ferment that can be used in subsequent batches of bread dough.

Rye sourdough

In all cases, a sourdough or *levain* can remain viable for generations. There are stories of breads being made today from starters that were begun in the 1800s, particularly in Northern California, where sourdough starters of the early settlers were used to ferment the sourdough bread for which that area of the country is famous.

Stiff *levain*: A salt-free dough with a hydration that is typically about 54 percent; must be fed at least once daily.

Liquid *levain*: A salt-free dough with a hydration that is typically about 100 percent; must be fed at least once daily.

Creating a Liquid *Levain*

A liquid *levain* begins simply as a mixture of flour and water. At The French Culinary Institute, the following guidelines are used to create a liquid *levain*.

○ Wild yeast, present in the flour and in the environment, populates the mixture. It is stronger and more stable than commercial yeast, as well as more resistant to acidity. Starch in the mixture is broken down into sugar by the yeast and enzymes, resulting in alcohol and carbon dioxide, the by-products of fermentation.

Starch > fructose/dextrose + alcohol + CO_2 (carbon dioxide)

○ On the first day of starting the culture, use rye flour (the coarser the better) because rye flour contains more wild yeast. If you must use wheat flour, sift before mixing to incorporate more air.

○ On Day 2, discard one-half of the total amount of the culture. Add water and flour to the mixture to continue the process.

○ On Day 3, yeast activity begins in the culture. (One gram of flour contains 13,000 cells of wild yeast and about 320 cells of lactic bacteria.)

○ Between Days 6 and 10, depending on the environment, acidity (lactic acid) starts to develop. This acidity inhibits bad bacteria (gray molds) that may be lurking.

The French Culinary Institute liquid *levain* is kept at 125 percent hydration because that is the hydration level at which the *levain* is most easily poured and cleaned from the machinery. *Levain* can be stiffer (solid *levain*) and can also be kept at a 1:1 ratio of flour to water.

Recipe for Creating a Liquid *Levain* Culture

	Ingredient	Amount
Day 1	Coarse rye flour	100 grams / 3½ ounces
	Water (~80°F / 27°C)	125 grams / 4½ ounces
	Mix 50 strokes by wooden spoon.	
Day 2	½ culture from Day 1	115 grams / 4 ounces
	Rye flour	100 grams / 3½ ounces
	Water (~80°F / 27°C)	125 grams / 4½ ounces
Days 3 through 9*	½ culture from Day 2	115 grams / 4 ounces
	Wheat flour	100 grams / 3½ ounces
	Water (~80°F / 27°C)	125 grams / 4½ ounces

* Repeat daily until the culture is ready to use. By Day 8, the mixture should have sufficient ripeness for leavening bread. However, to continue developing strength and complexity, it may be fed for 2 or 3 more days before use.

When the culture is ready, it turns concave and has the right acidity and yeast content to leaven bread. At The French Culinary Institute, we continue to call it a culture, but in other artisanal bakeries, a mature culture becomes known as the "mother" or starter and is no longer called a culture.

Day 10 and beyond	To continue *levain* upkeep, the basic refreshment ratio is 100 percent wheat flour, 125 percent water, and 20 percent liquid *levain*. This should be added to compensate for the quantity removed (i.e., if 500 grams are removed, they should be replaced with 500 grams of refresher using the ratio above). If the *levain* is not used regularly, cover it and store in the refrigerator. It will last for several months under refrigeration.

Recipe for Feeding a Liquid *Levain*

If desired for large-scale baking, the following recipe can be doubled to yield approximately 1,000 grams of liquid *levain*. It can be stored, covered, and refrigerated for several weeks. The gray water that forms on top of the *levain* may be stirred back into it. If mold forms on a liquid *levain*, the *levain* must be discarded and made again.

Makes 500 grams / 1 pound 1½ ounces

Ingredient	Amount	Baker's Percentage
Liquid *levain* (see Note)	50 grams / 1¾ ounces	20%
Flour	240 grams / 8½ ounces	100%
Water	300 grams / 10½ ounces	125%
TOTAL	590 grams / 1 pound 4¾ ounces	245%

Note: Of the total 590 grams (1 pound 4¾ ounces) of "fed" liquid *levain*, **save at least 50 grams** (1¾ ounces) for the next baking.

Session 6

Exercises in Baker's Percentage

Baker's percentage is a method of proportioning ingredients by their total weight in relation to the weight of the flour, which is always 100 percent (as a result, the flour in combination with the remaining ingredients will amount to more than 100 percent).

For instance, if a recipe calls for 10 pounds of flour and 5 pounds of liquid, the resulting percentages will be 100 percent and 50 percent respectively. This method of measuring enables the baker quickly to recalculate a recipe, depending upon his or her needs on any given day. In addition, percentage measurements based entirely on weight ensure that the recipe is always precise, which in turn guarantees a perfect baked loaf.

The following exercises in baker's percentage will help the novice baker learn the necessary calculations to make using the system second nature.

Formula in Baker's Percentage

(You know the percentages in a formula and you want to calculate the actual ingredient weights.)

Example:

Flour	100%
Water	65%
Salt	2%
Yeast	1.5%
Total	**168.5%**

A. Beginning with the amount of flour you want to use:

Example: 50 kg or lb of flour

Example problem:

Flour	100%	50 kg or lb
Water	65%	? kg or lb
Salt	2%	? kg or lb
Yeast	1.5%	? kg or lb
Total	**168.5%**	**? kg or lb**

Calculate the other ingredients:

Water	50 x 65%	= 32.5 kg or lb
Salt	50 x 2%	= 1 kg or lb
Yeast	50 x 1.5%	= .75 kg or lb

Formula using 50 kg or lb of flour:

Flour	100%	50 kg or lb
Water	65%	32.5 kg or lb
Salt	2%	1 kg or lb
Yeast	1.5%	.75 kg or lb
Total	**168.5%**	**84.25 kg or lb**

B. Beginning with the amount of dough you want to make:

Example: 50 kg or lb of dough

Example problem:

Flour	100%	? kg or lb
Water	65%	? kg or lb
Salt	2%	? kg or lb
Yeast	1.5%	? kg or lb
Total	**168.5%**	**50 kg or lb**

Calculate the amount of flour:

100 (flour %) is to 168.5 (total %) as z (unknown) is to 50

$$\frac{100}{168.5} = \frac{z}{50}$$

50 x 100 / 168.5 = z

z = 29.7 (rounded to the nearest tenth)

Calculate the other ingredients as in A above:

Water	29.7 x 65%	= 19.3 kg or lb
Salt	29.7 x 2%	= .594 kg or lb
Yeast	29.7 x 1.5%	= .445 kg or lb

Formula to make 50 kg or lb of dough:

Flour	100%	29.7 kg or lb
Water	65%	19.3 kg or lb
Salt	2%	.594 kg or lb
Yeast	1.5%	.445 kg or lb
Total	**168.5%**	**50 kg or lb**

Formula with Actual Ingredient Weights

(You know the actual ingredient weights in a formula and you want to know the percentages.)

Example problem:

Flour	? %	75 kg or lb
Water	? %	47.25 kg or lb
Salt	? %	1.5 kg or lb
Yeast	? %	1.31 kg or lb
Total	**? %**	**125.06 kg or lb**

Flour is 100%; calculate what % of flour each ingredient is:

Water	47.25 ÷ 75	= .63 = 63%
Salt	1.5 ÷ 75	= .02 = 2%
Yeast	1.31 ÷ 75	= .0175 = 1.75%

Formula using baker's percentage:

Flour	100%	75 kg or lb
Water	63%	47.25 kg or lb
Salt	2%	1.5 kg or lb
Yeast	1.75%	1.31 kg or lb
Total	**166.75%**	**125.06 kg or lb**

Calculating Baker's Percentage from Scratch

Before calculating your formula, determine the following:

1. **T**otal **A**mount of **F**lour (weight), including the flour in the starter:_____ (**TAF**)

2. Percentage (**%**) of **W**ater in **S**tarter:_____ (**%WS**)

3. Percentage (**%**) of **F**ermented **F**lour:_____ (**%FF**)

4. Percentage (**%**) of **S**alt:_____ (**%S**)

Determining Percentage (%)

(**%F**) **Flour**:   The total percentage of flour **must always** equal 100%.

(**%W**) **Water**:   Water is determined by the baker based on flour absorption, type of dough desired (wet or dry dough), leavener used, etc. Percentages range from 55% to 75%.

(**%S**) **Salt**:   Salt is also determined by the baker. Depending on the type of dough desired, percentages range from 1.8% to 2.2%.

Example:

	Percentage **%**	**A**ctual **Q**uantity	**A**ctual **S**tarter	**F**inal **Q**uantity
F: **F**lour	%F 100%			
W: **W**ater	%W			
S: **S**alt	%S			
Starter				

Determining Final Quantity (FQ)

(FQF) Flour: Subtract Actual Flour in Starter **(AFS)** from Actual Quantity of Flour **(AQF)**.

AQF – AFS = FQF

(FQW) Water: Subtract Actual Water in Starter **(AWS)** from Actual Quantity of Water **(AWF)**.

AQW – AWS = FQW

(FQS) Salt: Carry Actual Quantity of Salt **(AQS)** over to Final Quantity of Salt **(FQS)**.

AQS = FQS

(FQST) Starter: Add Actual Flour in Starter **(AFS)** to Actual Water in Starter **(AWS)**.

AFS + AWS = Final Quantity of STarter (FQST)

Example:

	Percentage %	Actual Quantity	Actual Starter	Final Quantity
F: Flour	%F 100%			**FQF = AQF – AFS**
W: Water	%W			**FQW = AQW – AWS**
S: Salt	%S			**FQS = AQS**
Starter				**FQST = AFS – AWS**

Determining <u>A</u>ctual <u>Q</u>uantity (<u>AQ</u>)

(AQF) Flour: Take the <u>T</u>otal <u>A</u>mount of <u>F</u>lour **(TAF)** multiplied by the percentage (<u>%</u>) of <u>F</u>lour **(%F)**.
TAF x %F = AQF

(AQW) Water: Take the <u>T</u>otal <u>A</u>mount of <u>F</u>lour **(TAF)** multiplied by the percentage (<u>%</u>) of <u>W</u>ater **(%W)**.
TAF x %W = AQW

(AQS) Salt: Take the <u>T</u>otal <u>A</u>mount of <u>F</u>lour **(TAF)** multiplied by the percentage (<u>%</u>) of <u>S</u>alt **(%S)**.
TAF x %S = AQS

Example:

	Percentage <u>%</u>	<u>A</u>ctual <u>Q</u>uantity	<u>A</u>ctual <u>S</u>tarter	<u>F</u>inal <u>Q</u>uantity
F: <u>F</u>lour	%F 100%	**AQF – TAF x %F**		
W: <u>W</u>ater	%W	**AQW = TAF x %W**		
S: <u>S</u>alt	%S	**AQS = TAF x %S**		
Starter				

Determining <u>A</u>ctual <u>S</u>tarter (<u>AS</u>)

(AFS) Flour: Take the <u>T</u>otal <u>A</u>mount of <u>F</u>lour **(TAF)** multiplied by the percentage (<u>%</u>) of <u>F</u>ermented <u>F</u>lour **(%FF)**.
TAF x %FF = AFS

(AWS) Water: Take the <u>A</u>ctual <u>F</u>lour in <u>S</u>tarter **(AFS)** multiplied by the percentage (<u>%</u>) of <u>W</u>ater in <u>S</u>tarter **(%WS)**.
AFS x %WS = AWS

Example:

	Percentage <u>%</u>	<u>A</u>ctual <u>Q</u>uantity	<u>A</u>ctual <u>S</u>tarter	<u>F</u>inal <u>Q</u>uantity
F: <u>F</u>lour	%F 100%	AQF – TAF x %F	**AFS = TAF x %FF**	
W: <u>W</u>ater	%W	AQW = TAF x %W	**AWS = AFS x %WS**	
S: <u>S</u>alt	%S	AQS = TAF x %S		
Starter				

Completed Baker's Percentage Chart:

	Percentage **%**	**A**ctual **Q**uantity	**A**ctual **S**tarter	**F**inal **Q**uantity
F: **F**lour	%F 100%*	AQF – TAF x %F	AFS = TAF x %FF	FQF = AQF – AFS
W: **W**ater	%W**	AQW = TAF x %W	AWS = AFS x %WS	FQW = AQW – AWS
S: **S**alt	%S**	AQS = TAF x %S		FQS = AQS
Starter				FQST = AFS + AWS

* Flour percentage is **always** 100%.
** These numbers, determined by the baker, are based on flour absorption, type of dough desired, leavener used, etc.

Baker's Percentage Chart:

	Percentage **%**	**A**ctual **Q**uantity	**A**ctual **S**tarter	**F**inal **Q**uantity
Flour #1				
Flour #2				
Flour #3				
Water				
Salt				
Starter				
Ingredients				
Ingredients				

Total amount of flour:_____

Percentage (%) of water in starter:_____

Percentage (%) of fermented flour:_____

1.

2.

3.

4.

1. Selecting Ingredients

Even though there are only four basic ingredients—flour, salt, yeast, and water—in basic bread dough, there are many variations within those four that need to be considered. For instance, what type of flour is being used? What type of yeast—fresh, active dry, or instant dry? How coarse is the salt being used? What is the water temperature? Without answers to those questions, it will be difficult to achieve the desired result.

2. Scaling Ingredients

Accurate scaling (weighing), especially for the ratios of yeast and salt to flour, is crucial for effective fermentation. Inaccuracies will lead to less than desirable results. In bread making, all ingredients are scaled out by weight, not by volume.

3. Mixing

The mixing technique used and whether you incorporate an autolyse (a resting period during the mixing process) depends on the type of product you are making.

4. Bulk Fermentation

Bulk fermentation, the period during which the yeast produces carbon dioxide and alcohol and the dough's gluten network continues to develop, can take anywhere from 10 minutes to overnight. The amount of time will be determined by the type of product you are making and the ratios in your formula.

5.

5. Folding/Turning

Halfway through the bulk fermentation, almost all doughs are folded or turned. In home-style recipes for bread making, the process is often referred to as a punch. The fold/turn has four purposes. It strengthens the dough's structure, evens out the temperature, redistributes and feeds the yeast by giving it access to new food (sugars), and aids in slowing down fermentation and the release of carbon dioxide in the dough.

Folding is done by first picking up and stretching the top side of the dough (while it is still in the bowl) and folding it toward the center. After the bowl is spun 180°, the top side is again stretched out and folded in. After a quarter turn of the bowl, the top is once again stretched out and folded in. The bowl is turned another 180° and, for the last time, the top is stretched out and folded in. Finally, the entire piece of dough is picked up and turned upside down into the bowl.

6. Dividing

The dough is divided immediately after the bulk fermentation is complete. A bench knife is used to divide the dough and a scale is used to confirm that each piece is the correct weight according to the formula.

6.

7.

7. Pre-shaping

Pre-shaping gives the baker the opportunity to set
the structure of the final loaf and helps make the
final shaping easier (see pages 68–70). The type of
pre-shape depends on the final shape desired. Both
bâtards and *boules* start with a round pre-shape, while
a baguette is generally formed into a loglike pre-shape.
All breads benefit from pre-shaping.

8. Bench Rest/Intermediate Fermentation

After pre-shaping, bread doughs must be rested so
that the gluten network can relax before the final shape
is formed. This is called a bench rest or intermediate
fermentation and typically takes 15 to 20 minutes.
The duration of the rest depends on the condition of
the dough, the temperature and moisture levels of the
bakery, and how tightly the baker has formed the pre-
shape. A tighter pre-shape will take more time to relax
than a looser one because the gluten structure is more
elastic, and the baker will have to wait longer before
final shaping.

9. Final Shaping

The final shape of the dough is determined by the type
of finished loaf desired (see pages 68–70). In classic
French bread making there are four basic shapes: the
baguette, the *bâtard*, the *boule*, and the loaf (formed
in a loaf-shaped pan).

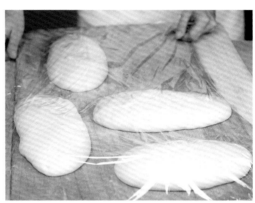

8.

9.

10. 11. 12. 13.

10. Final Fermentation/Proofing

Although the yeast in bread dough has been working throughout the bread-making process, this is the last chance it has to complete the fermentation. The final proof can last anywhere from 5 minutes to overnight, depending upon the condition of the dough, the type of loaf being made, and temperature and moisture levels in the bakery.

11. Scoring

Scoring simply means cutting marks into the top of the dough to allow the bread to expand properly during baking. Although utilitarian, the marks also give a decorative appearance to the top of the baked bread (see pages 63–65). Most breads are scored just before they are loaded into the oven.

12. Baking

Baking time is determined by the type of dough being baked. Most lean doughs (doughs without fat or sugar) are baked at around 475°F (246°C) with steam. The steam is important, as it allows the bread to spring in the oven, giving it a shiny, crisp crust. Although they are lean, artisanal breads are usually baked for a longer period of time to develop the desired thick, crisp, and flavorful crust. Doneness is determined by the amount of time baked, the color of the crust, and the hollow sound that results when you knock on the bottom of the finished loaf.

13. Cooling

Bread cut directly upon removal from the oven will have a wet, spongy crumb and a gassy flavor from the carbon dioxide still present in the loaf. Therefore, bread should be cooled completely before being served or eaten. During the cooling period, the crumb is set and excess gas and moisture dissipate.

14. Storing

The shelf life of bread depends as much on its shape and size as it does on the type of bread and the manner in which it is stored. A small loaf or a loaf with an expansive surface (such as a baguette) has a very short shelf life, a day at most. Larger loaves can last longer if stored properly. Proper storage is crucial to maintaining both the quality of a bread and the loaf's longevity. Breads that are meant to be crisp and crusty should not be stored in plastic or under refrigeration; a paper bag or a bread box is the best place to store these. Enriched bread may be stored in a resealable plastic bag, but when refrigerated these breads can become quite hard. Both lean and enriched breads usually last from 3 to 4 days at room temperature. If double-wrapped in plastic film so that it is airtight, most bread can be frozen for up to 3 months.

14.

Session 8

Classic French Breads

These are the most classic of all of the French breads. The history and lore of many of them is captured in "A Brief History of Bread" (pages 8–11), so here we proceed with those basic recipes that comprise the traditional repertoire of the esteemed French bread baker.

Bordelaise
Liquid *Levain* Baguette
Pâte Fermentée Baguette
Poolish Baguette
Pain de Mie
Petits Pains de Restaurant
Pain aux Céréales
Pain Brioche
Fougasse aux Olives
Pain au Levain, Raisins, et Noix
Pain au Fromage
Pain Normand
Pain au Citron
Pain au Lait
Pain de Mie Complet
Pain Viennois
Straight Baguette
Rye Bread (using *Pâte Fermentée*)

Demonstration

Bordelaise

Makes 1 loaf

Estimated time to complete: 21 hours
Improved mix
Desired dough temperature (DDT): 75°F (25°C)

Ingredient	Amount	Baker's Percentage
For the liquid *levain*:		
Bread flour	63 grams / 2¼ ounces	100%
Cool water	79 grams / 2¾ ounces	125%
Liquid *levain* culture (see pages 75–76)	6 grams / ¼ ounce	10%
Total	**148 grams / 5¼ ounces**	**235%**
For the final dough:		
Bread flour or all-purpose flour	334 grams / 11¾ ounces	90%
Coarse rye flour	30 grams / 1 ounce	8%
Whole wheat flour	7 grams / ¼ ounce	2%
Water	222 grams / 7¾ ounces	60%
Liquid *levain*	148 grams / 5¼ ounces	40%
Salt	9 grams / ⅓ ounce	2.4%
Total	**750 grams / 1 pound 10⅓ ounces**	**202.4%**

Oil for greasing bowl
Flour for dusting
Ice for steam

Equipment

Scale	Large cutting board
Digital thermometer	*Couche*
Large mixing bowl	Baking stone(s) or tiles
Wooden spoon	Cast-iron or stainless steel roasting pan
Bowl scraper	*Lame* or razor
Plastic film	Peel
Standing electric mixer fitted with the hook	Wire rack
Large bowl or container	

Prepare the *mise en place* for the liquid *levain*, taking care that the water is about 75°F (25°C).

To make the liquid *levain*, combine the bread flour and water with the culture in a large mixing bowl, stirring with a wooden spoon to blend. When blended, scrape down the edge of the bowl, cover with plastic film, and set aside to ferment at 70°F (20°C) for 12 to 14 hours.

When ready to make the final dough, prepare the *mise en place*.

Combine the bread, coarse rye, and whole wheat flours with the water and liquid *levain* in the bowl of a standing electric mixer fitted with the hook. Mix on low speed until blended. Stop the mixer and autolyse for 15 minutes.

Add the salt and mix on low for 5 minutes. Increase the mixer speed to medium and mix until the dough begins to pull away from the sides of the bowl, feels elastic, and gives some resistance when tugged.

Lightly oil a large bowl or container.

Scrape the dough into the prepared bowl. Cover the bowl with plastic film and set aside to ferment for 1 hour.

Uncover and fold the dough. Again, cover with plastic film and set aside to ferment for 2 hours.

Lightly flour a clean, flat work surface.

Uncover the dough and form it into a neat round on the floured surface (see page 68). Cover with plastic film and bench rest for 15 minutes.

Cover a large cutting board with a *couche* and dust the *couche* with flour.

Uncover the dough and, if necessary, lightly flour the work surface. Gently press on the dough to degas and carefully shape into a *bâtard* (see pages 68–69). Place the *bâtard* on the *couche*-covered board. Cover with plastic film and proof for 2½ to 3 hours, or until the dough has finished proofing (see page 70). (Alternatively, place the dough in the refrigerator for 12 hours and when ready to bake, transfer the loaves directly to the oven.)

About an hour before you are ready to bake the loaf, place the baking stone(s) or tiles into the oven and preheat to 470°F (243°C). If using a pan to create steam (see page 70), place it in the oven now.

Uncover the dough and, using a *lame* or a razor, immediately score the loaf as directed on pages 64–65. To make the required steam, add 1 cup of ice to the hot pan in the oven. Using a peel, immediately transfer the loaves to the hot baking stone(s) in the preheated oven.

Bake, with steam, for 45 minutes, or until the crust is a deep brown color and the sides are firm to the touch. If the crust darkens before the bread is finished baking, reduce the oven temperature to 440°F (227°C).

Remove from the oven and transfer to a wire rack to cool.

Demonstration

Liquid *Levain* Baguette

Makes 4 loaves

Estimated time to complete: 18 hours
Improved mix
Desired dough temperature (DDT): 75°F (25°C)

Ingredient	Amount	Baker's Percentage
For the liquid *levain*:		
Bread flour	33 grams / 1⅛ ounces	100%
Cool water	41 grams / 1½ ounces	125%
Liquid *levain* culture (see pages 75–76)	3 grams / ⅛ ounce	10%
Total	**77 grams / 2¾ ounces**	**235%**
For the final dough:		
Bread flour	777 grams / 1 pound 11½ ounces	90%
Water	524 grams / 1 pound 2½ ounces	60%
Salt	15 grams / ½ ounce	2.4%
Liquid *levain*	78 grams / 2¾ ounces	40%
Fresh yeast	6 grams / ¼ ounce	0.75%
Total	**1400 grams / 3 pounds 1½ ounces**	**193.15%**

Oil for greasing bowl

Flour for dusting

Ice for steam

Equipment

Scale	Large bowl or container
Digital thermometer	Baking stone(s) or tiles
Large mixing bowl	Large cast-iron or stainless steel roasting pan
Wooden spoon	4 baguette pans
Bowl scraper	*Lame* or razor
Plastic film	Wire racks
Standing electric mixer fitted with the hook	

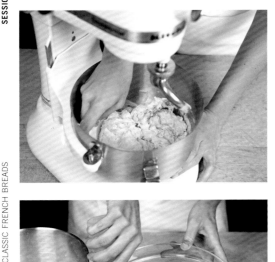
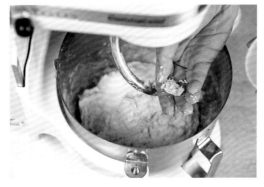

Prepare the *mise en place* for the liquid *levain*, taking care that the water is about 70°F (20°C).

To make the liquid *levain*, combine the bread flour and water with the culture in a large mixing bowl, stirring with a wooden spoon to blend. When blended, scrape down the edge of the bowl, cover with plastic film, and set aside to ferment at 70°F (20°C) for 12 to 14 hours.

When ready to make the final dough, prepare the *mise en place*.

Combine the bread flour with the water in the bowl of a standing electric mixer fitted with the hook. Mix on low speed until blended. Stop the mixer and autolyse for 15 minutes.

Add the salt along with the liquid *levain* and yeast and mix on low for 5 minutes. Increase the mixer speed to medium and mix for about 8 minutes, or until the dough has come together but remains slightly sticky.

Check the gluten development by pulling a window (see page 64).

Lightly oil a large bowl or container.

Scrape the dough into the prepared bowl. Cover the bowl with plastic film and set aside to ferment for 1 hour.

Uncover and fold the dough. Again, cover with plastic film and set aside to ferment for 1 hour.

About an hour before you are ready to bake the loaves, place the baking stone(s) or tiles into the oven and pre-heat to 470°F (243°C). If using a pan to create steam (see page 70), place it in the oven now.

Lightly flour a clean, flat work surface.

Uncover the dough and divide it into four 350-gram / 12½-ounce logs on the floured surface. Cover with

plastic film and bench rest for 15 minutes.

Uncover the dough and, if necessary, lightly flour the work surface. Gently press on the dough to degas and carefully shape each log into a baguette (see page 69). Place each baguette, seam side down, into a baguette pan. Cover with plastic film and proof for 30 minutes.

Uncover the dough and, using a *lame* or a razor, immediately score the loaves as directed on pages 64–65. To make the required steam, add 1 cup of ice to the

hot pan in the oven. Immediately transfer the bread pans to the hot baking stone(s) in the preheated oven.

Bake, with steam, for 25 minutes, or until the crust is a deep golden-brown color, the sides are firm to the touch, and the loaves make a hollow sound when tapped on the bottom.

Remove from the oven and transfer to wire racks to cool.

Demonstration

Pâte Fermentée Baguette

Makes 4 loaves

Estimated time to complete: 4½ hours
Improved mix
Desired dough temperature (DDT): 75°F (25°C)

Ingredient	Amount	Baker's Percentage
Bread flour	766 grams / 1 pound 11 ounces	100%
Water	536 grams / 1 pound 3 ounces	70%
Salt	15 grams / ½ ounce	2%
Fresh yeast	6 grams / ¼ ounce	0.75%
Pâte fermentée (see pages 111–12)	77 grams / 2¾ ounces	10%
Total	**1400 grams / 3 pounds 1½ ounces**	**182.75%**

Oil for greasing bowl
Flour for dusting
Ice for steam

Equipment

Scale	Baking stone(s) or tiles
Standing electric mixer fitted with the hook	Cast-iron or stainless steel roasting pan
Large bowl or container	4 baguette pans
Bowl scraper	*Lame* or razor
Plastic film	Wire racks

Prepare the *mise en place*.

Combine the bread flour with the water in the bowl of a standing electric mixer fitted with the hook. Mix on low speed until blended. Stop the mixer and autolyse for 15 minutes.

Add the salt along with the yeast and *pâte fermentée* and mix on low for 5 minutes. Increase the mixer speed to medium and mix for about 8 minutes, or until the dough has come together but remains slightly sticky. Check the gluten development by pulling a window (see page 64).

Lightly oil a large bowl or container.

Scrape the dough into the prepared bowl. Cover the bowl with plastic film and set aside to ferment for 1 hour.

Uncover and fold the dough. Again, cover with plastic film and set aside to ferment for 1 hour.

About an hour before you are ready to bake the loaves, place the baking stone(s) or tiles into the oven and preheat to 470°F (243°C). If using a pan to create steam (see page 70), place it in the oven now.

Lightly flour a clean, flat work surface.

Uncover the dough and divide it into four 350-gram / 12½-ounce logs on the floured surface. Cover with plastic film and bench rest for 15 minutes.

Uncover the dough and, if necessary, lightly flour the work surface. Gently press on the dough to degas and carefully shape each log into a baguette (see page 69).

Place each baguette, seam side down, into a baguette pan. Cover with plastic film and proof for 30 minutes.

Uncover the dough and, using a *lame* or a razor, immediately score the loaves as directed on pages 64–65. To make the required steam, add 1 cup of ice to the hot pan in the oven. Immediately transfer the bread pans to the hot baking stone(s) in the preheated oven.

Bake, with steam, for 25 minutes, or until the crust is a deep golden-brown color and the sides are firm to the touch.

Remove from the oven and transfer to wire racks to cool.

Demonstration

Poolish Baguette

Makes 4 loaves

Estimated time to complete: 18 hours
Improved mix
Desired dough temperature (DDT): 75°F (25°C)

Ingredient	Amount	Baker's Percentage
For the poolish:		
Bread flour	56 grams / 2 ounces	100%
Cool water	56 grams / 2 ounces	100%
Fresh yeast	1 gram / pinch	0.1%
Total	**113 grams / 4 ounces**	**200.1%**
For the final dough:		
Bread flour	754 grams / 1 pound 10⅔ ounces	100%
Water	511 grams / 1 pound 2 ounces	67.7%
Salt	16 grams / ½ ounce	2.15%
Fresh yeast	6 grams / ¼ ounce	0.75%
Poolish	113 grams / 4 ounces	15%
Total	**1400 grams / 3 pounds 1½ ounces**	**185.6%**

Oil for greasing bowl
Flour for dusting
Ice for steam

Equipment

Scale	Large bowl or container
Digital thermometer	Baking stone(s) or tiles
Large mixing bowl	Cast-iron or stainless steel roasting pan
Wooden spoon	4 baguette pans
Bowl scraper	*Lame* or razor
Plastic film	Wire racks
Standing electric mixer fitted with the hook	

Prepare the *mise en place* for the poolish, taking care that the water is about 75°F (25°C).

To make the poolish, combine the bread flour and water with the yeast in a large mixing bowl, stirring with a wooden spoon to blend. When blended, scrape down the edge of the bowl, cover with plastic film, and set aside to ferment at 70°F (20°C) for 12 to 14 hours.

When ready to make the final dough, prepare the *mise en place*.

Combine the bread flour with the water in the bowl of a standing electric mixer fitted with the hook. Mix on low speed until blended. Stop the mixer and autolyse for 15 minutes.

Add the salt along with the yeast and poolish and mix on low for 5 minutes. Increase the mixer speed to medium and mix for about 8 minutes, or until the dough has come together but remains slightly sticky. Check the gluten development by pulling a window (see page 64).

Lightly oil a large bowl or container.

Scrape the dough into the prepared bowl. Cover the bowl with plastic film and set aside to ferment for 1 hour.

Uncover and fold the dough. Again, cover with plastic film and set aside to ferment for 1 hour.

About an hour before you are ready to bake the loaves, place the baking stone(s) or tiles into the oven and preheat to 470°F (243°C). If using a pan to create steam (see page 70), place it in the oven now.

Lightly flour a clean, flat work surface.

Uncover the dough and divide it into four 350-gram / 12½-ounce logs on the floured surface. Cover with plastic film and bench rest for 15 minutes.

Uncover the dough and, if necessary, lightly flour the work surface. Gently press on the dough to degas and carefully shape each log into a baguette (see page 69). Place each baguette, seam side down, into a baguette pan. Cover with plastic film and proof for 45 minutes.

Uncover the dough and, using a *lame* or a razor, immediately score the loaves as directed on pages 63–65. To make the required steam, add 1 cup of ice to the hot pan in the oven. Immediately transfer the bread pans to the hot baking stone(s) in the preheated oven.

Bake, with steam, for 25 minutes, or until the crust is a deep golden-brown color and the sides are firm to the touch.

Remove from the oven and transfer to wire racks to cool.

Demonstration

Pain de Mie

Makes 2 loaves

Estimated time to complete: 4 hours
Improved mix
Desired dough temperature (DDT): 75°F (25°C)

Ingredient	Amount	Baker's Percentage
Unsalted butter	55 grams / 2 ounces	10%
Bread flour	553 grams / 1 pound 3½ ounces	100%
Cold milk	331 grams / 11⅔ ounces	60%
Fresh yeast	28 grams / 1 ounce	5%
Sugar	22 grams / ¾ ounce	4%
Salt	11 grams / ⅓ ounce	2%
Total	**1000 grams / 2 pounds 3¼ ounces**	**181%**

Oil for greasing bowl
Flour for dusting
Butter for greasing pans
1 large egg for egg wash

Equipment

Scale	Plastic film
Parchment paper	Two 9-inch loaf pans
Rolling pin	Small bowl
Standing electric mixer fitted with the hook	Whisk
Large bowl or container	Pastry brush
Bowl scraper	Wire racks

Prepare the *mise en place.*

Place the butter on a sheet of parchment paper and, using a rolling pin, lightly pound on it to soften.

Combine the bread flour, milk, softened butter, yeast, sugar, and salt in the bowl of a standing electric mixer fitted with the hook. Mix on low speed for 5 minutes.

Increase the mixer speed to medium and mix for about 8 minutes, or until the dough has come together but remains slightly sticky. Check the gluten development by pulling a window (see page 64).

Lightly oil a large bowl or container.

Scrape the dough into the prepared bowl. Cover the bowl

About *Pain de Mie*

A *pain de mie* is a slightly sweet loaf whose name translates to "bread of crumb." It is also commonly known as a pullman or white sandwich loaf and is most frequently used to make sandwiches or for toasting. The sugar and butter it contains create a bread much richer and sweeter than most other French breads.

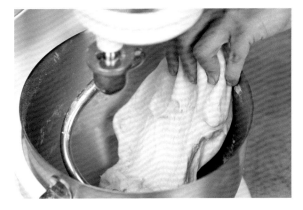

with plastic film and set aside to ferment for 1 hour.

Lightly flour a clean, flat work surface.

Uncover the dough and divide it into two 500-gram / 18-ounce rounds (see page 68) on the floured surface. Cover with plastic film and bench rest for 15 minutes.

Lightly butter two 9-inch loaf pans.

Uncover the dough and, if necessary, lightly flour the work surface. Gently press on the dough to degas and carefully shape each round into a *bâtard* (see pages 68–69). Place each *bâtard* into a prepared loaf pan. Cover with plastic film and proof for 90 minutes.

About a half hour before you are ready to bake the loaves, preheat the oven to 425°F (220°C).

To make the egg wash, combine the egg with 14 grams / 1 tablespoon water in a small bowl, whisking to blend.

Uncover the dough and, using a pastry brush, lightly coat the top of each loaf with the egg wash.

Transfer the loaves to the preheated oven. Bake for 35 minutes, or until the crust is golden brown and shiny, the sides are firm to the touch.

Remove from the oven and transfer to wire racks to cool.

Demonstration

Petits Pains de Restaurant

Makes 2 dozen rolls

Estimated time to complete: 4 hours

Improved mix

Desired dough temperature (DDT): 75°F (25°C)

Ingredient	Amount	Baker's Percentage
Bread flour	778 grams / 1 pound 11½ ounces	100%
Water	529 grams / 1 pound 2⅔ ounces	65%
Fresh yeast	16 grams / ½ ounce	2%
Salt	16 grams / ½ ounce	2%
Unsalted butter	16 grams / ½ ounce	2%
Total	**1355 grams / 3 pounds**	**185%**

Oil for greasing bowl

Flour for dusting

Ice for steam

Equipment

Scale	Two 12 x 18-inch sheet pans
Standing electric mixer fitted with the hook	Parchment paper
Large bowl or container	Cast-iron or stainless steel roasting pan
Bowl scraper	Kitchen shears
Plastic film	Wire racks

Prepare the *mise en place*.

Combine the bread flour with the water in the bowl of a standing electric mixer fitted with the hook. Mix on low speed until blended. Stop the mixer and autolyse for 15 minutes.

Add the yeast, salt, and butter and mix on low for 5 minutes. Increase the mixer speed to medium and mix for about 8 minutes, or until the dough has come together but remains slightly sticky. Check the gluten development by pulling a window (see page 64).

Lightly oil a large bowl or container.

Scrape the dough into the prepared bowl. Cover the bowl with plastic film and set aside to ferment for 45 minutes.

Uncover and fold the dough. Again, cover with plastic film and set aside to ferment for 45 minutes.

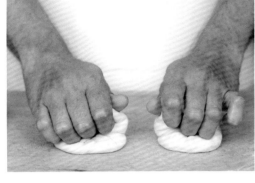
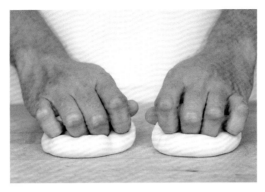
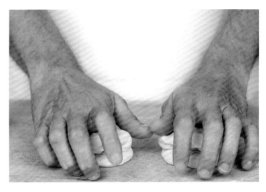

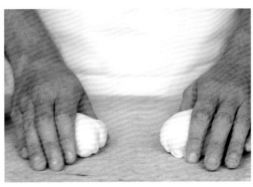

Line two 12 x 18-inch pans with parchment paper. Set aside.

Lightly flour a clean, flat work surface.

Uncover the dough and divide it into 60-gram / 2-ounce pieces on the floured surface, shaping each one into a small round (see page 68). Cover with plastic film and bench rest for 15 minutes.

Uncover the dough and, if necessary, lightly flour the work surface. Gently press on the dough to degas and again form each piece into a small round shape. Place the rolls on the prepared sheet pans. Cover with plastic film and proof for 1 hour.

About an hour before you are ready to bake the rolls, preheat the oven to 470°F (243°C). If using a pan to create steam (see page 70), place it in the oven now.

Uncover the dough and, using kitchen shears, snip a small cut at about a 45-degree angle and about ½ inch deep in the center of each roll. To make the required steam, add 1 cup of ice to the hot pan in the oven. Immediately place the rolls in the preheated oven.

Bake, with steam, for 22 minutes, or until the rolls are a golden-brown color, the sides are firm to the touch, and the rolls make a hollow sound when tapped on the bottom.

Remove from the oven and transfer to wire racks to cool.

Demonstration

Pain aux Céréales

Makes 2 loaves

Estimated time to complete: 12 hours
Improved mix
Desired dough temperature (DDT): 75°F (25°C)

Ingredient	Amount	Baker's Percentage
For the *pâte fermentée*:		
Bread flour	97 grams / 3½ ounces	100%
Cool water	66 grams / 2⅓ ounces	68%
Fresh yeast	2 grams / .07 ounce	2%
Salt	2 grams / .07 ounce	2%
Total	**167 grams / 5¾ ounces**	**172%**
For the final dough:		
Bread flour	443 grams / 15⅔ ounces	100%
Water	310 grams / 11 ounces	70%
Salt	9 grams / ⅓ ounce	2.1%
Fresh yeast	4 grams / ⅛ ounce	1%
Diastatic malt	18 grams / ⅔ ounce	0.75%
Pâte fermentée	167 grams / 5¾ ounces	37.5%
Sesame seeds	27 grams / 1 ounce	6%
Flax seeds	22 grams / ¾ ounce	5%
Total	**1000 grams / 2 pounds 3⅓ ounces**	**222.35%**

Oil for greasing bowl
Flour for dusting
Sesame seeds for topping
Flax seeds for topping
Ice for steam

Equipment

Scale	*Couche*
Digital thermometer	Plate
Standing electric mixer fitted with the hook	Plastic spray bottle filled with cool water
Bowl scraper	Baking stone(s) or tiles
Medium mixing bowl	Cast-iron or stainless steel pan
Plastic film	*Lame* or razor
Large bowl or container	Peel
Large cutting board	Wire racks

Prepare the *mise en place* for the *pâte fermentée,* taking care that the water is about 75°F (25°C).

To make the *pâte fermentée*, combine the bread flour and water with the yeast and salt in the bowl of a standing electric mixer fitted with the hook. Mix on low speed until completely blended; the mix will be quite stiff. When blended, scrape the mixture into a lightly oiled medium mixing bowl, cover with plastic film, and refrigerate for 8 hours or overnight.

When ready to make the final dough, prepare the *mise en place*.

Combine the bread flour with the water in the bowl of a standing electric mixer fitted with the hook. Mix on low speed until blended. Stop the mixer and autolyse for 15 minutes.

Add the salt along with the yeast, diastatic malt, and *pâte fermentée* and mix on low for 5 minutes. Increase the mixer speed to medium and mix for about 8 minutes, or until the dough has come together but remains slightly sticky. Check the gluten development by pulling a window (see page 64). Decrease the mixer speed to low and add the sesame and flax seeds, mixing until integrated.

Lightly oil a large bowl or container.

Scrape the dough into the prepared bowl. Cover the bowl

with plastic film and set aside to ferment for 45 minutes.

Uncover and fold the dough. Again, cover with plastic film and set aside to ferment for 45 minutes.

Cover a large cutting board with a *couche* and dust the *couche* with flour.

Lightly flour a clean, flat work surface.

Uncover the dough and divide it into two 500-gram / 18-ounce rounds (see page 68) on the floured surface. Cover with plastic film and bench rest for 15 minutes.

Place the sesame and flax seeds for topping on a plate.

Uncover the dough and, if necessary, lightly flour the work surface. Gently press on the dough to degas and carefully shape each round into a *bâtard* (see pages 68–69).

Lightly spray the top of each loaf with water. Then, press the top of each loaf gently onto the plate with the sesame and flax seeds, coating neatly. The moisture will help the seeds adhere to the loaf as it bakes.

Place one *bâtard* on one side of the *couche*-covered board, fold the *couche* up to make a double layer of cloth to serve as a divider between the loaves, and place the remaining loaf next to the fold. Cover with plastic film and proof for 1 hour.

About an hour before you are ready to bake the loaves, place the baking stone(s) or tiles into the oven and pre-heat to 450°F (232°C). If using a pan to create steam (see page 70), place it in the oven now.

Uncover the loaves and, using a *lame* or a razor, imme-diately score the loaves as directed on pages 63–65.

To make the required steam, add 1 cup of ice to the hot pan in the oven. Using a peel, immediately transfer the loaves to the hot baking stone(s) in the preheated oven.

Bake, with steam, for 40 minutes, or until the crust is a deep reddish-brown color, the sides are firm to the touch, and the loaves make a hollow sound when tapped on the bottom.

Remove from the oven and transfer to wire racks to cool.

Demonstration

Pain Brioche

Makes 3 loaves

Estimated time to complete: 5 hours
Improved mix
Desired dough temperature (DDT): 75°F (25°C)

Ingredient	Amount	Baker's Percentage
Bread flour	662 grams / 1 pound 7⅓ ounces	100%
Cool water	146 grams / 5⅛ ounces	22%
Cool milk	66 grams / 2⅓ ounces	10%
Cold eggs	146 grams / 5⅛ ounces	22%
Fresh yeast	26 grams / 1 ounce	4%
Sugar	79 grams / 2¾ ounces	2%
Salt	13 grams / ½ ounce	2%
Unsalted butter	212 grams / 7½ ounces	32%
Total	**1350 grams / 3 pounds**	**204%**

Oil for greasing bowl

Flour for dusting

Butter for greasing pans

1 large egg for egg wash

Equipment

Scale	Plastic film
Digital thermometer	Three 9-inch loaf pans
Standing electric mixer fitted with the hook	Small bowl
Parchment paper	Whisk
Rolling pin	Pastry brush
Large bowl or container	Wire racks
Bowl scraper	

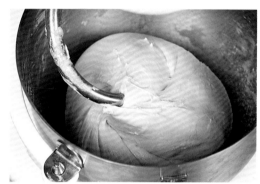

Prepare the *mise en place,* taking care that the water and the milk are about 75°F (25°).

Place the butter on a clean, flat work surface and, using a rolling pin, lightly pound on it to soften.

Combine the bread flour, water, milk, eggs, and yeast in the bowl of a standing electric mixer fitted with the hook. Mix on low speed for about 5 minutes, or until the dough is starting to become shaggy (mixed but not smooth in texture) and there is some gluten development. Add the sugar and salt, increase the mixer speed to medium, and continue mixing for about 5 minutes, or until the dough begins to come together into a mass.

With the mixer on low, add the butter, a little at a time, and mix for about 5 minutes, or until the dough has come together and pulls away from the bowl.

Lightly oil a large bowl or container.

Scrape the dough into the prepared bowl. Cover the bowl with plastic film and set aside to ferment for 45 minutes.

Uncover and fold the dough. Again, cover with plastic film and set aside to ferment for 45 minutes.

Lightly flour the work surface.

Uncover the dough and divide it into three 450-gram / 16-ounce rounds (see page 68) on the floured surface. Cover with plastic film and bench rest for 15 minutes.

Lightly butter three 9-inch loaf pans.

To make the egg wash, combine the egg with 14 grams / 1 tablespoon water in a small bowl, whisking to blend.

Uncover the dough and, if necessary, lightly flour the work surface. Gently press on the dough to degas and

carefully shape each round into a *bâtard* (see pages 68–69).

Place one *bâtard*, seam side down, in each prepared pan. Using a pastry brush, lightly coat the top of each loaf with the egg wash. (Do not discard the remaining egg wash.) Cover the loaves with plastic film and proof for 2 hours.

About a half hour before you are ready to bake the loaves, preheat the oven to 350°F (177°C).

Uncover the dough and again, using a pastry brush, lightly coat the top of each loaf with the remaining egg wash. (If desired, the pans can be set on sheet pans for baking, but this is not necessary.)

Transfer the loaves to the preheated oven. Bake for 35 minutes or until the crust is golden brown and shiny and the sides are firm to the touch.

Remove from the oven and transfer to wire racks to cool.

Demonstration

Fougasse aux Olives

Makes 2 loaves

Estimated time to complete: 21 hours
Improved mix
Desired dough temperature (DDT): 75°F (25°C)

Ingredient	Amount	Baker's Percentage
For the liquid *levain*:		
Bread flour	35 grams / 1¼ ounces	100%
Cool water	44 grams / 1½ ounces	125%
Liquid *levain* culture (see pages 75–76)	4 grams / ⅛ ounce	10%
Total	**83 grams / 3 ounces**	**235%**
For the final dough:		
Pitted olives	103 grams / 3⅔ ounces	25%
Bread flour	371 grams / 13 ounces	90%
Rye flour	41 grams / 1½ ounces	10%
Water	281 grams / 10 ounces	68%
Liquid *levain*	83 grams / 3 ounces	20%
Olive oil	8 grams / ⅓ ounce	2%
Salt	8 grams / ⅓ ounce	2%
Yeast	1 gram / pinch	0.25%
Fresh thyme leaves	4 grams / ⅛ ounce	1%
Total	**900 grams / 1 pound 15¾ ounces**	**218.25%**

Oil for greasing bowl
Flour for dusting
Ice for steam

Equipment

Scale	Large bowl or container
Digital thermometer	2 sheet pans
Large mixing bowl	Parchment paper
Wooden spoon	Baking stone(s) or tiles
Bowl scraper	Cast-iron or stainless steel roasting pan
Plastic film	Bench scraper
Fine-mesh sieve	Wire racks
Standing electric mixer fitted with the hook	

Note

Fougasse dough is sometimes used to make a sandwichlike handheld treat also known as *fougasse,* in which the dough is folded over cheese and meat (or even fruit and nuts) and baked.

Prepare the *mise en place* for the liquid *levain,* taking care that the water is about 75°F (25°C).

To make the liquid *levain,* combine the bread flour and water with the culture in a large mixing bowl, stirring with a wooden spoon to blend. When blended, scrape down the edge of the bowl, cover with plastic film, and set aside to ferment at 70°F (20°C) for 12 to 14 hours.

When ready to make the final dough, prepare the *mise en place.*

Place the olives in a fine-mesh sieve and rinse under cold running water. Pat dry and set aside.

Combine the bread and rye flours with the water in the bowl of a standing electric mixer fitted with the hook.

About *Fougasse*

Fougasse is typically found in the south of France, though it goes by different names in other areas of southern Europe and is known as *fouaisse* or *foisse* in the Burgundy region of France. It is a flat bread that is often flavored with olives, herbs, or other savory additions and is eaten as a snack or appetizer. It almost always has a decorative top or is sculpted into a decorative shape, with the most common decorative patterns being a leaf or a sheaf of wheat. In old times, a *fougasse* was the bread that the baker used to estimate the oven temperature and set the time frame necessary for baking the remainder of the day's loaves.

Mix on low speed until blended. Stop the mixer and autolyse for 15 minutes.

Add the liquid *levain* along with the olive oil, salt, and yeast and mix on low for 5 minutes. Increase the mixer speed to medium and mix for about 8 minutes, or until the dough has come together but remains slightly sticky. Check the gluten development by pulling a window (see page 64). If the gluten has developed sufficiently, mix in the olives and thyme on low speed.

Lightly oil a large bowl or container.

Scrape the dough into the prepared bowl. Cover the bowl with plastic film and set aside to ferment for 1 hour.

Uncover and fold the dough. Again, cover with plastic film and set aside to ferment for 2 hours.

Lightly flour a clean, flat work surface.

Uncover the dough and divide it into two 450-gram / 16-ounce rounds on the floured surface. Cover with plastic film and bench rest for 15 minutes.

Lightly oil one sheet pan.

Uncover the rounds and place them on the oiled sheet pan. Cover with plastic film and proof for 2½ to 3 hours.

About an hour before you are ready to bake the loaves, place the baking stone(s) or tiles into the oven and preheat to 470°F (243°C). If using a pan to create steam (see page 70), place it in the oven now.

Line a second sheet pan with parchment paper.

Uncover the rounds and place them on floured parchment paper. Gently press on the dough to degas and again shape each piece into a large round. Using a bench scraper, make a cut down the center of each round, leaving about 1 inch at each end uncut, and going all the way through the dough. Then, cut two lines on the diagonal on each side of the center cut, again going all the way through. Using your fingertips, gently stretch each cut to make openings about 2 inches wide to create a leaf pattern (see photo).

Using a peel, transfer the bread to the parchment-lined sheet pan.

To make the required steam, add 1 cup of ice to the hot pan in the oven. Transfer the sheet pans to the preheated oven.

Bake, with steam, for 25 minutes, or until the loaves are a deep golden brown and the crust is quite firm.

Remove from the oven and transfer to wire racks to cool.

Demonstration

Pain au Levain, Raisins, et Noix

Makes 3 loaves

Estimated time to complete: 19 hours
Improved mix
Desired dough temperature (DDT): 75°F (25°C)

Ingredient	Amount	Baker's Percentage
For the liquid *levain*:		
Bread flour	101 grams / 3½ ounces	100%
Water	126 grams / 4½ ounces	125%
Liquid *levain* culture (see pages 75–76)	10 grams / ⅓ ounce	10%
Total	**237 grams / 8⅓ ounces**	**235%**
For the final dough:		
Raisins	96 grams / 3⅓ ounces	15%
Walnut pieces	96 grams / 3⅓ ounces	15%
Bread flour	481 grams / 1 pound 1 ounce	75%
Whole wheat flour	160 grams / 5⅔ ounces	25%
Water	406 grams / 14⅓ ounces	63.3%
Liquid *levain*	237 grams / 8⅓ ounces	37%
Salt	18 grams / ⅔ ounce	2.8%
Yeast	6 grams / ¼ ounce	0.75%
Total	**1500 grams / 3 pounds 5 ounces**	**233.85%**

Oil for greasing bowl
Flour for dusting
Ice for steam

Equipment

Scale	Standing electric mixer fitted with the hook
Large mixing bowl	Large bowl or container
Wooden spoon	Large cutting board
Bowl scraper	*Couche*
Plastic film	Baking stone(s) or tiles
Digital thermometer	Cast-iron or stainless steel roasting pan
Small bowl	*Lame* or razor
Small baking dish	Peel
Fine-mesh sieve	Wire racks

Prepare the *mise en place* for the liquid *levain*.

To make the liquid *levain*, combine the bread flour and water with the culture in a large mixing bowl, stirring with a wooden spoon to blend. When blended, scrape down the edge of the bowl, cover with plastic film, and set aside to ferment at 70°F (20°C) for 12 to 14 hours.

When ready to make the final dough, preheat the oven to 470°F (243°C) and prepare the *mise en place*.

Place the raisins in a small, heat-proof bowl. Cover with hot water and set aside to rehydrate for 30 minutes.

While the raisins are rehydrating, place the walnuts in a single layer in a small baking dish. Place in the pre-heated oven and bake, turning occasionally, for about 8 minutes or until nicely colored and fragrant. Remove from the oven and set aside to cool.

Drain the raisins well and set aside.

Combine the bread and whole wheat flours with the water and liquid *levain* in the bowl of a standing electric mixer fitted with the hook. Mix on low speed until blended. Stop the mixer and autolyse for 15 minutes.

Add the salt and yeast and mix on low for 5 minutes. Increase the mixer speed to medium and mix for about 8 minutes, or until the dough has come together but

remains slightly sticky. Check the gluten development by pulling a window (see page 64). If the gluten has developed sufficiently, mix in the raisins and walnuts on low speed.

Lightly oil a large bowl or container.

Scrape the dough into the prepared bowl. Cover the bowl with plastic film and set aside to ferment for 1 hour.

Uncover and fold the dough. Again, cover with plastic film and set aside to ferment for 1 hour.

Cover a large cutting board with a *couche* and dust the *couche* with flour.

Lightly flour a clean, flat work surface.

Uncover the dough and divide it into three 500-gram / 18-ounce rounds on the floured surface. Cover with plastic film and bench rest for 15 minutes.

Uncover the dough and, if necessary, lightly flour the work surface. Gently press on the dough to degas and shape each piece into a round (see pages 68–69). Place one round on one side of the *couche*-covered board, fold the *couche* up to make a double layer of cloth to serve as a divider between the loaves, and place the remaining loaves in the same manner. Cover with plastic film and proof for 1 hour.

About an hour before you are ready to bake the loaves, place the baking stone(s) or tiles into the oven and pre-heat to 450°F (232°C). If using a pan to create steam (see page 70), place it in the oven now.

Uncover the dough and, using a *lame* or a razor, immediately score the loaves as directed on pages 63–65. To make the required steam, add 1 cup of ice to the hot pan in the oven. Using a peel, immediately transfer the loaves to the hot baking stone(s) in the preheated oven.

Bake, with steam, for 25 minutes, or until the crust is caramel colored, the sides are firm to the touch, and the loaves make a hollow sound when tapped on the bottom.

Remove from the oven and transfer to wire racks to cool.

Demonstration

Pain au Fromage

Makes 3 loaves

Estimated time to complete: 19 hours

Improved mix

Desired dough temperature (DDT): 75°F (25°C)

Ingredient	Amount	Baker's Percentage
For the liquid *levain*:		
Bread flour	132 grams / 4⅔ ounces	100%
Water	165 grams / 5¾ ounces	125%
Liquid *levain* culture (see pages 75–76)	13 grams / ½ ounce	10%
Total	**310 grams / 11 ounces**	**235%**
For the final dough:		
Bread flour	641 grams / 1 pound 6⅔ ounces	100%
Water	372 grams / 13 ounces	58%
Liquid *levain*	310 grams / 11 ounces	48.5%
Salt	14 grams / ½ ounce	2.2%
Yeast	3 grams / ⅛ ounce	0.5%
Grated cheese (see Note)	160 grams / 5⅔ ounces	25%
Total	**1500 grams / 3 pounds 5 ounces**	**234.2%**

Oil for greasing bowl

Flour for dusting

Ice for steam

Equipment

Scale	Large bowl or container
Large mixing bowl	Large cutting board
Wooden spoon	*Couche*
Bowl scraper	Baking stone(s) or tiles
Plastic film	Cast-iron or stainless steel roasting pan
Digital thermometer	*Lame* or razor
Standing electric mixer fitted with the hook	Peel
Grater	Wire racks

Lightly oil a large bowl or container.

Scrape the dough into the prepared bowl. Cover the bowl with plastic film and set aside to ferment for 1 hour.

Uncover and fold the dough. Again, cover with plastic film and set aside to ferment for 90 minutes.

Cover a large cutting board with a *couche* and dust the *couche* with flour.

Lightly flour a clean, flat work surface.

Uncover the dough and divide it into three 500-gram / 18-ounce rounds on the floured surface. Cover with plastic film and bench rest for 15 minutes.

Uncover the dough and, if necessary, lightly flour the work surface. Gently press on the dough to degas and again shape each piece into a round (see page 68). Place one round on one side of the *couche*-covered board, fold the *couche* up to make a double layer of cloth to serve as a divider between the loaves, and place the remaining loaves in the same manner. Cover with plastic film and proof for 1 hour.

About an hour before you are ready to bake the loaves, place the baking stone(s) or tiles into the oven and preheat it to 450°F (232°C). If using a pan to create steam (see page 70), place it in the oven now.

Uncover the dough and, using a *lame* or a razor, immediately score the loaves as directed on pages 63–65. To make the required steam, add 1 cup of ice to the hot pan in the oven. Using a peel, immediately transfer the loaves to the hot baking stone(s) in the preheated oven.

Bake, with steam, for 40 minutes, or until the crust is a reddish-brown color, the sides are firm to the touch, and the loaves make a hollow sound when tapped on the bottom.

Note

You can use Gruyère, Asiago, Parmigiano-Reggiano, or other firm or hard cheese.

Prepare the *mise en place* for the liquid *levain*.

To make the liquid *levain*, combine the bread flour and water with the culture in a large mixing bowl, stirring with a wooden spoon to blend. When blended, scrape down the edge of the bowl, cover with plastic film, and set aside to ferment at 70°F (20°C) for 12 to 14 hours.

When ready to make the final dough, prepare the *mise en place*.

Combine the bread flour, water, and liquid *levain* in the bowl of a standing electric mixer fitted with the hook. Mix on low speed until blended. Stop the mixer and autolyse for 15 minutes.

Add the salt and yeast and mix on low for 5 minutes. Increase the mixer speed to medium and mix for about 8 minutes, or until the dough has come together but remains slightly sticky. Check the gluten development by pulling a window (see page 64). If the gluten has developed sufficiently, mix in the cheese on low speed.

Demonstration

Pain Normand

Makes 4 loaves

Estimated time to complete: 19 hours
Improved mix
Desired dough temperature (DDT): 75°F (25°C)

Ingredient	Amount	Baker's Percentage
For the liquid *levain*:		
Bread flour	30 grams / 1 ounce	100%
Water	37 grams / 1⅓ ounces	125%
Liquid *levain* culture (see pages 75–76)	3 grams / ⅛ ounce	10%
Total	**70 grams / 2½ ounces**	**235%**
For the final dough:		
Dried apples	70 grams / 2½ ounces	15%
Apple cider	187 grams / 6⅔ ounces	40%
Bread flour	398 grams / 14 ounces	85%
Whole wheat flour	47 grams / 9⅓ ounces	10%
Rye flour	24 grams / ¾ ounce	5%
Water	187 grams / 6⅔ ounces	40%
Liquid *levain*	70 grams / 2½ ounces	15%
Salt	10 grams / ⅓ ounce	2.2%
Yeast	7 grams / 2 ounces	1.5%
Total	**1000 grams / 2 pounds 12¾ ounces**	**213.7%**

Oil for greasing bowl

Flour for dusting

57 grams (2 ounces) apple cider for brushing loaves

1 apple, thinly sliced into rounds, for garnish

Ice for steam

Equipment

Scale

Large mixing bowl

Wooden spoon

Bowl scraper

Plastic film

Digital thermometer

Sharp knife or mandoline

Small bowl

Fine-mesh sieve

Standing electric mixer fitted with the hook

Large bowl or container

Sheet pan

Parchment paper

Pastry brush

Baking stone(s) or tiles

Cast-iron or stainless steel roasting pan

Peel

Wire racks

About *Pain Normand*

Pain Normand probably originated in Normandy, where apples and apple cider are favored ingredients in both savory and sweet dishes. Some bakers incorporate chopped dried apples into the dough before baking to give an additional apple flavor to the baked bread.

Prepare the *mise en place* for the liquid *levain*.

To make the liquid *levain*, combine the bread flour and water with the culture in a large mixing bowl, stirring with a wooden spoon to blend. When blended, scrape down the edge of the bowl, cover with plastic film, and set aside to ferment at 75°F (25°C) for 12 to 14 hours.

When ready to make the final dough, prepare the *mise en place*.

Using a sharp knife, coarsely chop the dried apples. Place them in a small bowl and cover with the apple cider. Allow to soak for 45 minutes.

Strain the apples through a fine-mesh sieve, reserving any remaining cider. Set the soaked apples and reserved cider aside.

Combine the bread, whole wheat, and rye flours with the water, liquid *levain*, and reserved cider in the bowl of a standing electric mixer fitted with the hook. Mix on low speed until blended. Stop the mixer and autolyse for 15 minutes.

Add the salt and yeast and mix on low for 5 minutes. Increase the mixer speed to medium and mix for about 8 minutes, or until the dough has come together but remains slightly sticky. Check the gluten development by pulling a window (see page 64). If the gluten has developed sufficiently, mix in the soaked apples on low speed.

Lightly oil a large bowl or container.

Scrape the dough into the prepared bowl. Cover the bowl with plastic film and set aside to ferment for 1 hour.

Uncover and fold the dough. Again, cover with plastic film and set aside to ferment for 90 minutes.

Lightly flour a clean, flat work surface.

Uncover the dough and divide it into four 250-gram / 9-ounce rounds on the floured surface. Cover with plastic film and bench rest for 15 minutes.

Line a sheet pan with parchment paper.

Uncover the dough and, if necessary, lightly flour the work surface. Gently press on the dough to degas and again shape each piece into a round (see page 68). Place the rounds on the parchment-lined sheet pan, leaving about 3 inches between each one. Cover with plastic film and proof for 1 hour.

About an hour before you are ready to bake the loaves, place the baking stone(s) or tiles into the oven and pre-heat to 450°F (232°C). If using a pan to create steam (see page 70), place it in the oven now.

Uncover the loaves and, using a pastry brush, lightly coat each loaf with apple cider. Garnish the top of each loaf with an apple slice and brush each slice with the apple cider.

To make the required steam, add 1 cup of ice to the hot pan in the oven. Immediately transfer the breads to the preheated oven.

Bake, with steam, for 30 minutes, or until the crust is a reddish-brown color, the sides are firm to the touch, and the loaves make a hollow sound when tapped on the bottom.

Remove from the oven and transfer to wire racks to cool.

Demonstration

Pain au Citron

Makes 4 loaves

Estimated time to complete: 12 hours
Improved mix
Desired dough temperature (DDT): 75°F (25°C)

Ingredient	Amount	Baker's Percentage
For the *pâte fermentée*:		
Bread flour	55 grams / 2 ounces	100%
Cool water	35 grams / 1¼ ounces	65%
Fresh yeast	1 gram / pinch	2%
Salt	1 gram / pinch	2%
Total	**92 grams / 3¼ ounces**	**169%**
For the final dough:		
Bread flour	770 grams / 1 pound 11 ounces	100%
Water	477 grams / 1 pound ¾ ounce	62%
Fresh lemon juice	35 grams / 1¼ ounces	4.5%
Salt	15 grams / ½ ounce	2%
Fresh yeast	7 grams / ¼ ounce	1%
Pâte fermentée	92 grams / 3¼ ounces	12%
Fresh lemon zest	4 grams / ⅛ ounce	0.5%
Total	**1400 grams / 3 pounds 1½ ounces**	**182%**

Oil for greasing bowl
Flour for dusting
Ice for steam

Equipment

Scale	2 large cutting boards
Digital thermometer	*Couche* for two boards
Standing electric mixer fitted with the hook	Baking stone(s) or tiles
Bowl scraper	Cast-iron or stainless steel roasting pan
Medium mixing bowl	*Lame* or razor
Plastic film	Peel
Large bowl or container	Wire racks

Prepare the *mise en place* for the *pâte fermentée*, taking care that the water is about 75°F (25°C).

To make the *pâte fermentée*, combine the bread flour and water with the yeast and salt in the bowl of a standing electric mixer fitted with the hook. Mix on low speed until completely blended; the mix will be quite stiff. When blended, scrape the mixture into a medium mixing bowl, cover with plastic film, and refrigerate for 8 hours or overnight.

When ready to make the final dough, prepare the *mise en place*.

Combine the bread flour with the water and lemon juice in the bowl of a standing electric mixer fitted with the hook. Mix on low speed until blended. Stop the mixer and autolyse for 15 minutes.

Add the salt, yeast, *pâte fermentée,* and zest and mix on low for 5 minutes. Increase the mixer speed to medium and mix for about 8 minutes, or until the dough has come together but remains slightly sticky. Check the gluten development by pulling a window (see page 64).

Lightly oil a large bowl or container.

Scrape the dough into the prepared bowl. Cover the bowl with plastic film and set aside to ferment for 45 minutes.

Uncover and fold the dough. Again, cover with plastic film and set aside to ferment for 45 minutes.

Cover the cutting boards with the *couche* and dust the *couche* with flour.

Lightly flour a clean, flat work surface.

Uncover the dough and divide it into four 350-gram / 12½-ounce rounds on the floured surface. Cover with plastic film and bench rest for 15 minutes.

Uncover the dough and, if necessary, lightly flour the work surface. Gently press on the dough to degas and carefully shape each round into a plump *bâtard* (see pages 68–69) so they look like large lemons.

Place one loaf on one side of a *couche*-covered board, fold the *couche* up to make a double layer of cloth to serve as a divider between the loaves, and place the second loaf next to the fold. Repeat with the third and fourth loaves on the second *couche*-covered board. Cover with plastic film and proof for 1 hour.

About an hour before you are ready to bake the loaves, place the baking stone(s) or tiles into the oven and preheat to 470°F (243°C). If using a pan to create steam (see page 70), place it in the oven now.

Uncover the dough and, using a *lame* or a razor, immediately score the loaves as directed on pages 63–65.

To make the required steam, add 1 cup of ice to the hot pan in the oven. Using a peel, immediately transfer the loaves to the hot baking stone(s) in the preheated oven.

Bake, with steam, for 40 minutes, or until the crust is a deep golden-brown color, the sides are firm to the touch, and the loaves make a hollow sound when tapped on the bottom.

Remove from the oven and transfer to wire racks to cool.

Demonstration

Pain au Lait

Makes 14 rolls

Estimated time to complete: 5 hours
Improved mix
Desired dough temperature (DDT): 75°F (25°C)

Ingredient	Amount	Baker's Percentage
Bread flour	543 grams / 1 pound 3 ounces	100%
Cold milk	405 grams / 14¼ ounces	75%
Fresh yeast	12 grams / ½ ounce	2%
Honey	12 grams / ½ ounce	2%
Salt	12 grams / ½ ounce	2%
Cold unsalted butter	65 grams / 2¼ ounces	12%
Total	**1049 grams / 2 pounds 5 ounces**	**193%**

Oil for greasing bowl

Flour for dusting

1 large egg for egg wash

Equipment

Scale	Parchment paper
Standing electric mixer fitted with the hook	Small bowl
Large bowl or container	Whisk
Bowl scraper	Pastry brush
Plastic film	Wire racks
12 x 18-inch sheet pan	

Prepare the *mise en place*.

Combine the bread flour with the milk, yeast, honey, and salt in the bowl of a standing electric mixer fitted with the hook. Mix on low speed for about 4 minutes, or until blended. Increase the mixer speed to medium and mix for about 8 minutes, or until the dough begins to pull away from the sides of the bowl, feels elastic, and gives some resistance when tugged. Check the gluten development by pulling a window (see page 64).

Place the butter on a clean, flat work surface and, using a rolling pin, lightly pound on it to soften.

With the mixer on low, add the butter, a little at a time, and mix for about 5 minutes, or until the dough has come together and pulls away from the bowl.

Lightly oil a large bowl or container.

Scrape the dough into the prepared bowl. Cover the bowl with plastic film and set aside to ferment for 1 hour.

Uncover and fold the dough. Again, cover with plastic film and set aside to ferment for 1 hour.

Lightly flour a clean, flat work surface.

Uncover the dough and divide it into fourteen 75-gram / 2¾-ounce rounds (see page 68) on the floured surface. Cover with plastic film and bench rest for 15 minutes.

Line a 12 x 18-inch sheet pan with parchment paper.

Uncover the dough and, if necessary, lightly flour the work surface. Gently press on the dough to degas and carefully shape each round into a round, a *bâtard*, or any decorative shape you desire. Place the rolls onto the prepared pan, seam side down. Cover with plastic film and proof for 90 minutes.

About an hour before you are ready to bake the rolls, preheat the oven to 425°F (220°C).

To make the egg wash, combine the egg with 14 grams / 1 tablespoon water in a small bowl, whisking to blend.

Uncover the dough and, using a pastry brush, lightly coat the top of each roll with the egg wash.

Transfer the rolls to the preheated oven. Bake for 20 minutes, or until the crust is golden brown, the sides are firm to the touch, and the rolls make a hollow sound when tapped on the bottom.

Remove from the oven and transfer to wire racks to cool.

Demonstration

Pain de Mie Complet

Makes 2 loaves

Estimated time to complete: 5½ hours
Improved mix
Desired dough temperature (DDT): 75°F (25°C)

Ingredient	Amount	Baker's Percentage
Bread flour	276 grams / 9¾ ounces	50%
Fine whole wheat flour	276 grams / 9¾ ounces	50%
Water	359 grams / 12⅔ ounces	65%
Powdered milk	22 grams / ¾ ounce	4.06%
Unsalted butter	28 grams / 1 ounce	5%
Cool heavy cream	17 grams / ⅔ ounce	3%
Salt	14 grams / ½ ounce	2.5%
Fresh yeast	8 grams / ⅛ ounce	1.56%
Total	**1000 grams / 2 pounds 3⅓ ounces**	**181.12%**

Oil for greasing bowl
Flour for dusting
Butter for greasing pans
1 large egg for egg wash

Equipment

Scale	Two 9-inch loaf pans
Digital thermometer	Small bowl
Standing electric mixer fitted with the hook	Whisk
Large bowl or container	Pastry brush
Bowl scraper	Wire racks
Plastic film	

Prepare the *mise en place*, taking care that the cream is about 60°F (15°C).

Combine the bread and fine whole wheat flours with the water, powdered milk, butter, heavy cream, salt, and yeast in the bowl of a standing electric mixer fitted with the hook. Mix on low speed for about 4 minutes, or until blended. Increase the mixer speed to medium and mix for about 8 minutes, or until the dough is smooth and almost shiny. Check the gluten development by pulling a window (see page 64).

Lightly oil a large bowl or container.

Scrape the dough into the prepared bowl. Cover the bowl with plastic film and set aside to ferment for 1 hour.

Lightly flour a clean, flat work surface.

Uncover the dough and divide it into two 500-gram / 18-ounce rounds on the floured surface. Cover with plastic film and bench rest for 15 minutes.

Lightly butter two 9-inch loaf pans.

Uncover the dough and, if necessary, lightly flour the work surface. Gently press on the dough to degas and carefully shape each round into a *bâtard* (see pages 68–69). Place each *bâtard* into a prepared loaf pan, seam side down. Cover with plastic film and proof for 90 minutes.

About an hour before you are ready to bake the loaves, preheat the oven to 350°F (177°C).

To make the egg wash, combine the egg with 14 grams / 1 tablespoon water in a small bowl, whisking to blend.

Uncover the dough and, using a pastry brush, lightly coat the top of each loaf with the egg wash.

Transfer the loaves to the preheated oven. Bake for 35 minutes, or until the crust is golden brown and shiny and the sides are firm to the touch.

Remove from the oven. Then, turn the loaves from the pans and transfer to wire racks to cool.

Demonstration

Pain Viennois

Makes 1 dozen rolls
Estimated time to complete: 4½ hours
Intensive mix
Desired dough temperature (DDT): 75°F (25°C)

Ingredient	Amount	Baker's Percentage
Bread flour	1000 grams / 2 pounds 3 ounces	100%
Cold milk	600 grams / 11¼ ounces	60%
Sugar	60 grams / 2 ounces	6%
Fresh yeast	40 grams / 1½ ounces	4%
Salt	20 grams / ¾ ounce	2%
Unsalted butter	200 grams / 7 ounces	20%
Total	**1920 grams / 3 pounds 9½ ounces**	**192%**

Oil for greasing bowl
Flour for dusting
1 large egg for egg wash

Equipment

Scale	Two 12 x 18-inch sheet pans
Standing electric mixer fitted with the hook	Small bowl
Parchment paper	Whisk
Rolling pin	Pastry brush
Large bowl or container	Baking stone(s) or tiles
Bowl scraper	Wire racks
Plastic film	

Prepare the *mise en place*.

Combine the bread flour, milk, sugar, yeast, and salt in the bowl of a standing electric mixer fitted with the hook. Mix on low speed for about 5 minutes, or until the dough is starting to become shaggy and there is some gluten development. Increase the mixer speed to medium and mix for about 12 minutes, or until the dough becomes smooth and almost shiny. Check the gluten development by pulling a window (see page 64).

Place the butter on a clean, flat work surface and, using a rolling pin, lightly pound on it to soften.

With the mixer on low, add the butter, a little at a time,

and mix for about 5 minutes, or until the butter is completely incorporated into the dough.

Lightly oil a large bowl or container.

Scrape the dough into the prepared bowl. Cover the bowl with plastic film and set aside to ferment for 1 hour.

Lightly flour a clean, flat work surface.

Uncover the dough and divide it into twelve 150-gram / 5¼-ounce pieces on the floured surface and shape each piece into a small *bâtard* (see pages 68–69). Cover with plastic film and bench rest for 15 minutes.

Line two 12 x 18-inch sheet pans with parchment paper.

Uncover the dough and, if necessary, lightly flour the work surface. Gently press on the dough to degas and carefully shape each *bâtard* into a baguette (see page 69). Place 6 loaves on each prepared sheet pan.

To make the egg wash, combine the egg with 14 grams / 1 tablespoon water in a small bowl, whisking to blend.

Using a pastry brush, lightly coat the top of each loaf with the egg wash. (Do not discard the remaining egg wash.) Cover the loaves with plastic film and proof for 2 hours.

About an hour before you are ready to bake the loaves, place the baking stone(s) or tiles into the oven and preheat to 425°F (220°C).

Uncover the dough and, using a *lame* or a razor, immediately score the loaves as directed on pages 63–65, and again, using a pastry brush, lightly coat the top of each loaf with the remaining egg wash.

Transfer the loaves to the preheated oven. Bake for 40 minutes, or until the crust is golden brown, the sides are firm to the touch, and the loaves make a hollow sound when tapped on the bottom.

Remove from the oven and transfer to wire racks to cool.

Demonstration

Straight Baguette

Makes 4 loaves

Estimated time to complete: 5 hours

Short mix

Desired dough temperature (DDT): 75°F (25°C)

Ingredient	Amount	Baker's Percentage
Bread flour	766 grams / 1 pound 11 ounces	100%
Water	567 grams / 1 pound 4 ounces	74%
Salt	14 grams / ½ ounce	1.8%
Fresh yeast	5 grams / ⅛ ounce	0.6%
Total	**1352 grams / 3 pounds**	**176.4%**

Oil for greasing bowl

Flour for dusting

Ice for steam

Equipment

Scale	Cast-iron or stainless steel roasting pan
Standing electric mixer fitted with the hook	4 baguette pans
Large bowl or container	*Lame* or razor
Bowl scraper	Peel
Plastic film	Wire racks
Baking stone(s) or tiles	

Prepare the *mise en place*.

Combine the bread flour with the water in the bowl of a standing electric mixer fitted with the hook. Mix on low speed until blended. Stop the mixer and autolyse for 15 minutes.

Add the salt and yeast and mix on low for 5 minutes.

Lightly oil a large bowl or container.

Scrape the dough into the prepared bowl. Cover the bowl with plastic film and set aside to ferment for 20 minutes.

Uncover and fold the dough. Again, cover with plastic film and set aside to ferment for 20 minutes.

Uncover and fold the dough. Cover with plastic film and set aside a third time to ferment for 20 minutes.

Finally, uncover and fold the dough. Cover with plastic

film and set aside to ferment for 2 hours.

About an hour before you are ready to bake the loaves, place the baking stone(s) or tiles into the oven and preheat to 470°F (243°C). If using a pan to create steam (see page 70), place it in the oven now.

Lightly flour a clean, flat work surface.

Uncover the dough and divide it into four 338-gram / 12-ounce logs on the floured surface. Cover with plastic film and bench rest for 15 minutes.

Uncover the dough and, if necessary, lightly flour the work surface. Gently press on the dough to degas and carefully shape each log into a baguette (see page 69).

Place each baguette, seam side down, into a baguette pan. Cover with plastic film and proof for 30 minutes.

Uncover the dough and, using a *lame* or a razor, immediately score the loaves as directed for baguette on pages 63–65. To make the required steam, add 1 cup of ice to the hot pan in the oven. Immediately transfer the loaves to the hot baking stone(s) in the preheated oven.

Bake, with steam, for 25 minutes or until the crust is a deep golden-brown color and the sides are firm to the touch.

Remove from the oven and transfer to wire racks to cool.

Demonstration

Rye Bread (using *Pâte Fermentée*)

Makes 3 loaves

Estimated time to complete: 21 hours
Improved mix
Desired dough temperature (DDT): 75°F (25°C)

Ingredient	Amount	Baker's Percentage
For the *pâte fermentée*:		
Bread flour	280 grams / 10 ounces	100%
Water	191 grams / 6¾ ounces	68%
Yeast	6 grams / ⅕ ounce	2%
Salt	6 grams / ⅕ ounce	2%
Total	**483 grams / 1 pound 1¼ ounces**	**172%**
For the final dough:		
Rye flour	550 grams / 1 pound 3½ ounces	97%
Bread flour	17 grams / ¾ ounce	3%
Water	420 grams / 14¾ ounces	74%
Pâte fermentée	483 grams / 1 pound 1¼ ounces	85%
Fresh yeast	11 grams / ½ ounce	2%
Salt	11 grams / ½ ounce	2%
Wine vinegar	8 grams / ⅓ ounce	1.5%
Total	**1500 grams / 3 pounds 5 ounces**	**264.5%**

Oil for greasing bowl

Flour for dusting

Coarse rye flour for dusting

Ice for steam

Equipment

Scale	Bowl scraper
Digital thermometer	Plastic film
Large mixing bowl	Standing electric mixer fitted with the hook
Wooden spoon	Large bowl or container

Large cutting board

Couche

Baking stone(s) or tiles

Cast-iron or stainless steel roasting pan

Lame or razor

Peel

Wire racks

Prepare the *mise en place* for the *pâte fermentée*, taking care that the water is about 75°F (25°C).

To make the *pâte fermentée*, combine the bread flour and water with the yeast and salt in a large mixing bowl, stirring with a wooden spoon to blend. When blended, scrape down the edge of the bowl, cover with plastic film, and set aside to ferment at 75°F (25°C) for 5 hours or at 39°F (4°C) for 18 hours.

When ready to make the final dough, prepare the *mise en place*.

Combine the rye and bread flours with the water, *pâte fermentée,* yeast, salt, and vinegar in the bowl of a standing electric mixer fitted with the hook. Mix on low speed until blended. Stop the mixer and autolyse for 15 minutes.

Increase the mixer speed to medium and mix for about 7 minutes, or until the dough begins to pull away from the sides of the bowl, feels elastic, and gives some resistance when tugged.

Lightly oil a large bowl or container.

Scrape the dough into the prepared bowl. Cover the bowl with plastic film and set aside to ferment for 50 minutes.

Cover the cutting board with the *couche* and dust the *couche* with flour.

Lightly flour a clean, flat work surface.

Uncover the dough and divide it into three 500-gram / 18-ounce rounds on the floured surface. Cover with plastic film and bench rest for 20 minutes.

About an hour before you are ready to bake the loaves, place the baking stone(s) or tiles into the oven and preheat it to 450°F (232°C). If using a pan to create steam (page 70), place it in the oven now.

Uncover the dough and, if necessary, lightly flour the work surface. Gently press on the dough to degas and carefully shape each round into a *bâtard* (see pages 68–69). Place one *bâtard* on one side of the *couche*-covered board. Fold the *couche* up to make a double layer of cloth to serve as a divider between the loaves, and place one of the remaining loaves next to the fold. Repeat for the remaining loaf.

Dust the tops with coarse rye flour and, using a *lame* or a razor, immediately score the loaves as directed on pages 63–65.

Cover with plastic film and proof for 1 hour.

When ready to bake, to make the required steam, add 1 cup of ice to the hot pan in the oven. Uncover the dough and, using a peel, immediately transfer the loaves to the hot baking stone(s) in the preheated oven.

Bake for 40 minutes, or until the crust is very brown, the sides are firm to the touch, and the loaves make a hollow sound when tapped on the bottom.

Remove from the oven and transfer to wire racks to cool.

Session 9

Traditional Italian Breads

In Italy, throughout recorded history, bread of one type or another has always been a source of nourishment for both peasant and grandee. In ancient times, breads were often made with farro or spelt wheat, both of which were almost extinct by the twentieth century and have only recently been rediscovered. Most breads were baked in the village bakery, a tradition that still exists in some small towns in the countryside. But today, most Italian breads are commercially made.

Since professional bakers have been part of daily life since the second century, Italians are almost equal to the French in their love of good bread. No table is considered complete without a freshly baked loaf. However, the typical Italian family loaf is longer and thicker than the classic French baguette and was originally developed to keep one family in bread for a week. And, with typical Italian passion, there is no debate about what that loaf should be—low in salt, unsweetened, yeast leavened, and thin crusted.

The standard Italian loaf is generally made with a long fermentation period, allowing the yeast to work to its most expansive. The interior is filled with holes and is quite moist, a perfect foil for absorbing fragrant olive oil and savory toppings. Throughout Italy, not only does each region have its own style of cooking, but also its own type of bread, and in this section we will learn many of them.

In America, Italian bread was, at the earliest point of Italian immigration in the eighteenth century, fairly straightforward—flour, water, and yeast. But, through the years and particularly with the growth of artisanal bakeries, there are now a wide variety of Italian or Italian-style breads, including the ubiquitous pizza. It is now common to find sandwiches made from *ciabatta*, *foccacia*, or Tuscan breads in chain restaurants, delicatessens, and diners.

Carta di Musica	Thin Crispy Foccacia
Ciabatta	Straight Dough Ciabatta
Pane al' Olio	Pane al Segale con Pancetta
Pane Pugliese	Puccia
Pane alle Patate	La Mouna
Ciabatta with Liquid Levain	Panettone
Pane Siciliano Semolina	Panmarino
Pane al' Olive	Pizza
Pane Toscano	Ciriole
Foccacia (Soft Style)	Pane Francese
Grissini	Pane alla Cioccolata

Demonstration

Carta di Musica

Makes 1 dozen flatbreads
Estimated time to complete: 2 hours or up to 26 hours
Intensive mix
Desired dough temperature (DDT): 75°F (25°C)

Ingredient	Amount	Baker's Percentage
Durum flour	533 grams / 1 pound 2¾ ounces	100%
Water	357 grams / 12½ ounces	67%
Fresh yeast	5 grams / ⅕ ounce	1%
Salt	5 grams / ⅕ ounce	1%
Total	**900 grams / 1 pound 15¾ ounces**	**169%**

Flour for dusting

Equipment

Scale	Plastic film
12 x 18-inch sheet pan or bagel board	Rolling pin
Parchment paper	Peel
Standing electric mixer fitted with the hook	Wire racks
Bowl scraper	

Prepare the *mise en place*.

Line a 12 x 18-inch sheet pan with parchment paper or flour a bagel board. Set aside.

Combine the flour with the water, yeast, and salt in the bowl of a standing electric mixer fitted with the hook. Mix on low speed until blended. Increase the mixer speed to medium and mix for about 8 minutes, or until the dough has come together but remains slightly sticky. Check the gluten development by pulling a window (see page 64).

Using a bowl scraper, immediately scrape the dough

from the bowl onto a clean, lightly floured work surface and form it into twelve 75-gram / 2¾-ounce rounds. Place the rounds on the prepared sheet pan or bagel board, cover with plastic film, and bench rest for 30 minutes.

Transfer the dough to the refrigerator for at least 30 minutes, but for no more than 24 hours.

About an hour before you are ready to bake the flatbreads, place the baking stone(s) or tiles into the oven and preheat to 500°F (260°C). If you are using a pan to create steam (see page 70), place it in the oven now.

About *Carta di Musica*

Carta di Musica, translated to "paper of music," is a paper-thin flatbread that often is used as a partner for cheese and fruit. The name refers either to its tissue-like appearance or to the fact that a sheet of music can be read through a properly made loaf.

Lightly flour a clean, flat work surface.

Remove the dough from the refrigerator. Uncover and, working with one piece at a time, place the dough on the floured work surface. Using a rolling pin, roll out each piece to a 9-inch (23-centimeter) circle.

Using a peel, immediately transfer the flatbreads to the hot baking stone(s) in the preheated oven and bake for

4 minutes, or until crisp and dry. The breads will puff while baking and collapse once they are removed from the oven.

Remove from the oven and transfer to wire racks to cool.

Demonstration

Ciabatta

Makes 4 loaves

Estimated time to complete: 18 hours
Improved mix
Desired dough temperature (DDT): 75°F (25°C)

Ingredient	Amount	Baker's Percentage
For the poolish:		
Bread flour	78 grams / 2¾ ounces	100%
Water	78 grams / 2¾ ounces	100%
Fresh yeast	0.1 gram / pinch	0.1%
Total	**156 grams / 5½ ounces**	**200.1%**
For the final dough:		
Bread flour	705 grams / 1 pound 9 ounces	100%
Water	517 grams / 1 pound 2¼ ounces	73.3%
Poolish	156 grams / 5½ ounces	22.2%
Salt	16 grams / ½ ounce	2.2%
Fresh yeast	6 grams / ¼ ounce	0.8%
Total	**1400 grams / 3 pounds 1½ ounces**	**198.5%**

Oil for greasing bowl

Flour for dusting

Ice for steam

Equipment

Scale	Baking stone(s) or tiles
Large mixing bowl	Cast-iron or stainless steel roasting pan
Wooden spoon	Large cutting board
Bowl scraper	*Couche* or bagel or bread board
Plastic film	Peel
Digital thermometer	Parchment paper
Standing electric mixer fitted with the hook	Wire racks
Large bowl or container	

Prepare the *mise en place* for the poolish.

To make the poolish, combine the bread flour and water with the yeast in a large mixing bowl, stirring with a wooden spoon to blend. When blended, scrape down the edge of the bowl, cover with plastic film, and set aside to ferment at 75°F (25°C) for 12 to 14 hours.

When ready to make the final dough, prepare the *mise en place*.

Combine the bread flour with 465 grams / 16½ ounces of the water in the bowl of a standing electric mixer fitted with the hook. Mix on low speed until blended. Stop the mixer and autolyse for 15 minutes.

Add the poolish along with the salt and yeast and mix on low for 5 minutes. Increase the mixer speed to medium and mix for about 8 minutes, or until the dough has come together but remains slightly sticky. Drizzle in the remaining water and continue to mix until the dough is smooth and almost shiny. Check the gluten development by pulling a window (see page 64).

Lightly oil a large bowl or container.

Scrape the dough into the prepared bowl. Cover the bowl with plastic film and set aside to ferment for 1 hour.

Uncover and fold the dough. Again, cover with plastic film and set aside to ferment for 1 hour.

About an hour before you are ready to bake the loaves, place the baking stone(s) or tiles into the oven and preheat to 470°F (243°C). If using a pan to create steam (see page 70), place it in the oven now.

Cover the cutting board with the *couche* and dust the *couche* with flour, or lightly flour a bagel or bread board.

Uncover the dough and transfer it to the floured surface. Carefully divide it into four 350-gram / 12½-ounce rectangular pieces (they need not be perfectly shaped). Place on the *couche*-covered board or bagel or bread board. Cover with plastic film and proof for 30 minutes.

Line a peel with parchment paper.

Uncover the dough and invert it onto the prepared peel.

When ready to bake, to make the required steam, add 1 cup of ice to the hot pan in the oven. Using the peel, immediately transfer the loaves to the hot baking stone(s) in the preheated oven.

Bake, with steam, for 35 minutes, or until the bread is a golden-brown color, the sides are firm to the touch, and the loaves make a hollow sound when tapped on the bottom.

Remove from the oven and transfer to wire racks to cool.

About *Ciabatta*

Ciabatta is a flat, rustic Italian bread that is substantially wider and flatter than a regular loaf. Its Italian translation is "slipper," which is indicative of its baked shape. It is made in almost every region of Italy, with each region having its own style.

Depending upon the locale, the texture can range from a firm, slightly tough crust and a soft, chewy interior to a very crisp crust with a light, holey interior. *Ciabatta* dough can be seasoned with salt, olives, herbs, or extra-virgin olive oil, each of which will change its texture somewhat. If made with whole wheat flour, it is known as *ciabatta integrale*; with milk, *ciabatta al latte*. In the United States, *ciabatta* is most often made with a sourdough starter and a very wet dough that produces a sour-tasting loaf with a very open crumb. No matter the style, *ciabatta* makes an excellent sandwich loaf and is often used to make *panino,* the classic grilled Italian sandwich.

Demonstration

Pane al' Olio

Makes 2 dozen rolls

Estimated time to complete: 18 hours
Intensive mix
Desired dough temperature (DDT): 75°F (25°C)

Ingredient	Amount	Baker's Percentage
For the biga:		
Bread flour	222 grams / 7¾ ounces	100%
Water	189 grams / 6⅔ ounces	85%
Fresh yeast	0.2 gram / pinch	0.1%
Total	**411 grams / 1 pound 13½ ounces**	**185.1%**
For the final dough:		
Bread flour	821 grams / 1 pound 13 ounces	100%
Water	452 grams / 16 ounces	55%
Biga	411 grams / 14½ ounces	50%
Salt	18 grams / ⅔ ounce	2.2%
Fresh yeast	16 grams / ½ ounce	2%
Olive oil	82 grams / 3 ounces	10%
Total	**1800 grams / 4 pounds**	**219.2%**

Oil for greasing bowl
Flour for dusting
Ice for steam

Equipment

Scale	Large bowl or container
Large mixing bowl	Two 12 x 18-inch sheet pans
Wooden spoon	Parchment paper
Bowl scraper	Baking stone(s) or tiles
Plastic film	Cast-iron or stainless steel roasting pan
Digital thermometer	Kitchen shears
Standing electric mixer fitted with the hook	Wire racks

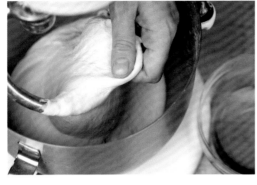

Prepare the *mise en place* for the biga.

To make the biga, combine the bread flour and water with the yeast in a large mixing bowl, stirring with a wooden spoon to blend. When blended, scrape down the edge of the bowl, cover with plastic film, and set aside to ferment at 75°F (25°C) for 12 to 14 hours.

When ready to make the final dough, prepare the *mise en place*.

Combine the bread flour with the water and biga in the bowl of a standing electric mixer fitted with the hook. Mix on low speed until blended.

Add the salt and yeast and mix on low for 5 minutes. Increase the mixer speed to medium and mix for 5 minutes, or until the dough is smooth. Check the gluten development by pulling a window (see page 64). If the gluten is fully developed, mix in the olive oil on low speed.

Lightly oil a large bowl or container.

Scrape the dough into the prepared bowl. Cover the bowl with plastic film and set aside to ferment for 30 minutes.

Uncover and fold the dough. Again, cover with plastic film and set aside to ferment for 1 hour.

Line the sheet pans with parchment paper.

Lightly flour a clean, flat work surface.

Uncover the dough and divide it into twenty-four 75-gram / 2¾-ounce rounds on the floured surface. Cover with plastic film and bench rest for 15 minutes.

Uncover the dough and, if necessary, lightly flour the work surface. Gently press on the dough to degas and carefully shape each round into a neat round roll. Place 12 rolls, seam side down, on each of the prepared sheet pans. Cover with plastic film and proof for 1 hour.

About an hour before you are ready to bake the rolls, place the baking stone(s) or tiles into the oven and pre-heat to 450°F (232°C). If using a pan to create steam (see page 70), place it in the oven now.

Uncover the dough and, using kitchen shears, snip a small cut at about a 45° angle and about ½ inch deep in the center of each roll to make a point. To make the required steam, add 1 cup of ice to the hot pan in the oven. Immediately place the rolls in the preheated oven.

Bake, with steam, for 22 minutes, or until the rolls are a golden-brown color, the sides are firm to the touch, and the rolls make a hollow sound when tapped on the bottom.

Remove from the oven and transfer to wire racks to cool.

Demonstration

Pane Pugliese

Makes 2 loaves

Estimated time to complete: 18 hours
Improved mix
Desired dough temperature (DDT): 75°F (25°C)

Ingredient	Amount	Baker's Percentage
For the biga:		
Bread flour	358 grams / 12⅔ ounces	100%
Water	179 grams / 6⅓ ounces	50%
Fresh yeast	0.4 gram / pinch	0.1%
Total	**537 grams / 1 pound 3 ounces**	**150.1%**
For the final dough:		
Bread flour	358 grams / 12⅔ ounces	100%
Water	322 grams / 11⅓ ounces	90%
Biga	537 grams / 1 pound 3 ounces	150%
Salt	14 grams / ½ ounce	4%
Fresh yeast	4 grams / ⅛ ounce	1%
Total	**1235 grams / 2 pounds 11½ ounces**	**345%**

Oil for greasing bowl
Flour for dusting

Equipment

Scale	Large cutting board
Large mixing bowl	*Couche*
Wooden spoon	Baking stone(s) or tiles
Bowl scraper	Cast-iron or stainless steel roasting pan
Plastic film	*Lame* or razor
Digital thermometer	Peel
Standing electric mixer fitted with the hook	Wire racks
Large bowl or container	

About *Pane Pugliese*
_____

Pane Pugliese is a simple peasant bread
from the Puglia area in southeastern
Italy. It has a deep flavor and, unlike
many Italian breads, is a good keeper
with an excellent shelf life.

Prepare the *mise en place* for the biga.

To make the biga, combine the bread flour and water
with the yeast in a large mixing bowl, stirring with a
wooden spoon to blend. When blended, scrape down
the edge of the bowl, cover with plastic film, and set
aside to ferment at 70°F (20°C) for 12 to 14 hours.

When ready to make the final dough, prepare the *mise
en place*.

Combine the bread flour with the water and biga in the
bowl of a standing electric mixer fitted with the hook.
Mix on low speed until blended. Stop the mixer and
autolyse for 15 minutes.

Add the salt and yeast and mix on low for 5 minutes.
Increase the mixer speed to medium and mix for about
12 minutes, or until the dough has come together but
remains slightly sticky. Check the gluten development
by pulling a window (see page 64).

Lightly oil a large bowl or container.

Scrape the dough into the prepared bowl. Cover the
bowl with plastic film and set aside to ferment for
30 minutes.

Uncover and fold the dough. Again, cover with plastic
film and set aside to ferment for 1 hour.

Cover the cutting board with the *couche* and dust the
couche with flour.

Lightly flour a clean, flat work surface.

Uncover the dough and divide it into two 600-gram /
21½-ounce rounds on the floured surface. Cover with
plastic film and bench rest for 15 minutes.

Uncover the dough and, if necessary, lightly flour the
work surface. Gently press on the dough to degas and
carefully shape each round into a long, pointy *bâtard*
(see pages 68–69).

Place one *bâtard* on one side of the *couche*-covered
board, fold the *couche* up to make a double layer of
cloth to serve as a divider between the loaves, and
place the remaining loaf next to the fold. Cover with
plastic film and proof for 1 hour.

About an hour before you are ready to bake the loaves,
place the baking stone(s) or tiles into the oven and preheat to 450°F (232°C). If using a pan to create steam
(see page 70), place it in the oven now.

Uncover the loaves and, using a *lame* or a razor, immediately score the loaves as directed on pages 63–65.
To make the required steam, add 1 cup of ice to the
hot pan in the oven. Using a peel, immediately transfer
the loaves to the hot baking stone(s) in the preheated
oven. Bake, with steam, for 40 minutes, or until the
crust is deep brown and crisp.

Remove from the oven and transfer to wire racks to cool.

Demonstration

Pane alle Patate

Makes 2 loaves

Estimated time to complete: 19 hours
Improved mix
Desired dough temperature (DDT): 75°F (25°C)

Ingredient	Amount	Baker's Percentage
For the biga:		
Bread flour	33 grams / 1⅛ ounces	100%
Water	28 grams / 1 ounce	85%
Fresh yeast	0.03 gram / pinch	0.1%
Total	**61 grams / 2⅛ ounces**	**185.1%**
For the final dough:		
Bread flour	474 grams / 1 pound ¾ ounce	100%
Water	237 grams / 8⅓ ounces	50%
Biga	61 grams / 2⅛ ounces	13%
Salt	16 grams / ½ ounce	3.3%
Fresh yeast	5 grams / ⅛ ounce	1%
Roughly mashed potatoes	355 grams / 12½ ounces	75%
Olive oil	24 grams / 1 ounce	5%
Minced garlic	19 grams / ⅔ ounce	4%
Minced fresh flat-leaf parsley	9 grams / ⅓ ounce	2%
Total	**1200 grams / 2 pounds 10¼ ounces**	**253.3%**

Oil for greasing bowl

Flour for dusting

Ice for steam

Equipment

Scale	Large cutting board
Large mixing bowl	*Couche*
Wooden spoon	Baking stone(s) or tiles
Bowl scraper	Cast-iron or stainless steel roasting pan
Plastic film	*Lame* or razor
Digital thermometer	Peel
Standing electric mixer fitted with the hook	Wire racks
Large bowl or container	

Prepare the *mise en place* for the biga.

To make the biga, combine the bread flour and water with the yeast in a large mixing bowl, stirring with a wooden spoon to blend. When blended, scrape down the edge of the bowl, cover with plastic film, and set aside to ferment at 70°F (20°C) for 12 to 14 hours.

When ready to make the final dough, prepare the *mise en place*.

Combine the bread flour with the water in the bowl of a standing electric mixer fitted with the hook. Mix on low speed until blended. Stop the mixer and autolyse for 15 minutes.

Lightly flour a clean, flat work surface.

Uncover the dough and divide it into two 600-gram / 21½-ounce rounds on the floured surface. Cover with plastic film and bench rest for 15 minutes.

Uncover the dough and, if necessary, lightly flour the work surface. Gently press on the dough to degas and carefully shape each piece into a neat round loaf. Place one loaf on one side of the *couche*-covered board, fold the *couche* up to make a double layer of cloth to serve as a divider between the loaves, and place the remaining loaf next to the fold. Cover with plastic film and proof for 1 hour.

About an hour before you are ready to bake the loaves, place the baking stone(s) or tiles into the oven and preheat to 450°F (232°C). If using a pan to create steam (see page 70), place it in the oven now.

Uncover the loaves and, using a *lame* or a razor, immediately score the loaves as directed on pages 63–65. To make the required steam, add 1 cup of ice to the hot pan in the oven. Using a peel, immediately transfer the loaves to the hot baking stone(s) in the preheated oven.

Bake, with steam, for 40 minutes or until the loaves are reddish brown and crisp.

Remove from the oven and transfer to wire racks to cool.

Add the biga, salt, and yeast and mix on low for 5 minutes. Increase the mixer speed to medium and mix for about 12 minutes, or until the dough has come together but remains slightly sticky. Check the gluten development by pulling a window (see page 64). If the gluten has developed sufficiently, mix in the potatoes, olive oil, garlic, and parsley on low speed.

Lightly oil a large bowl or container.

Scrape the dough into the prepared bowl. Cover the bowl with plastic film and set aside to ferment for 45 minutes.

Uncover and fold the dough. Again, cover with plastic film and set aside to ferment for 1 hour.

Cover the cutting board with the *couche* and dust the *couche* with flour.

Demonstration

Ciabatta with Liquid *Levain*

Makes 4 loaves

Estimated time to complete: 18 hours
Improved mix
Desired dough temperature (DDT): 75°F (25°C)

Ingredient	Amount	Baker's Percentage
For the liquid *levain*:		
Bread flour	67 grams / 2⅓ ounces	100%
Water	84 grams / 3 ounces	125%
Liquid *levain* culture (see pages 75–76)	7 grams / ¼ ounce	10%
Total	**158 grams / 5⅔ ounces**	**235%**
For the final dough:		
Bread flour	705 grams / 1 pound 9 ounces	100%
Water	517 grams / 1 pound 2¼ ounces	73.3%
Liquid *levain*	158 grams / 5⅔ ounces	22.5%
Salt	16 grams / ½ ounce	2.2%
Fresh yeast	4 grams / ⅛ ounce	0.5%
Total	**1400 grams / 3 pounds 1½ ounces**	**198.5%**

Oil for greasing bowl

Flour for dusting

Ice for steam

Equipment

Scale	Standing electric mixer fitted with the hook
Large mixing bowl	Large bowl or container
Wooden spoon	Baking stone(s) or tiles
Bowl scraper	Cast-iron or stainless steel roasting pan
Plastic film	Peel
Digital thermometer	Wire racks

Prepare the *mise en place* for the liquid *levain*.

To make the liquid *levain*, combine the bread flour and water with the culture in a large mixing bowl, stirring with a wooden spoon to blend. When blended, scrape down the edge of the bowl, cover with plastic film, and set aside to ferment at 75°F (25°C) for 12 to 14 hours.

When ready to make the final dough, prepare the *mise en place*.

Combine the bread flour with 465 grams / 16½ ounces of the water in the bowl of a standing electric mixer fitted with the hook. Mix on low speed until blended.

Add the liquid *levain* along with the salt and yeast and mix on low for 5 minutes. Increase the mixer speed to medium and mix for about 8 minutes, or until the dough has come together but remains slightly sticky. Drizzle in the remaining water and continue to mix until the dough is smooth and almost shiny. Check the gluten development by pulling a window (see page 64).

Lightly oil a large bowl or container.

Scrape the dough into the prepared bowl. Cover the bowl with plastic film and set aside to ferment for 1 hour.

Uncover and fold the dough. Again, cover with plastic film and set aside to ferment for 1 hour.

About an hour before you are ready to bake the loaves, place the baking stone(s) or tiles into the oven and preheat to 470°F (243°C). If using a pan to create steam (see page 70), place it in the oven now.

Lightly flour a clean, flat work surface.

Uncover the dough and divide it into four 350-gram / 12½-ounce rectangular pieces on the floured surface (they need not be perfectly shaped). Cover with plastic film and proof for 30 minutes.

Uncover the dough and, if necessary, lightly flour the work surface. Gently press on the dough to degas and carefully shape each piece of dough into a fairly even rectangle.

To make the required steam, add 1 cup of ice to the hot pan in the oven. Using a peel, immediately transfer the loaves to the hot baking stone(s) in the preheated oven.

Bake, with steam, for 35 minutes, or until the crust is golden brown and crisp and the loaves make a hollow sound when tapped on the bottom.

Remove from the oven and transfer to wire racks to cool.

Demonstration

Pane Siciliano Semolina

Makes 4 loaves

Estimated time to complete: 19 hours
Improved mix
Desired dough temperature (DDT): 75°F (25°C)

Ingredient	Amount	Baker's Percentage
For the poolish:		
Bread flour	260 grams / 9⅛ ounces	100%
Water	260 grams / 9⅛ ounces	100%
Fresh yeast	0.3 gram / pinch	0.1%
Total	**520 grams / 1 pound 2¼ ounces**	**200.1%**
For the final dough:		
Durum flour	649 grams / 1 pound 7 ounces	91%
Semolina flour	64 grams / 2¼ ounces	9%
Water	425 grams / 15 ounces	59.5%
Poolish	520 grams / 1 pound 2¼ ounces	72.7%
Salt	19 grams / ⅔ ounce	2.7%
Fresh yeast	4 grams / ⅛ ounce	0.6%
Toasted sesame seeds	19 grams / ⅔ ounce	2.7%
Total	**1700 grams / 3 pounds 12 ounces**	**238.2%**

Oil for greasing bowl
Flour for dusting
Semolina flour for finishing
Ice for steam

Equipment

Scale	2 large cutting boards
Large mixing bowl	*Couche* for two boards
Wooden spoon	12 x 18-inch sheet pan
Bowl scraper	Damp kitchen towel
Plastic film	Baking stone(s) or tiles
Digital thermometer	Cast-iron or stainless steel roasting pan
Standing electric mixer fitted with the hook	Peel
Large bowl or container	Wire racks

Prepare the *mise en place* for the poolish.

To make the poolish, combine the bread flour and water with the yeast in a large mixing bowl, stirring with a wooden spoon to blend. When blended, scrape down the edge of the bowl, cover with plastic film, and set aside to ferment at 75°F (25°C) for 12 to 14 hours.

When ready to make the final dough, prepare the *mise en place*.

Combine the durum and semolina flours with the water and poolish in the bowl of a standing electric mixer fitted with the hook. Mix on low speed until blended. Stop the mixer and autolyse for 15 minutes.

Add the salt along with the yeast and mix on low for 5 minutes. Increase the mixer speed to medium and mix for about 8 minutes, or until the dough has come together but remains slightly sticky. Check the gluten development by pulling a window (see page 64). If the gluten has developed sufficiently, mix in the sesame seeds on low speed.

Lightly oil a large bowl or container.

Scrape the dough into the prepared bowl. Cover the bowl with plastic film and set aside to ferment for 1 hour.

Uncover and fold the dough. Again, cover with plastic film and set aside to ferment for 1 hour.

Cover the cutting boards with the *couche* and dust the *couche* with flour.

Lightly flour a clean, flat work surface.

Uncover the dough and divide it into four 425-gram / 15-ounce logs on the floured surface. Cover with plastic film and bench rest for 15 minutes.

Sprinkle the semolina flour for finishing on a sheet pan.

Uncover the dough and, if necessary, lightly flour the work surface. Carefully shape each log into a baguette (see page 69) on the floured surface. Briefly wrap the damp kitchen towel around each loaf to help the semolina adhere. Then, roll each loaf in the semolina flour and form it into an S shape. Place one S-shaped loaf on one side of one of the *couche*-covered boards, fold the *couche* up to make a double layer of cloth to serve as a divider between the loaves, and place another loaf next to the fold. Repeat the process with the remaining two loaves on the second *couche*-covered board. Cover with plastic film and proof for 1 hour.

About an hour before you are ready to bake the loaves, place the baking stone(s) or tiles into the oven and preheat to 450°F (232°C). If using a pan to create steam (see page 70), place it in the oven now.

To make the required steam, add 1 cup of ice to the hot pan in the oven. Using a peel, immediately

About *Pane Siciliano Semolina*

Pane Siciliano Semolina, when formed into smaller loaves, is often used for *panini,* traditional Italian sandwiches. The semolina flour gives a deep yellow hue to the baked loaf and the sesame seeds add a hint of nuttiness.

transfer the loaves to the hot baking stone(s) in the preheated oven.

Bake, with steam, for 40 minutes, or until the crust is golden brown and crisp and the loaves make a hollow sound when tapped on the bottom

Remove from the oven and transfer to wire racks to cool.

Demonstration

Pane al' Olive

Makes 7 loaves

Estimated time to complete: 19 hours
Improved mix
Desired dough temperature (DDT): 75°F (25°C)

Ingredient	Amount	Baker's Percentage
For the biga:		
Bread flour	72 grams / 2½ ounces	100%
Water	61 grams / 2¼ ounces	85%
Fresh yeast	0.07 gram / pinch	0.1%
Total	**133 grams / 4¾ ounces**	**185.1%**
For the final dough:		
Bread flour	893 grams / 2 pounds	100%
Water	500 grams / 1 pound 2 ounces	56%
Biga	133 grams / 4¾ ounces	15%
Salt	118 grams / 4 ounces	2.2%
Fresh yeast	80 grams / 2⅔ ounces	1.5%
Olive oil	643 grams / 1 pound 7 ounces	12%
Pitted and chopped black olives	803 grams / 1 pound 12 ounces	15%
Total	**3170 grams / 7 pounds**	**201.7%**

Oil for greasing bowl
Flour for dusting
Ice for steam

Equipment

Scale	2 large cutting boards
Large mixing bowl	*Couche* for two boards
Wooden spoon	Baking stone(s) or tiles
Bowl scraper	Cast-iron or stainless steel roasting pan
Plastic film	*Lame* or razor
Digital thermometer	Peel
Standing electric mixer fitted with the hook	Wire racks
Large bowl or container	

Prepare the *mise en place* for the biga.

To make the biga, combine the bread flour and water with the yeast in a large mixing bowl, stirring with a wooden spoon to blend. When blended, scrape down the edge of the bowl, cover with plastic film, and set aside to ferment at 75°F (25°C) for 12 to 14 hours.

When ready to make the final dough, prepare the *mise en place*.

Combine the bread flour with the water and biga in the bowl of a standing electric mixer fitted with the hook. Mix on low speed until blended. Stop the mixer and autolyse for 15 minutes.

Add the salt and yeast and mix on low for 5 minutes. Increase the mixer speed to medium and mix for about 12 minutes, or until the dough has come together but remains slightly sticky. Check the gluten development by pulling a window (see page 64). If the gluten is fully developed, mix in the olive oil and then the olives on low speed.

Lightly oil a large bowl or container.

Scrape the dough into the prepared bowl. Cover the bowl with plastic film and set aside to ferment for 45 minutes.

Uncover and fold the dough. Again, cover with plastic film and set aside to ferment for 1 hour and 15 minutes.

Lightly flour a clean, flat work surface.

Uncover the dough and divide it into seven 450-gram / 16-ounce rounds on the floured surface. Cover with plastic film and bench rest for 15 minutes.

Cover the cutting boards with the *couche* and dust the *couche* with flour.

Uncover the dough and, if necessary, lightly flour the work surface. Gently press on the dough to degas and carefully shape each piece into a neat round. Place one loaf on one side of one of the *couche*-covered boards, fold the *couche* up to make a double layer of cloth to serve as a divider between the loaves, and place a second loaf next to the fold. Repeat the process with the remaining two loaves and the second *couche*-covered board. Cover with plastic film and proof for 1 hour.

About an hour before you are ready to bake the loaves, place the baking stone(s) or tiles into the oven and pre-heat to 450°F (232°C). If using a pan to create steam (see page 70), place it in the oven now.

Uncover the loaves and, using a *lame* or a razor, immediately score the loaves as directed on pages 63–65. To make the required steam, add 1 cup of ice to the hot pan in the oven. Using a peel, immediately transfer the loaves to the hot baking stone(s) in the preheated oven.

Bake, with steam, for 40 minutes, or until the crust is golden brown, the sides are firm to the touch, and the loaves make a hollow sound when tapped on the bottom.

Remove from the oven and transfer to wire racks to cool.

Demonstration

Pane Toscano

Makes 4 loaves

Estimated time to complete: 19 hours
Improved mix
Desired dough temperature (DDT): 75°F (25°C)

Ingredient	Amount	Baker's Percentage
For the biga:		
Bread flour	426 grams / 15 ounces	100%
Water	277 grams / 9¾ ounces	65%
Fresh yeast	0.4 gram / pinch	0.1%
Total	**703 grams / 1 pound 8½ ounces**	**165.1%**
For the final dough:		
Bread flour	639 grams / 1 pound 5⅓ ounces	100%
Water	448 grams / 15 ounces	70%
Biga	703 grams / 1 pound 8¾ ounces	110%
Fresh yeast	10 grams / ⅓ ounce	1.5%
Total	**1800 grams / 3 pounds 13 ounces**	**281.5%**

Oil for greasing bowl
Flour for dusting
Ice for steam

Equipment

Scale	2 large cutting boards
Large mixing bowl	*Couche* for two boards
Wooden spoon	Baking stone(s) or tiles
Bowl scraper	Cast-iron or stainless steel roasting pan
Plastic film	*Lame* or razor
Digital thermometer	Peel
Standing electric mixer fitted with the hook	Wire racks
Large bowl or container	

About *Pane Toscano*

For centuries, Tuscans have made salt-free breads. One theory for this is that the population has always been particularly penurious and, in early years when there was a salt tax, they simply refused to pay the tax and so made due without salt in their breads. Others theorize that the cuisine of the region is so tasty and deeply flavored that the bread is bland to marry well with the zest of the main dishes. Whatever the reason, *Pane Toscano*, though lacking in salt, is still quite crusty with a coarse crumb.

Prepare the *mise en place* for the biga.

To make the biga, combine the bread flour and water with the yeast in a large mixing bowl, stirring with a wooden spoon to blend. When blended, scrape down the edge of the bowl, cover with plastic film, and set aside to ferment at 75°F (25°C) for 12 to 14 hours.

When ready to make the final dough, prepare the *mise en place*.

Combine the bread flour with the water in the bowl of a standing electric mixer fitted with the hook. Mix on low speed until blended.

Add the biga and yeast and mix on low for 5 minutes. Increase the mixer speed to medium and mix for about 12 minutes, or until the dough has come together but remains slightly sticky. Check the gluten development by pulling a window (see page 64).

Lightly oil a large bowl or container.

Scrape the dough into the prepared bowl. Cover the bowl with plastic film and set aside to ferment for 45 minutes.

Uncover and fold the dough. Again, cover with plastic film and set aside to ferment for 1 hour and 15 minutes.

Cover the cutting boards with the *couche* and dust the *couche* with flour.

Lightly flour a clean, flat work surface.

Uncover the dough and divide it into four 450-gram / 16-ounce rounds on the floured surface. Cover with plastic film and bench rest for 15 minutes.

Uncover the dough and, if necessary, lightly flour the work surface. Gently press on the dough to degas and carefully shape each piece into a neat round. Place one loaf on one side of one of the *couche*-covered boards, fold the *couche* up to make a double layer of cloth to serve as a divider between the loaves, and place a second loaf next to the fold. Repeat the process with the remaining two loaves and the second *couche*-covered board. Cover with plastic film and proof for 1 hour.

About an hour before you are ready to bake the loaves, place the baking stone(s) or tiles into the oven and preheat to 450°F (232°C). If using a pan to create steam (see page 70), place it in the oven now.

Uncover the loaves and, using a *lame* or a razor, immediately score the loaves as directed on pages 63–65. To make the required steam, add 1 cup of ice to the hot pan in the oven. Using a peel, immediately transfer the loaves to the hot baking stone(s) in the preheated oven.

Bake, with steam, for 40 minutes, or until the crust is golden brown, the sides are firm to the touch, and the loaves make a hollow sound when tapped on the bottom.

Remove from the oven and transfer to wire racks to cool.

Demonstration

Foccacia (Soft Style)

Makes 2 sheets

Estimated time to complete: 5 hours

Intensive mix

Desired dough temperature (DDT): 75°F (25°C)

Ingredient	Amount	Baker's Percentage
Bread flour	1326 grams / 2 pounds 14¼ ounces	100%
Water	862 grams / 1 pound 14½ ounces	65%
Salt	27 grams / 1 ounce	2%
Fresh yeast	13 grams / ½ ounce	1%
Olive oil	172 grams / 6 ounces	13%
Total	**2400 grams / 5 pounds 4¼ ounces**	**181%**

Oil for greasing pans

Flour for dusting

Olive oil, tomato slices, rosemary, and coarse salt for topping (see also "About *Foccacia*")

Equipment

Scale	Bowl scraper
Standing electric mixer fitted with the hook	Plastic film
Two 12 x 18-inch sheet pans	Wire racks
Parchment paper	

Prepare the *mise en place*.

Combine the bread flour with the water, salt, and yeast in the bowl of a standing electric mixer fitted with the hook. Mix on low speed until blended. Increase the mixer speed to medium and mix for about 7 minutes, or until the dough is smooth and shiny. Check the gluten development by pulling a window (see page 64). If the gluten is fully developed, mix in the olive oil on low speed.

Line the sheet pans with parchment paper and lightly coat both sides of the paper with olive oil.

Lightly flour a clean, flat work surface.

Scrape the dough onto the floured surface and divide it into two pieces about 1200 grams / 2 pounds 10¾ ounces each. Place a piece of dough in the center of each of the prepared sheet pans. Cover with plastic film and set aside to ferment for 3 hours.

Uncover the dough and carefully stretch and flatten it with your fingertips to push it into the corners of the pan. Using your fingertips, gently dot the top of the dough with shallow holes (this is called dimpling). If desired, top with

About *Foccacia*

Modern *foccacia* has evolved from *panis focacius*, a flat bread baked in the ashes of the hearth in the bakeries of ancient Rome. It remains a flat bread, but in modern bakeries, it is usually flavored with olive oil and often herbs. *Foccacia* is classically topped with only olive oil, rosemary, and a sprinkling of coarse salt, but it can also be topped with cheese, herbs, aromatics such as garlic and onion, cured meats, tomatoes, or vegetables.

Foccacia dough can be rolled out or simply pressed into a baking pan. Prior to baking, the dough is usually marked with the baker's fingertips or slashed to keep it from forming bubbles at it bakes. Wells formed by fingertips can hold surface olive oil and thereby keep the surface soft, moist, and pliable.

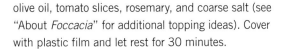

olive oil, tomato slices, rosemary, and coarse salt (see "About *Foccacia*" for additional topping ideas). Cover with plastic film and let rest for 30 minutes.

About a half hour before you are ready to bake the sheets, preheat the oven to 450°F (232°C).

Uncover the dough and transfer the pans to the pre-heated oven. Bake for 25 minutes, or until the crust is golden brown.

Remove from the oven and transfer to wire racks to cool.

Demonstration

Grissini

Makes 3 dozen breadsticks

Estimated time to complete: 17 hours or up to 25 hours
Intensive mix
Desired dough temperature (DDT): 75°F (25°C)

Ingredient	Amount	Baker's Percentage
For the biga:		
Bread flour	109 grams / 3¾ ounces	100%
Water	91 grams / 3¼ ounces	91%
Fresh yeast	0.1 gram / pinch	0.1%
Total	**200 grams / 7 ounces**	**191.1%**
For the final dough:		
Bread flour	1000 grams / 2 pounds 3⅓ ounces	100%
Water	480 grams / 1 pound 1 ounce	48%
Biga	200 grams / 7½ ounces	20%
Salt	22 grams / ¾ ounce	2.2%
Fresh yeast	20 grams / ¾ ounce	2%
Olive oil	100 grams / 3½ ounces	10%
Unsalted butter, at room temperature	100 grams / 3½ ounces	10%
Total	**1922 grams / 4 pounds 4 ounces**	**192.2%**

Oil for greasing bowl

Flour for dusting

Coarse salt, sesame seeds, or grated Parmesan cheese for topping (optional)

Equipment

Scale	Large bowl or container
Large mixing bowl	Three 12 x 18-inch sheet pans
Wooden spoon	Parchment paper
Bowl scraper	Rolling pin
Plastic film	Spray bottle filled with cool water
Digital thermometer	Pastry wheel or chef's knife
Standing electric mixer fitted with the hook	Wire racks

About *Grissini*

Originating in Turin and its surrounding areas sometime around the fourteenth century, *grissini* are extremely thin—almost chopstick-sized—sticks of very dry, crisp bread. There are three types of *grissini*: *stirato* (straight); *torinese* (the traditional kind made in Turin which are softer than the dry, crisp *grissini*, and are often twisted); and *rubatà* (hand rolled).

Prepare the *mise en place* for the biga.

To make the biga, combine the bread flour and water with the yeast in a large mixing bowl, stirring with a wooden spoon to blend. When blended, scrape down the edge of the bowl, cover with plastic film, and set aside to ferment at 75°F (25°C) for 12 to 14 hours.

When ready to make the final dough, prepare the *mise en place*.

Combine the bread flour with the water in the bowl of a standing electric mixer fitted with the hook. Mix on low speed until blended.

Add the biga, salt, and yeast and mix on low for 5 minutes. Increase the mixer speed to medium and mix about 5 minutes, or until the dough is smooth. Check the gluten development by pulling a window (see page 64). If the gluten is fully developed, mix in the olive oil and butter on low speed.

Lightly oil a large bowl or container.

Scrape the dough into the prepared bowl. Cover the bowl with plastic film and set aside to ferment for 1 hour.

Uncover and fold the dough. Again, cover with plastic film and refrigerate for at least 1 hour or up to 8 hours.

Line the baking sheets with parchment paper.

Lightly flour a clean, flat work surface.

About an hour before you are ready to bake the breadsticks, preheat the oven to 375°F (191°C).

Uncover the dough and place it on the floured surface. Using a rolling pin, roll out the dough to a rectangle about ¼ inch (6 millimeters) thick. Spray the surface of the dough with cool water to help the topping adhere. Sprinkle with coarse salt, seeds, or cheese, if desired.

Using a pastry wheel or chef's knife, cut the dough into strips about ½ inch (12 millimeters) wide. Arrange the strips on the prepared baking sheets. Cover with plastic film and proof for 30 minutes.

Uncover the dough and transfer the pans to the preheated oven. Bake for 15 to 18 minutes, depending upon the thickness, or until the breadsticks are light brown and crisp.

Remove from the oven and transfer to wire racks to cool.

Demonstration

Thin Crispy *Foccacia*

Makes 4 loaves

Estimated time to complete: 19 hours

Short mix

Desired dough temperature (DDT): 75°F (25°C)

Ingredient	Amount	Baker's Percentage
For the liquid *levain*:		
Bread flour	36 grams / 1¼ ounces	100%
Water	44 grams / 1½ ounces	125%
Liquid *levain* culture (see pages 75–76)	4 grams / ⅛ ounce	10%
Total	**84 grams / 2⅞ ounces**	**235%**
For the final dough:		
Bread flour	835 grams / 1 pound 13½ ounces	100%
Water	643 grams / 1 pound 6¾ ounces	77%
Liquid *levain*	84 grams / 2⅞ ounces	48.5%
Salt	17 grams / ⅔ ounce	2%
Yeast	4 grams / ⅛ ounce	0.5%
Olive oil	17 grams / ⅔ ounce	2%
Total	**1600 grams / 3 pounds 8½ ounces**	**230%**

Oil for greasing bowl

Flour for dusting

Olive oil, herbs, grated cheese, or olives for topping (optional; see Note)

Ice for steam

Equipment

Scale	Large bowl or container
Large mixing bowl	Baking stone(s) or tiles
Wooden spoon	Cast-iron or stainless steel roasting pan
Bowl scraper	2 large cutting boards
Plastic film	Pastry brush
Digital thermometer	Peel
Standing electric mixer fitted with the hook	Wire racks

Note

Thin crispy *foccacia* can be drizzled with olive oil and salt, sprinkled with grated cheese or herbs, or, in fact, lightly covered with anything the baker desires.

Prepare the *mise en place* for the liquid *levain*.

To make the liquid *levain*, combine the bread flour and water with the culture in a large mixing bowl, stirring with a wooden spoon to blend. When blended, scrape down the edge of the bowl, cover with plastic film, and set aside to ferment at 75°F (25°C) for 12 to 14 hours.

When ready to make the final dough, prepare the *mise en place*.

Combine the bread flour and water in the bowl of a standing electric mixer fitted with the hook. Mix on low speed until blended. Add the liquid *levain* along with the salt, yeast, and olive oil and mix on low for 5 minutes, or until the dough has come together.

Lightly oil a large bowl or container.

Scrape the dough into the prepared bowl. Cover the bowl with plastic film and set aside to ferment for 20 minutes.

Uncover and fold the dough. Again, cover with plastic film and set aside to ferment for 20 minutes.

Uncover and fold the dough. Cover with plastic film and set aside a third time to ferment for 20 minutes.

Finally, uncover and fold the dough, cover with plastic film, and set aside to ferment for 2 hours.

About an hour before you are ready to bake the loaves, place the baking stone(s) or tiles into the oven and preheat it to 500°F (260°C). If using a pan to create steam (see page 70), place it in the oven now.

Lightly flour a clean, flat work surface.

Uncover the dough and divide it into four 400-gram / 14-ounce rounds on the floured surface. Cover with plastic film and bench rest for 15 minutes.

Lightly dust two large cutting boards with flour.

Uncover the dough and, if necessary, lightly flour the work surface. Gently press on the dough to degas and carefully shape each piece into a neat round on the floured surface. Place two rounds on each of the pre-pared cutting boards. Cover with plastic film and proof for 45 minutes.

Uncover the dough and gently stretch each piece into a disk about 10 inches (25 centimeters) in diameter. Brush the disks with olive oil and sprinkle with herbs, grated cheese, or olives, if desired.

To make the required steam, add 1 cup of ice to the hot pan in the oven. Using a peel, immediately transfer the loaves to the hot baking stone(s) in the preheated oven.

Bake, with steam, for 10 minutes, or until the loaves are golden brown and crisp around the edges.

Remove from the oven and transfer to wire racks to cool.

Demonstration

Straight Dough *Ciabatta*

Makes 4 loaves

Estimated time to complete: 5 hours

Short mix

Desired dough temperature (DDT): 75°F (25°C)

Ingredient	Amount	Baker's Percentage
Bread flour	776 grams / 1 pound 11½ ounces	100%
Water	606 grams / 1 pound 5⅓ ounces	78%
Salt	14 grams / ½ ounce	1.8%
Fresh yeast	4 grams / ⅛ ounce	0.5%
Total	**1400 grams / 3 pounds 1½ ounces**	**180.3%**

Oil for greasing bowl

Flour for dusting

Ice for steam

Equipment

Scale	Baking stone(s) or tiles
Standing electric mixer fitted with the hook	Cast-iron or stainless steel roasting pan
Large bowl or container	Peel
Bowl scraper	Wire racks
Plastic film	

Prepare the *mise en place*.

Combine the bread flour with the water in the bowl of a standing electric mixer fitted with the hook. Mix on low speed until blended.

Add the salt and yeast and mix on low for 5 minutes, or until the dough has come together but remains slightly sticky.

Lightly oil a large bowl or container

Scrape the dough into the prepared bowl. Cover the bowl with plastic film and set aside to ferment for 20 minutes.

Uncover and fold the dough. Again, cover with plastic film and set aside to ferment for 20 minutes.

Uncover and fold the dough. Cover with plastic film and set aside a third time to ferment for 20 minutes.

Finally, uncover and fold the dough, cover with plastic film, and set aside to ferment for 2 hours.

About an hour before you are ready to bake the loaves, place the baking stone(s) or tiles into the oven and pre-heat to 470°F (243°C). If using a pan to create steam (see page 70), place it in the oven now.

Lightly flour a clean, flat work surface.

Uncover the dough and divide it into four 350-gram / 12½-ounce rectangular pieces on the floured surface (they need not be perfectly shaped). Cover with plastic film and bench rest for 30 minutes.

Uncover the dough and, if necessary, lightly flour the work surface. Gently press on the dough to degas and carefully shape each piece of dough into a fairly even rectangle.

To make the required steam, add 1 cup of ice to the hot pan in the oven. Using a peel, immediately transfer the loaves to the hot baking stone(s) in the preheated oven.

Bake, with steam, for 35 minutes, or until the crust is golden brown and firm and the loaves make a hollow sound when tapped on the bottom.

Remove from the oven and transfer to wire racks to cool.

Demonstration

Pane al Segale con Pancetta

Makes 4 loaves

Estimated time to complete: 17½ hours
Improved mix
Desired dough temperature (DDT): 75°F (25°C)

Ingredient	Amount	Baker's Percentage
For the biga:		
Bread flour	401 grams / 14 ounces	100%
Water	340 grams / 12 ounces	85%
Fresh yeast	0.4 gram / pinch	0.1%
Total	**741 grams / 1 pound 10 ounces**	**185.1%**
For the final dough:		
Rye flour	495 grams / 1 pound 1½ ounces	100%
Water	267 grams / 9½ ounces	54%
Biga	741 grams / 1 pound 10⅛ ounces	150%
Salt	25 grams / 1 ounce	5%
Olive oil	20 grams / ⅔ ounce	4%
Fresh yeast	5 grams / ¼ ounce	1%
Diced pancetta, rendered and drained	247 grams / 8¾ ounces	50%
Total	**1800 grams / 3 pounds 15½ ounces**	**364%**

Oil for greasing bowl

Flour for dusting

Ice for steam

Equipment

Scale	2 large cutting boards
Large mixing bowl	*Couche* for two boards
Wooden spoon	Baking stone(s) or tiles
Bowl scraper	Cast-iron or stainless steel roasting pan
Plastic film	*Lame* or razor
Digital thermometer	Peel
Standing electric mixer fitted with the hook	Wire racks
Large bowl or container	

Prepare the *mise en place* for the biga.

To make the biga, combine the bread flour and water with the yeast in a large mixing bowl, stirring with a wooden spoon to blend. When blended, scrape down the edge of the bowl, cover with plastic film, and set aside to ferment at 75°F (25°C) for 12 to 14 hours.

When ready to make the final dough, prepare the *mise en place*.

Combine the rye flour with the water, biga, salt, olive oil, and yeast in the bowl of a standing electric mixer fitted with the hook. Mix on low speed until blended.

Increase the mixer speed to medium and mix until the dough is smooth. Check the gluten development by pulling a window (see page 64). If the gluten is fully developed, mix in the pancetta on low speed.

Lightly oil a large bowl or container.

Scrape the dough into the prepared bowl. Cover the bowl with plastic film and set aside to ferment for 30 minutes.

Uncover and fold the dough. Again, cover with plastic film and set aside to ferment for 30 minutes.

Lightly flour a clean, flat work surface.

Uncover the dough and divide it into four 450-gram /

16-ounce rounds on the floured surface. Cover with plastic film and bench rest for 15 minutes.

Cover the cutting boards with the *couche* and dust the *couche* with flour.

Uncover the dough and, if necessary, lightly flour the work surface. Carefully shape each round into a long *bâtard* (see pages 68–69). Place one loaf on one side of one of the *couche*-covered boards, fold the *couche* up to make a double layer of cloth to serve as a divider between the loaves, and place a second loaf next to the fold. Repeat the process with the remaining two loaves and the second *couche*-covered board. Cover with plastic film and proof for 1 hour.

About an hour before you are ready to bake the loaves, place the baking stone(s) or tiles into the oven and preheat it to 450°F (232°C). If using a pan to create steam (see page 70), place it in the oven now.

Uncover the dough and, using a *lame* or a razor, immediately score the loaves as directed on pages 63–65. To make the required steam, add 1 cup of ice to the hot pan in the oven. Using a peel, immediately transfer the loaves to the hot baking stone(s) in the preheated oven.

Bake, with steam, for 40 minutes, or until the crust is deep brown and crisp and the loaves make a hollow sound when tapped on the bottom.

Remove from the oven and transfer to wire racks to cool.

Demonstration

Puccia

Makes 2 dozen rolls

Estimated time to complete: 18 hours

Improved mix

Desired dough temperature (DDT): 75°F (25°C)

Ingredient	Amount	Baker's Percentage
For the durum biga:		
Durum flour	103 grams / 3⅔ ounces	100%
Water	56 grams / 2 ounces	54%
Fresh yeast	0.5 gram / pinch	0.5%
Total	**159 grams / 5⅔ ounces**	**154.5%**
For the final dough:		
Bread flour	638 grams / 1 pound 6½ ounces	80%
Coarse whole wheat flour	160 grams / 5⅔ ounces	20%
Water	574 grams / 1 pound 4¼ ounces	72%
Durum biga	159 grams / 5⅔ ounces	20%
Salt	18 grams / ⅔ ounce	2.2%
Fresh yeast	12 grams / ½ ounce	1.5%
Pitted and chopped olives	239 grams / 8½ ounces	30%
Total	**1800 grams / 3 pounds 15½ ounces**	**225.7%**

Oil for greasing bowl

Flour for dusting

Ice for steam

Equipment

Scale	Large bowl or container
Large mixing bowl	Two 12 x 18-inch sheet pans
Wooden spoon	Parchment paper
Bowl scraper	Cast-iron or stainless steel roasting pan
Plastic film	*Lame* or razor
Digital thermometer	Peel
Standing electric mixer fitted with the hook	Wire racks

Prepare the *mise en place* for the durum biga.

To make the durum biga, combine the durum flour and water with the yeast in a large mixing bowl, stirring with a wooden spoon to blend. When blended, scrape down the edge of the bowl, cover with plastic film, and set aside to ferment at 75°F (25°C) for 12 to 14 hours.

When ready to make the final dough, prepare the *mise en place*.

Combine the bread and whole wheat flours with the water in the bowl of a standing electric mixer fitted with the hook. Mix on low speed until blended.

Add the durum biga, salt, and yeast and mix on low for 5 minutes. Increase the mixer speed to medium and mix for about 5 minutes, or until the dough is smooth. Check the gluten development by pulling a window (see page 64). If the gluten is fully developed, mix in the olives on low speed.

Lightly oil a large bowl or container.

Scrape the dough into the prepared bowl. Cover the bowl with plastic film and set aside to ferment for 45 minutes.

Uncover and fold the dough. Again, cover with plastic film and set aside to ferment for 45 minutes.

Lightly flour a clean, flat work surface.

Uncover the dough and divide it into twenty-four 75-gram / 2¾-ounce rounds on the floured surface. Cover with plastic film and bench rest for 15 minutes.

Line the sheet pans with parchment paper.

Uncover the dough and, if necessary, lightly flour the work surface. Gently press on the dough to degas and carefully shape each round into a neat ball.

Place 12 rolls on each of the prepared sheet pans. Cover with plastic film and proof for 1 hour.

About 1 hour before you are ready to bake the rolls, preheat the oven to 470°F (243°C). If using a pan to create steam (see page 70), place it in the oven now.

Uncover the dough and, using a *lame* or a razor, immediately score the rolls as directed on pages 63–65. To make the required steam, add 1 cup of ice to the hot pan in the oven. Immediately transfer the sheet pans to the preheated oven.

Bake, with steam, for 20 minutes, or until the crust is golden brown and crisp and the rolls make a hollow sound when tapped on the bottom.

Remove from the oven and transfer to wire racks to cool.

Demonstration

La Mouna

Makes 2 loaves

Estimated time to complete: 14 hours
Improved mix
Desired dough temperature (DDT): 75°F (25°C)

Ingredient	Amount	Baker's Percentage
For the soaker:		
Diced candied orange peel	177 grams / 6⅓ ounces	100%
Orange liqueur	35 grams / 1¼ ounces	20%
Total	**212 grams / 7½ ounces**	**120%**
For the quick sponge:		
Bread flour	254 grams / 9 ounces	100%
Milk	142 grams / 5 ounces	56%
Fresh yeast	35 grams / 1¼ ounces	14%
Total	**431 grams / 15¼ ounces**	**170%**
For the final dough:		
Bread flour	445 grams / 15⅔ ounces	100%
Cold eggs	267 grams / 9½ ounces	60%
Quick sponge	431 grams / 15¼ ounces	97%
Salt	13 grams / ½ ounce	2.9%
Orange flower water	42 grams / 1½ ounces	9.5%
Sugar	177 grams / 6¼ ounces	40%
Unsalted butter, at room temperature	213 grams / 7½ ounces	48%
Soaker	212 grams / 7½ ounces	47.7%
Total	**1800 grams / 3 pounds 15½ ounces**	**405.1%**

Oil for greasing bowl
Flour for dusting
1 large egg for egg wash
Pearl sugar for sprinkling

Equipment

Scale	Large bowl or container
2 small bowls	2 sheet pans
Wooden spoon	Parchment paper
Plastic film	Baking stone(s) or tiles
Standing electric mixer fitted with the hook	Pastry brush
Bowl scraper	Peel
Large mixing bowl	Wire racks

Prepare the *mise en place* for the soaker.

To make the soaker, combine the candied orange peel and liqueur in a small bowl, stirring with a wooden spoon to blend. Cover with plastic film and set aside to soak at room temperature for at least 8 hours.

When ready to make the final dough, prepare your *mise en place* for both the sponge and the final dough.

To make the quick sponge, combine the bread flour and milk with the yeast in the bowl of a standing electric mixer fitted with the hook. Mix on low speed until blended. When blended, scrape the sponge into a large mixing bowl, cover with plastic film, and set aside to ferment for 30 minutes.

To make the final dough, combine the bread flour with the eggs, quick sponge, salt, and orange flower water

Lightly flour a clean, flat work surface.

Uncover the dough and divide it into two 900-gram / 2-pound rounds on the floured surface. Cover with plastic film and bench rest for 15 minutes.

Uncover the dough and, if necessary, lightly flour the work surface. Carefully mold the dough into 2 neat rounds. Cover with plastic film and bench rest for 10 minutes.

Using your thumb, punch a hole in the center of each round and stretch the hole out to form a circle about 4 inches (10 centimeters) in diameter. Cover with plastic film and proof for 2 hours.

About an hour before you are ready to bake the loaves, place the baking stone(s) or tiles into the oven and preheat to 350°F (177°C).

in the bowl of a standing electric mixer fitted with the hook. Mix on low speed until blended.

Increase the mixer speed to medium and mix just until some gluten has developed and the dough has some elasticity. Begin adding the sugar, 3 tablespoons at a time, incorporating well after each addition. Continue to mix until the dough is smooth. Check the gluten development by pulling a window (see page 64). If the gluten is fully developed, mix in the butter on low speed, making sure that the butter is well incorporated. Then, mix in the soaker, again on low speed.

Lightly oil a large bowl or container

Scrape the dough into the prepared bowl. Cover the bowl with plastic film and set aside to ferment for 45 minutes.

Uncover and fold the dough. Again, cover with plastic film and set aside to ferment for 45 minutes.

To make the egg wash, combine the egg with 14 grams / 1 tablespoon water in a small bowl, whisking to blend.

Line two sheet pans with parchment paper and set aside.

Uncover the dough and carefully transfer one loaf to each prepared sheet pan. Using a pastry brush, lightly coat the top of each loaf with egg wash. Sprinkle the top of each loaf with pearl sugar.

Transfer the sheet pans to the hot baking stone(s) in the preheated oven. Bake for 45 minutes, or until the crust is golden brown and shiny.

Remove from the oven and transfer to wire racks to cool.

Demonstration

Panettone

Makes 2 loaves

Estimated time to complete: 20 hours or up to 27 hours
Improved mix
Desired dough temperature (DDT): 75°F (25°C)

Ingredient	Amount	Baker's Percentage
For the soaker:		
Dark raisins	121 grams / 4¼ ounces	100%
Candied orange peel	39 grams / 1⅓ ounces	32.13%
Candied lemon peel	39 grams / 1⅓ ounces	32.13%
Freshly grated orange zest	7 grams / ¼ ounce	1%
Freshly grated lemon zest	7 grams / ¼ ounce	0.67%
Water	77 grams / 2¾ ounces	64%
Pure vanilla extract	7 grams / ¼ ounce	0.67%
Total	**297 grams / 10½ ounces**	**230.6%**
For the liquid *levain*:		
Bread flour	62 grams / 2⅛ ounces	100%
Water	62 grams / 2⅛ ounces	100%
Liquid *levain* culture (see pages 75–76)	92 grams / 3¼ ounces	150%
Total	**216 grams / 7½ ounces**	**350%**
For the final dough:		
Bread flour	374 grams / 13¼ ounces	100%
Levain	215 grams / 7½ ounces	57.5%
Cold egg yolks	225 grams / 8 ounces	60%
Fresh yeast	15 grams / ½ ounce	4%
Salt	6 grams / ¼ ounce	1.4%
Diastatic malt	6 grams / ¼ ounce	1.4%
Honey	6 grams / ¼ ounce	1.4%
Sugar	120 grams / 4¼ ounces	32%
Cold unsalted butter, cut into bits	116 grams / 4 ounces	31%
Soaker	297 grams / 10 ounces	74.73%
Total	**1380 grams / 3 pounds**	**363.43%**

Oil for greasing bowl

Flour for dusting

1 large egg for egg wash

Equipment

Scale	Large bowl or container
Plastic container with lid	Bowl scraper
Wooden spoon	2 *panettone* papers or molds (see Note)
Digital thermometer	Small bowl
Large mixing bowl	Whisk
Bowl scraper	Pastry brush
Plastic film	Kitchen shears
Standing electric mixer fitted with the hook	Wire racks

About *Panettone*

Although it originated in Milan, *panettone* is a traditional Christmas sweet bread throughout Italy and Latin America. It rises up in a cylindrical shape usually about a foot tall. In addition to the traditional raisins, candied fruits, and citrus zests, *panettone* can also contain chocolate bits. It is usually served with a sweet wine or a warm sweet beverage.

Prepare the *mise en place* for the soaker.

To make the soaker, combine the raisins, orange and lemon peel, and orange and lemon zest in a plastic container with a lid. Add the water and vanilla, stirring with a wooden spoon to blend. Cover with the lid and set aside to soak at room temperature for at least 8 hours.

Prepare the *mise en place* for the *levain*, taking care that the water is about 85°F (29°C).

To make the *levain*, combine the bread flour and water with the culture in a large mixing bowl, stirring with a wooden spoon to blend. When blended, scrape down the edge of the bowl, cover with plastic film, and set aside to ferment for 5 hours at 85°F (29°C).

When ready to make the final dough, prepare the *mise en place*.

Combine the bread flour with the *levain*, egg yolks, yeast, salt, malt, and honey in the bowl of a standing electric mixer fitted with the hook. Mix on low speed until blended. Increase the mixer speed to medium and mix until the gluten is fully developed. Check the gluten development by pulling a window (see page 64).

With the mixer on medium speed, begin adding the sugar, 2 tablespoons at a time, incorporating well after each addition. When the sugar has been incorporated, add the butter, continuing to mix until the dough is smooth. Finally, add the soaker and mix until well blended.

Lightly oil a large bowl or container.

Note

Panettone can be made in *panettone* molds or in papers of the same shape. Both are available from bakery and kitchen supply stores. If using a mold, it should be generously greased.

Scrape the dough into the prepared bowl. Cover the bowl with plastic film and set aside to ferment for 5 hours at 85°F (29°C).

Lightly flour a clean, flat work surface.

Uncover the dough and divide it into two 690-gram / 24½-ounce rounds on the floured surface. Cover with plastic film and bench rest for 15 minutes.

Set up the two *panettone* papers or molds.

Uncover the dough and, if necessary, lightly flour the work surface. Gently press on the dough to degas and carefully form each piece into a neat round. Place each round, seam side down, into a *panettone* paper or greased mold. Cover with plastic film and proof for 5 hours at 85°F (29°C).

About an hour before you are ready to bake the *panettone*, preheat the oven to 350°F (177°C).

To make the egg wash, combine the egg with 14 grams / 1 tablespoon water in a small bowl, whisking to blend. Using a pastry brush, lightly coat the top of each loaf with the egg wash.

Using kitchen shears, cut a deep cross in the center top of each loaf.

Place the *panettone* in the preheated oven and bake for 45 minutes, or until the crust is golden brown and shiny.

Remove from the oven and transfer to wire racks to cool.

Demonstration

Panmarino

Makes 4 loaves

Estimated time to complete: 20 hours

Improved mix

Desired dough temperature (DDT): 75°F (25°C)

Ingredient	Amount	Baker's Percentage
For the biga:		
Bread flour	143 grams / 5 ounces	100%
Water	122 grams / 4¼ ounces	85%
Fresh yeast	0.1 gram / pinch	0.1%
Total	**265 grams / 9¼ ounces**	**185.1%**
For the final dough:		
Bread flour	884 grams / 1 pound 15 ounces	100%
Water	477 grams / 1 pound 1 ounce	54%
Milk	44 grams / 1½ ounces	5%
Biga	265 grams / 9⅓ ounces	30%
Salt	23 grams / ¾ ounce	2.6%
Fresh yeast	0.4 gram / pinch	1%
Olive oil	88 grams / 3 ounces	10%
Chopped fresh rosemary	9 grams / ⅓ ounce	1%
Total	**1800 grams / 3 pounds 15 ounces**	**203.6%**

Oil for greasing bowl

Flour for dusting

Ice for steam

Equipment

Scale	2 large cutting boards
Large mixing bowl	*Couche* for two boards
Wooden spoon	Baking stone(s) or tiles
Bowl scraper	Cast-iron or stainless steel roasting pan
Plastic film	*Lame* or razor
Digital thermometer	Peel
Standing electric mixer fitted with the hook	Wire racks
Large bowl or container	

Prepare the *mise en place* for the biga.

To make the biga, combine the bread flour and water with the yeast in a large mixing bowl, stirring with a wooden spoon to blend. When blended, scrape down the edge of the bowl, cover with plastic film, and set aside to ferment at 75°F (25°C) for 14 to 16 hours.

When ready to make the final dough, prepare the *mise en place*.

Combine the bread flour with the water, milk, and biga in the bowl of a standing electric mixer fitted with the hook. Mix on low speed until blended.

Add the salt and yeast and mix on low for 5 minutes. Increase the mixer speed to medium and mix for about 7 minutes, or until the dough is smooth. Check the gluten development by pulling a window (see page 64).

If the gluten is fully developed, mix in the olive oil and rosemary on low speed.

Lightly oil a large bowl or container.

Scrape the dough into the prepared bowl. Cover the bowl with plastic film and set aside to ferment for 45 minutes.

Uncover and fold the dough. Again, cover with plastic film and set aside to ferment for 45 minutes.

Lightly flour a clean, flat work surface.

Uncover the dough and divide it into four 450-gram / 16-ounce rounds on the floured surface. Cover with plastic film and bench rest for 15 minutes.

Cover the cutting boards with the *couche* and dust the *couche* with flour.

Uncover the dough and, if necessary, lightly flour the work surface. Gently press on the dough to degas and carefully shape each piece into a tight, neat round. Place one loaf on one side of one of the *couche*-covered boards, fold the *couche* up to make a double layer of cloth to serve as a divider between the loaves, and place a second loaf next to the fold. Repeat the process with the remaining two loaves and the second *couche*-covered board. Cover with plastic film and proof for 1 hour.

About an hour before you are ready to bake the loaves, place the baking stone(s) or tiles into the oven and pre-heat to 450°F (232°C). If using a pan to create steam (see page 70), place it in the oven now.

Uncover the dough and, using a *lame* or razor, score the top of each loaf as directed on pages 63–65. To make the required steam, add 1 cup of ice to the hot pan in the oven. Using a peel, immediately transfer the rounds to the hot baking stone(s) in the preheated oven.

Bake, with steam, for 40 minutes, or until the crust is light brown and crisp and the loaves make a hollow sound when tapped on the bottom.

Remove from the oven and transfer to wire racks to cool.

Demonstration

Pizza

Makes 1240 grams (2 pounds 11¾ ounces), enough for three 10-inch pizzas
Estimated time to complete: 16 hours or up to 18 hours
Improved mix
Desired dough temperature (DDT): 75°F (25°C)

Ingredient	Amount	Baker's Percentage
For the liquid *levain*:		
Bread flour	28 grams / 1 ounce	100%
Water	35 grams / 1¼ ounces	125%
Liquid *levain* culture (see pages 75–76)	3 grams / 1 teaspoon	10%
Total	**66 grams / 2⅓ ounces**	235%
For the final dough:		
Bread flour	666 grams / 1 pound 7½ ounces	100%
Water	452 grams / 16 ounces	68%
Liquid *levain*	66 grams / 2⅓ ounces	10%
Olive oil	33 grams / 1⅛ ounces	5%
Salt	16 grams / ½ ounce	2.4%
Fresh yeast	7 grams / ¼ ounce	1%
Total	**1240 grams / 2 pounds 11¾ ounces**	**186.4%**

Flour for dusting

219 grams (7¾ ounces) tomato sauce for topping (optional; see also "About Pizza")

171 grams (6 ounces) grated mozzarella cheese for topping (optional; see also "About Pizza")

Fresh whole basil leaves for topping

Equipment

Scale	Standing electric mixer fitted with the hook
Large mixing bowl	Two 12 x 18-inch sheet pans
Wooden spoon	Baking stone(s) or tiles
Bowl scraper	Peel
Plastic film	Wire racks
Digital thermometer	

Note

Whatever topping you choose for your pizza, it is best that it be applied lightly; too much topping will render the baked crust soggy rather than give it the desired crisp, chewy texture.

Prepare the *mise en place* for the *levain*.

To make the *levain*, combine the bread flour and water with the culture in a large mixing bowl, stirring with a wooden spoon to blend. When blended, scrape down the edge of the bowl, cover with plastic film, and set aside to ferment at 70°F (20°C) for 12 to 14 hours.

When ready to make the final dough, prepare the *mise en place*.

Combine the bread flour with the water, liquid *levain*, olive oil, salt, and yeast in the bowl of a standing electric mixer fitted with the hook. Mix on low speed until blended. Increase the mixer speed to medium and

About Pizza

Although little is known about the early history of pizza, we do know that by the sixteenth century, a flat bread known as pizza was served as a street food to the poor population in Naples. The original topping was a type of béchamel sauce and a basic oil; cheese and tomato topping came next. By the late nineteenth century, the Pizza Margherita, featuring tomatoes, mozzarella cheese, and basil to honor the colors of the Italian flag, was devised to pay homage to the Queen consort of Italy, Margherita of Savoy. Another style, Pizza Marinara, is topped with tomatoes (or occasionally tomato sauce), basil, oregano, and garlic, and is drizzled with extra-virgin olive oil. Although over the years many, many toppings have come to be accepted, Neapolitans say that there are only two honest pizzas—Pizza Margherita and Pizza Marinara.

There are specific rules regarding the proper execution of a baked pizza. The *Associazione Verace Pizza Napoletana* (True Neapolitan Pizza Association) sets the guidelines for honorable pizza making. The dough for a true Neapolitan pizza must be hand-kneaded and rolled and not exceed 13 inches (33 centimeters) in diameter nor be more than ⅛ inch (3 millimeters) thick at the center. The topped pizza round must be baked in a wood-fired, domed oven at 930°F (499°C) for no more than 90 seconds.

mix for about 8 minutes, or until the dough has come together but remains slightly sticky. Check the gluten development by pulling a window (see page 64).

Lightly dust a clean, flat work surface.

Scrape the dough from the bowl onto the floured surface. For three 10-inch (25-centimeter) pizzas, divide the dough into three 413-gram / 14½-ounce rounds on the floured surface. Cover with plastic film and set aside to ferment for 2 hours at room temperature.

Transfer to the refrigerator and proof for 1 hour or up to overnight.

About an hour before you are ready to bake the pizzas, place the baking stone(s) or tiles into the oven and preheat to 650°F (343°C).

When ready to bake, remove the dough from the refrigerator, uncover, and, working with one piece at a time, use your hands to carefully stretch each dough round into a thin, evenly round circle about 10 inches (25 centimeters) in diameter.

Top with tomato sauce, cheese, and fresh basil (see "About Pizza" for additional topping ideas).

Using a peel, transfer the pizzas to the hot baking stone(s) in the preheated oven. Bake for 8 minutes, or until the topping is bubbling and the dough is crisp and crackling brown around the edges.

Remove from the oven and serve immediately.

Demonstration

Ciriole

Makes 2 dozen rolls

Estimated time to complete: 3½ hours

Intensive mix

Desired dough temperature (DDT): 75°F (25°C)

Ingredient	Amount	Baker's Percentage
Bread flour	1065 grams / 2 pounds 5⅔ ounces	100%
Water	586 grams / 1 pound 4⅔ ounces	55%
Malt syrup	53 grams / 2 ounces	5%
Olive oil	48 grams / 1¾ ounces	4.5%
Fresh yeast	27 grams / 1 ounce	2.5%
Salt	21 grams / ¾ ounce	2%
Total	**1800 grams / 3 pounds 15¾ ounces**	**169%**

Oil for greasing bowl

Flour for dusting

Ice for steam

Equipment

Scale	Cast-iron or stainless steel roasting pan
Standing electric mixer fitted with the hook	Two 12 x 18-inch sheet pans
Large bowl or container	Parchment paper
Bowl scraper	Kitchen shears
Plastic film	Wire racks
Baking stone(s) or tiles	

Prepare the *mise en place*.

Combine the bread flour with the water, malt syrup, olive oil, yeast, and salt in the bowl of a standing electric mixer fitted with the hook. Mix on low speed until blended. Increase the mixer speed to medium and mix for about 8 minutes, or until the dough has come together but remains slightly sticky. Check the gluten development by pulling a window (see page 64).

Lightly oil a large bowl or container.

Scrape the dough into the prepared bowl. Cover with plastic film and set aside to ferment for 1 hour.

Lightly flour a clean, flat work surface.

Uncover the dough and divide it into twenty-four 75-gram / 2¾-ounce rounds on the floured surface. Cover with plastic film and bench rest for 15 minutes.

About an hour before you are ready to bake the rolls, place the baking stone(s) or tiles into the oven and pre-heat to 450°F (232°C). If using a pan to create steam (see page 70), place it in the oven now.

Line the sheet pans with parchment paper.

Uncover the dough and, if necessary, lightly flour the work surface. Carefully shape each round into either a small neat round for round rolls or into small *bâtards* (see pages 68–69) for oblong rolls. Place twelve of the rolls on each of the prepared sheet pans.

Cover with plastic film and set aside to proof for 1 hour.

Uncover the dough and, using kitchen shears, snip a small V about ½ inch deep in the center of each roll.

To make the required steam, add 1 cup of ice to the hot pan in the oven. Immediately transfer the sheet pans to the preheated oven. Bake, with steam, for 18 minutes for the *bâtard* rolls or 20 minutes for the round rolls, or until the rolls are a golden-brown color, the crust is crisp, and the rolls make a hollow sound when tapped on the bottom.

Remove from the oven and transfer to wire racks to cool.

Demonstration

Pane Francese

(Adapted from Michel Suas' Advanced Bread and Pastry)

Makes 4 loaves

Estimated time to complete: 21 hours

Short mix

Desired dough temperature (DDT): 75°F (25°C)

Ingredient	Amount	Baker's Percentage
For the poolish:		
Bread flour	157 grams / 5½ ounces	100%
Water	157 grams / 5½ ounces	100%
Fresh yeast	0.1 gram / pinch	0.1%
Total	**314 grams / 11 ounces**	**200.1%**
For the final dough:		
Bread flour	500 grams / 1 pound 1⅓ ounces	80%
Whole wheat flour	125 grams / 4½ ounces	20%
Water	450 grams / 1 pound	70%
Poolish	314 grams / 11 ounces	50%
Salt	12 grams / ½ ounce	2%
Fresh yeast	3 grams / ⅛ ounce	1%
Malt	6 grams / ¼ ounce	1%
Total	**1410 grams / 3 pounds 1¾ ounces**	**224%**

Oil for greasing bowl

Flour for dusting

Ice for steam

Equipment

Scale	Large bowl or container
Large mixing bowl	Baking stone(s) or tiles
Wooden spoon	Cast-iron or stainless steel roasting pan
Bowl scraper	Pastry wheel or chef's knife
Plastic film	Peel
Digital thermometer	Wire racks
Standing electric mixer fitted with the hook	

About *Pane Francese*

Pane Francese, which translates to "French bread," is a strong-flavored bread with a thin, crisp crust and an open crumb, perfect for the dinner table. It originated in Lombardy, where the influence of French cuisine is strongly felt even today.

Prepare the *mise en place* for the poolish.

To make the poolish, combine the bread flour and water with the yeast in a large mixing bowl, stirring with a wooden spoon to blend. When blended, scrape down the edge of the bowl, cover with plastic film, and set aside to ferment at 70°F (20°C) for 14 to 16 hours.

When ready to make the final dough, prepare the *mise en place*.

Combine the bread and whole wheat flours with the water in the bowl of a standing electric mixer fitted with the hook. Mix on low speed until blended.

Add the poolish along with the salt, yeast, and malt and mix on low for 5 minutes, or until the dough has come together but remains slightly sticky. Check the gluten development by pulling a window (see page 64).

Lightly oil a large bowl or container.

Scrape the dough into the prepared bowl. Cover the bowl with plastic film and set aside to ferment for 20 minutes.

Uncover and fold the dough. Again, cover with plastic film and set aside to ferment for 20 minutes.

Uncover and fold the dough. Cover with plastic film and set aside a third time to ferment for 20 minutes.

Finally, uncover and fold the dough, cover with plastic film, and set aside to ferment for 2 hours.

About an hour before you are ready to bake the loaves, place the baking stone(s) or tiles into the oven and pre-heat to 470°F (243°C). If using a pan to create steam (see page 70), place it in the oven now.

Lightly flour a clean, flat work surface.

Uncover the dough and place it on the floured surface. Using a pastry wheel or chef's knife, cut the dough into four 350-gram / 12½-ounce long, thin strips about 20 inches (51 centimeters) long and 3 inches (7.6 centimeters) wide.

Cover with plastic film and proof for 30 minutes.

Uncover the dough and, if necessary, lightly flour the work surface. Gently press on the strips to degas. To make the required steam, add 1 cup of ice to the hot pan in the oven. Using a peel, immediately transfer the strips to the hot baking stone(s) in the preheated oven.

Bake for 25 minutes, or until the crust is deep brown and crisp and the strips make a hollow sound when tapped on the bottom.

Remove from the oven and transfer to wire racks to cool.

Demonstration

Pane alla Cioccolata

Makes 2 loaves

Estimated time to complete: 21 hours or up to 23 hours
Improved mix
Desired dough temperature (DDT): 75°F (25°C)

Ingredient	Amount	Baker's Percentage
For the liquid *levain*:		
Bread flour	225 grams / 8 ounces	100%
Water	280 grams / 9¾ ounces	125%
Liquid *levain* culture (see pages 75–76)	25 grams / ¾ ounce	10%
Total	**530 grams / 18½ ounces**	235%
For the final dough:		
Bread flour	320 grams / 11¼ ounces	100%
Dutch-processed cocoa powder	32 grams / 1⅛ ounces	10%
Water	175 grams / 6⅛ ounces	54.5%
Liquid *levain*	530 grams / 1 pound 2⅔ ounces	15%
Eggs, at room temperature	30 grams / 1 ounce	9%
Milk	20 grams / ¾ ounce	6%
Unsalted butter, at room temperature	15 grams / ½ ounce	4.5%
Fresh yeast	10 grams / ⅓ ounce	3%
Sea salt	6 grams / ¼ ounce	2%
Sugar	70 grams / 2½ ounces	22%
Semisweet chocolate chunks	130 grams / 4½ ounces	40%
Dried cherries	50 grams / 1¾ ounces	15%
Total	**1388 grams / 3 pounds ¾ ounce**	281%

Oil for greasing bowl
Flour for dusting
Butter for greasing pans
1 large egg for egg wash
Ice for steam

Equipment

Scale

Large mixing bowl

Wooden spoon

Bowl scraper

Plastic film

Digital thermometer

Standing electric mixer fitted with the hook

Large bowl or container

Two 9-inch loaf pans

Baking stone(s) or tiles

Cast-iron or stainless steel roasting pan

Small bowl

Whisk

Pastry brush

Wire racks

Prepare the *mise en place* for the liquid *levain*.

To make the liquid *levain*, combine the bread flour and water with the culture in a large mixing bowl, stirring with a wooden spoon to blend. When blended, scrape down the edge of the bowl, cover with plastic film, and set aside to ferment at room-temperature or 75°F (25°C) for 14 to 16 hours.

When ready to make the final dough, prepare the *mise en place*, taking care that the eggs and butter are at room temperature.

Combine the bread flour and cocoa powder with the water, liquid *levain*, eggs, milk, butter, yeast, and sea salt in the bowl of a standing electric mixer fitted with the hook. Mix on low speed until combined. Increase the mixer speed to medium and mix until well blended.

Uncover the dough and, if necessary, lightly flour the work surface. Gently press on the dough to degas and carefully shape each piece into a *bâtard* (see pages 68 69). Place each *bâtard* into a prepared loaf pan, seam side down. Cover with plastic film and proof for 2 hours.

About an hour before you are ready to bake the rounds, place the baking stone(s) or tiles in the oven and preheat to 350°F (177°C). If using a pan to create steam (see page 70), place it in the oven now.

To make the egg wash, combine the egg with 14 grams / 1 tablespoon water in a small bowl, whisking to combine.

Using a pastry brush, lightly coat the top of each loaf with the egg wash.

To make the required steam, add 1 cup of ice to the hot pan in the oven. Immediately transfer the loaves to the preheated oven.

Bake for 35 minutes, or until the crust is deep brown and the sides are firm to the touch.

Remove from the oven. Then turn the loaves from the pans onto wire racks to cool.

Begin adding the sugar, about a tablespoon at a time, incorporating well after each addition. Continue mixing for about 10 minutes or until the gluten is fully developed. Check the gluten development by pulling a window (see page 64). If the gluten is sufficiently developed, mix in the chocolate and cherries on low speed.

Lightly oil a large bowl or container.

Scrape the dough into the prepared bowl. Cover with plastic film and set aside to ferment for 1 hour.

Uncover and fold the dough. Again, cover with plastic film and set aside to ferment for 1 hour.

Lightly flour a clean, flat work surface.

Uncover the dough and divide it into two 694-gram / 24¾-ounce pieces. Cover with plastic film and bench rest for 10 minutes.

Lightly butter two 9-inch loaf pans.

Session 10

German and Middle European Breads

Traditional German and Middle European breads are considered to be among the healthiest breads because they are usually made with whole grains and little sugar. The most common flour used is rye, frequently in combination with wheat or other flours. Since rye flour is low in gluten, the breads, for the most part, tend to be quite dense and chewy. In addition, seeds, nuts, and whole grains are also used to intensify flavor and add texture. In Germany, the most ancient method of making rye bread is first to allow the dough to rest for almost a week, turning it slightly sour and giving the baked bread a very strong flavor and a deep color. However, nowadays, due to time constraints, very few bakers follow this classic method.

Because many German and Middle European breads have a high moisture content, they also tend to have a long shelf life. In addition, the baking process—a long, slow bake in a steam-heated oven—creates not only a moist, dense texture, but also a nutty taste and a deep caramel color.

Caraway Rye Bread	Sourdough Bagels
Five-Grain Bread	*Leinsamenbrot*
Kaiser Rolls	Pretzels
Baguettebrotchen	*Vinchgauer*
Challah	66 Percent Sourdough Rye Bread
40 Percent Sourdough Rye Bread	*Krauterquarkbrot*
Sourdough Rye Bread with Walnuts	German Fruit Bread
Whole Wheat and Rye Sourdough Bread	*Landbrot mit Sauerkraut*
Haferbrot	Swedish *Limpa*
Kugelhopf	Pumpernickel Bread
Musli-Brotchen	Stollen

Demonstration

Caraway Rye Bread

Makes 2 loaves

Estimated time to complete: 21 hours

Improved mix

Desired dough temperature (DDT): 75°F (25°C)

Ingredient	Amount	Baker's Percentage
For the rye *levain*:		
Coarse rye flour	44 grams / 1½ ounces	100%
Water	37 grams / 1⅓ ounces	85%
Liquid *levain* culture (see pages 75–76)	2 grams / pinch	5%
Total	**83 grams / 3 ounces**	**190%**
For the final dough:		
Bread flour	522 grams / 1 pound 2½ ounces	85%
Rye flour	92 grams / 3¼ ounces	15%
Water	455 grams / 1 pound	74%
Rye *levain*	83 grams / 3 ounces	40%
Fresh yeast	6 grams / ¼ ounce	1%
Salt	13 grams / ½ ounce	2.4%
Toasted caraway seeds	9 grams / ⅓ ounce	1.5%
Total	**1180 grams / 2 pounds 9¾ ounces**	**218.9%**

Oil for greasing bowl

Flour for dusting

Ice for steam

Equipment

Scale	Large cutting board
Large mixing bowl	*Couche*
Wooden spoon	Baking stone(s) or tiles
Bowl scraper	Cast-iron or stainless steel roasting pan
Plastic film	*Lame* or razor
Digital thermometer	Peel
Standing electric mixer fitted with the hook	Wire racks
Large bowl or container	

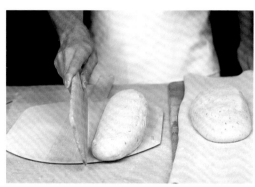
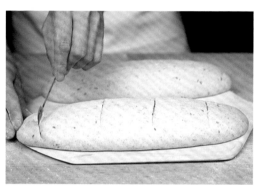

Prepare the *mise en place* for the rye *levain*.

To make the rye *levain*, combine the coarse rye flour and water with the culture in a large mixing bowl, stirring with a wooden spoon to blend. When blended, scrape down the edge of the bowl, cover with plastic film, and set aside to ferment at 70°F (20°C) for 14 to 16 hours.

When ready to make the final dough, prepare the *mise en place*.

Combine the bread and rye flours with the water and rye *levain* in the bowl of a standing electric mixer fitted with the hook. Mix on low speed until blended. Stop the mixer and autolyse for 15 minutes.

Add the yeast and salt and mix on low for 5 minutes. Increase the mixer speed to medium and mix for 5 to 10 minutes, or until the dough begins to pull away from the sides of the bowl, feels elastic, and gives some resistance when tugged. Mix in the caraway seeds on low speed.

Lightly oil a large bowl or container.

Scrape the dough into the prepared bowl. Cover the bowl with plastic film and set aside to ferment for 45 minutes.

Uncover and fold the dough. Again, cover with plastic film and set aside to ferment for 45 minutes.

Lightly flour a clean, flat work surface.

Uncover the dough and divide it into two 590-gram / 21-ounce rounds on the floured surface. Cover with plastic film and bench rest for 15 minutes.

Cover a large cutting board with a *couche* and dust the *couche* with flour.

Uncover and, if necessary, lightly flour the work surface. Gently press on the dough to degas and carefully shape each round into a *bâtard* (see pages 68–69). Place one loaf on one side of the *couche*-covered

board, fold the *couche* up to make a double layer of cloth to serve as a divider between the loaves, and place the remaining loaf next to the fold. Cover with plastic film and proof for 1½ to 2 hours.

About an hour before you are ready to bake the loaves, place the baking stone(s) or tiles into the oven and preheat to 470°F (243°C). If using a pan to create steam (see page 70), place it in the oven now.

Uncover the dough and, using a *lame* or a razor, immediately score the loaves as directed on pages 63–65. To make the required steam, add 1 cup of ice to the hot pan in the oven. Using a peel, immediately transfer the loaves to the hot baking stone(s) in the preheated oven.

Bake, with steam, for 45 minutes, or until the crust is a deep brown color, the sides are firm to the touch, and the loaves make a hollow sound when tapped on the bottom.

Remove from the oven and transfer to wire racks to cool.

Demonstration

Five-Grain Bread

(Adapted from The Bread Bakers Guild Team USA 1999)

Makes 2 loaves

Estimated time to complete: 19 hours or up to 21 hours
Improved mix
Desired dough temperature (DDT): 75°F (25°C)

Ingredient	Amount	Baker's Percentage
For the soaker:		
Flax seeds	39 grams / 1⅓ ounces	20%
Sesame seeds	39 grams / 1⅓ ounces	20%
Sunflower seeds	39 grams / 1⅓ ounces	20%
Pumpkin seeds	39 grams / 1⅓ ounces	20%
Rolled oats	39 grams / 1⅓ ounces	20%
Cold water	127 grams / 4½ ounces	64.8%
Total	**322 grams / 11¼ ounces**	**164.8%**
For the liquid *levain*:		
Bread flour	82 grams / 3 ounces	100%
Water	102 grams / 3½ ounces	125%
Liquid *levain* culture (see pages 75–76)	8 grams / ⅓ ounce	10%
Total	**192 grams / 6¾ ounces**	**235%**
For the final dough:		
Bread flour	254 grams / 9 ounces	60.1%
Whole wheat flour	127 grams / 4½ ounces	30%
Dark rye flour	42 grams / 1½ ounces	9.9%
Water	247 grams / 8⅔ ounces	58.4%
Liquid *levain*	192 grams / 6¾ ounces	45.5%
Fresh yeast	4 grams / ⅛ ounce	1.1%
Salt	12 grams / ½ ounce	2.8%
Soaker	322 grams / 11⅓ ounces	76.4%
Total	**1200 grams / 2 pounds 10⅓ ounces**	**284.2%**

Oil for greasing bowl

Flour for dusting

Flax seeds, sesame seeds, sunflower seeds, pumpkin seeds, and rolled oats for finishing

Ice for steam

Equipment

Scale	Large cutting board
Plastic container with lid	*Couche*
Wooden spoon	Damp kitchen towel
Large mixing bowl	12 x 18-inch sheet pan
Bowl scraper	Baking stone(s) or tiles
Plastic film	Cast-iron or stainless steel roasting pan
Digital thermometer	*Lame* or razor
Standing electric mixer fitted with the hook	Peel
Large bowl or container	Wire racks

Prepare the *mise en place* for the soaker.

To make the soaker, combine the flax, sesame, sunflower, and pumpkin seeds with the oats in a plastic container with a lid. Add the water, stirring with a wooden spoon to blend. Cover and set aside to soak at room temperature for 12 hours.

Prepare the *mise en place* for the liquid *levain*.

To make the liquid *levain*, combine the bread flour and water with the culture in a large mixing bowl, stirring with a wooden spoon to blend. When blended, scrape down the edge of the bowl, cover with plastic film, and set aside to ferment for 14 to 16 hours at room temperature or 75°C (25°C).

When ready to make the final dough, prepare the *mise en place*.

Combine the bread, whole wheat, and rye flours with the liquid *levain* and water in the bowl of a standing electric mixer fitted with the hook. Mix on low speed until blended. Stop the mixer and autolyse for 15 minutes.

Add the yeast and salt and mix on low for 5 minutes. Increase the mixer speed to medium and mix for about 7 minutes, or until the dough begins to pull away from the sides of the bowl, feels elastic, and gives some resistance when tugged. Decrease the mixer speed to low and mix in the soaker, including any remaining liquid.

Lightly oil a large bowl or container.

Scrape the dough into the prepared bowl. Cover the bowl with plastic film and set aside to ferment for 45 minutes.

Uncover and fold the dough. Again, cover with plastic film and set aside to ferment for 45 minutes.

Cover the cutting board with the *couche* and dust the *couche* with flour.

Lightly flour a clean, flat work surface.

Uncover the dough and divide it into two 600-gram / 21-ounce rounds on the floured surface. Cover with plastic film and bench rest for 10 minutes.

Uncover the dough and, if necessary, lightly flour the work surface. Gently press on the dough to degas and carefully shape each round into a *bâtard* (see pages 68–69). Place the damp kitchen towel on one half of the sheet pan. Place the seeds and oats for finishing on the other half. Working with one loaf at a time, roll the dough on the moistened towel, then roll the damp dough over and onto the seeds and oats. The dampness will help the seeds and oats adhere to the dough during baking. Place one loaf on one side of the *couche*-covered board, fold the *couche* up to make a double layer of cloth to serve as a divider between the loaves, and place the remaining loaf next to the fold. Cover with plastic film and proof for 1½ to 2 hours.

About an hour before you are ready to bake the loaves, place the baking stone(s) or tiles into the oven and pre-heat to 470°F (243°C). If using a pan to create steam (see page 70), place it in the oven now.

Uncover the dough and, using a *lame* or a razor, immediately score the loaves as directed on pages 63–65. To make the required steam, add 1 cup of ice to the hot pan in the oven. Using a peel, immediately transfer the loaves to the hot baking stone(s) in the preheated oven.

Bake, with steam, for 35 minutes, or until the crust is a deep brown color, the sides are firm to the touch, and the loaves make a hollow sound when tapped on the bottom.

Remove from the oven and transfer to wire racks to cool.

Demonstration

Kaiser Rolls

Makes 1 dozen rolls

Estimated time to complete: 3¾ hours

Intensive mix

Desired dough temperature (DDT): 75°F (25°C)

Ingredient	Amount	Baker's Percentage
Bread flour	812 grams / 1 pound 12⅔ ounces	100%
Water	430 grams / 15⅛ ounces	53%
Eggs	41 grams / 1½ ounces	5%
Fresh yeast	29 grams / 1 ounce	3.5%
Vegetable oil	19 grams / ⅔ ounce	2.4%
Malt syrup	16 grams / ½ ounce	2%
Salt	19 grams / ⅔ ounce	2.4%
Sugar	18 grams / ⅔ ounce	2.2%
Total	**1384 grams / 3 pounds ¾ ounce**	**170.5%**

Oil for greasing bowl

Flour for dusting

Equipment

Scale	Two 12 x 18-inch sheet pans
Standing electric mixer fitted with the hook	Parchment paper
Large bowl or container	Kaiser roll stamp (optional)
Bowl scraper	Wire racks
Plastic film	

Prepare the *mise en place*.

Combine the bread flour with the water, eggs, yeast, vegetable oil, and malt syrup in the bowl of a standing electric mixer fitted with the hook. Mix on low speed for about 4 minutes, or until blended.

Add the salt and sugar, increase the mixer speed to medium, and mix for about 8 minutes, or until the dough begins to pull away from the sides of the bowl, feels elastic, and gives some resistance when tugged.

Lightly oil a large bowl or container.

Scrape the dough into the prepared bowl. Cover the bowl with plastic film and set aside to ferment for 1 hour.

Lightly flour a clean, flat work surface.

About Kaiser Rolls

It is said that kaiser rolls were created in Vienna and named to honor Emperor Franz Josef. In America, they are also known as Vienna rolls, bulkies, or simply as hard rolls. A kaiser roll is a substantial, hard, crusty roll that may be sprinkled with poppy or sesame seeds before baking. The trademark kaiser roll shape can be made by forming a ball of dough and stamping the top with a kaiser roll stamp, or by using the technique described in the instructions at right.

Uncover the dough and divide it into twelve 115-gram / 4-ounce rounds on the floured surface. Cover with plastic film and bench rest for 15 minutes.

Line the sheet pans with parchment paper.

Uncover the dough and, if necessary, lightly flour the work surface. If you have a kaiser roll stamp, press the center of each roll with it. If you don't have a stamp, lightly press on the dough to degas and carefully shape each round into a baguette (see page 69) about 12 inches (30.5 centimeters) long. Working with one piece at a time, form each baguette into a loop, crossing the ends with the right end being on the bottom. Pull the right end up and over the center of the loop and then push it under in the same direction. The left loop end

should now be pointing right. Take the left end and pull it up and under the center hole and then connect it to the other end. You should now have a roll that is rather like a rosette. Place 6 rolls, seam side down, onto each of the prepared pans. Cover with plastic film and proof for 1 hour.

About an hour before you are ready to bake the rolls, preheat the oven to 400°F (205°C).

Uncover the dough and transfer the rolls to the pre-heated oven. Bake for 22 minutes, or until the rolls are golden brown and crisp.

Remove from the oven and transfer to wire racks to cool.

Demonstration

Baguettebrotchen

Makes 2 dozen rolls
Estimated time to complete: 3¾ hours
Intensive mix
Desired dough temperature (DDT): 75°F (25°C)

Ingredient	Amount	Baker's Percentage
Bread flour	795 grams / 1 pound 12 ounces	95%
Rye flour	42 grams / 1½ ounces	5%
Water	527 grams / 1 pound 2⅔ ounces	63%
Fresh yeast	25 grams / 1 ounce	3%
Malt syrup	17 grams / ⅔ ounce	2%
Unsalted butter at room temperature	17 grams / ⅔ ounce	2%
Salt	17 grams / ⅔ ounce	2%
Total	**1440 grams / 3 pounds 3 ounces**	**172%**

Oil for greasing bowl
Flour for dusting
Ice for steam

Equipment

Scale	Two 12 x 18-inch sheet pans
Standing electric mixer fitted with the hook	Parchment paper
Large bowl or container	Cast-iron or stainless steel roasting pan
Bowl scraper	*Lame* or razor
Plastic film	Wire racks

Prepare the *mise en place*, taking care that the butter is at room temperature.

Combine the bread and rye flours with the water, yeast, malt syrup, butter, and salt in the bowl of a standing electric mixer fitted with the hook. Mix on low speed for about 4 minutes, or until blended.

Increase the mixer speed to medium and mix for about 8 minutes, or until the dough begins to pull away from the sides of the bowl, feels elastic, and gives some resistance when tugged.

Lightly oil a large bowl or container.

Scrape the dough into the prepared bowl. Cover the bowl with plastic film and set aside to ferment for 1 hour.

Lightly flour a clean, flat work surface.

Uncover the dough and divide it into twenty-four 60-gram / 2-ounce rounds on the floured surface. Cover with plastic film and bench rest for 15 minutes.

Line the sheet pans with parchment paper.

Uncover the dough and, if necessary, lightly flour the work surface. Gently press on the dough to degas and carefully form each piece into a neat round. (Alternatively, the dough may be shaped into small *bâtards* [see pages 68–69].) Place 12 rolls, seam side down, onto each of the prepared sheet pans. Cover with plastic film and proof for 90 minutes.

About an hour before you are ready to bake the rolls, place the baking stone(s) or tiles into the oven and pre-heat to 450°F (232°C). If using a pan to create steam (see page 70), place it in the oven now.

Uncover the dough and, using a *lame* or a razor, imme-diately score each roll as directed on pages 63–65. To make the required steam, add 1 cup of ice to the hot pan in the oven. Immediately transfer the sheet pans to the preheated oven.

Bake, with steam, for 22 minutes for the round rolls or 20 minutes for the *bâtard*-shaped rolls, or until the rolls are golden brown and crisp.

Remove from the oven and transfer to wire racks to cool.

Demonstration

Challah

Makes four 3-strand braids or three 6-strand braids
Estimated time to complete: 5 hours
Improved mix
Desired dough temperature (DDT): 75°F (25°C)

Ingredient	Amount	Baker's Percentage
All-purpose flour	964 grams / 2 pounds 2 ounces	100%
Cold water	289 grams / 10¼ ounces	30%
Whole eggs, at room temperature	164 grams / 5¾ ounces	17%
Egg yolks, at room temperature	116 grams / 4 ounces	12%
Honey	39 grams / 1⅓ ounces	4%
Fresh yeast	29 grams / 1 ounce	3%
Salt	21 grams / ¾ ounce	2.2%
Sugar	67 grams / 2⅓ ounces	7%
Vegetable oil	111 grams / 4 ounces	11.5%
Total	**1800 grams / 3 pounds 15½ ounces**	**186.7%**

Butter for greasing bowl
Flour for dusting
1 large egg for egg wash

Equipment

Scale	Small bowl
Digital thermometer	Whisk
Standing electric mixer fitted with the hook	Pastry brush
Large bowl or container	Two 12 x 18-inch sheet pans
Bowl scraper	Parchment paper
Plastic film	Wire racks

Prepare the *mise en place*, taking care that the water is about 67°F (19 °C) and the whole eggs and egg yolks are at room temperature.

Combine the flour, water, whole eggs, egg yolks, honey, yeast, and salt in the bowl of a standing electric mixer fitted with the hook. Mix on low speed for about 5 minutes, or until the dough starts to become shaggy (mixed, but not smooth in texture).

Add the sugar, and continue to mix for 3 minutes.

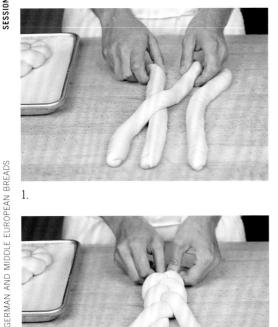
1.

2.

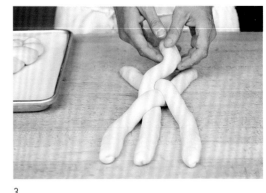
3.

4.

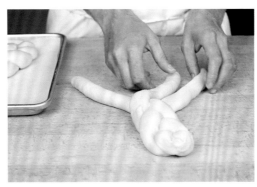
5.

6.

About Challah

Challah, traditionally a bread for the Jewish Sabbath, is a rich, slightly sweet, and beautiful bread. Although it does not have to be baked into a braid, the braids have enormous significance, as they symbolize the interweaving of heaven, earth, and mankind with God. Not quite as rich as a French brioche, the enrichments of eggs, sugar, honey, and oil make challah a special-occasion treat. Its beauty is found in its plump appearance and bright, shiny crust.

Increase the mixer speed to medium and mix for 5 minutes. Decrease the mixer speed to low and add the oil in a slow steady stream, mixing until fully incorporated.

Lightly butter a large bowl or container.

Scrape the dough into the prepared bowl. Cover the bowl with plastic film and set aside to ferment for 45 minutes.

Uncover, fold, and gently press on the dough to degas. Again, cover with plastic film and set aside to ferment for 45 minutes.

Lightly flour a clean, flat work surface.

Uncover the dough and divide it on the floured surface into twelve 150-gram / 5¼-ounce logs for 3-strand braids or eighteen 100-gram / 3½-ounce logs for

6-strand braids. Cover with plastic film and bench rest for 15 minutes.

Line the sheet pans with parchment paper.

Uncover the dough and, if necessary, lightly flour the work surface. Carefully roll each piece of dough into a neat cigar-shaped log about 14 inches (35 centimeters) long.

Working quickly to keep the dough from drying out:

To make a 3-strand braid, place 3 strands parallel to each other. Starting at the center, bring one outside strand over the center of the middle strand (photo 1). Grab the other outside strand and fold it over the new middle strand (noting that the first outside strand has become the middle strand, photo 2). Repeat this process until you reach the end of the strands (photo 3).

Pinch these ends together (photo 4). Flip the braided strands over so that the finished section is away from you. Continue braiding as before to completely braid the loaf (photo 5). Roll each end gently to seal (photo 6).

To make a 6-strand braid, pinch 6 of the logs together at the top and begin braiding the logs together, taking 1 to the top right and 6 to the top left, 1 down to the center and 2 to the top right, 6 down to the center and 5 to the top left, and so on, until you have completed the braid. Pinch the ends together to prevent them from separating during baking. Repeat the process for the remaining 12 pieces of dough.

To make the egg wash, combine the egg with 14 grams / 1 tablespoon water in a small bowl, whisking to blend.

Place two loaves on each of the prepared sheet pans (or two loaves on one pan and one on the other for 6-stand braids). Using a pastry brush, lightly coat the top of each loaf with the egg wash. (Do not discard the remaining egg wash.) Cover with plastic film and proof for 1½ hours.

About an hour before you are ready to bake the loaves, preheat the oven to 350°F (177°C).

Uncover the dough and again, using a pastry brush, lightly coat the top of each loaf with the remaining egg wash.

Transfer the pans to the preheated oven. Bake for 35 minutes, or until the crust is golden brown and shiny and the sides feel firm to the touch.

Remove from the oven and transfer to wire racks to cool.

Note

Challah can be made with three, four, or six braids, or even with no braids. For a simple unbraided loaf, divide the dough into four 450-gram (16-ounce) pieces and form each one into a *bâtard* (see pages 68–69). Place seam side down in four greased 9-inch loaf pans and bake as above.

Demonstration

40 Percent Sourdough Rye Bread

(Adapted from Jeffrey Hamelman's *Bread*)

Makes 2 loaves

Estimated time to complete: 16 hours or up to 18 hours
Improved mix
Desired dough temperature (DDT): 75°F (25°C)

Ingredient	Amount	Baker's Percentage
For the rye *levain*:		
Coarse rye flour	305 grams / 10¾ ounces	100%
Water	260 grams / 9¼ ounces	85%
Liquid *levain* culture (see pages 75–76)	15 grams / ½ ounce	5%
Total	**580 grams / 20½ ounces**	**190%**
For the final dough:		
Bread flour	475 grams / 1 pound ¾ ounce	100%
Water	281 grams / 10 ounces	59%
Rye *levain*	580 grams / 1 pound 4½ ounces	122%
Salt	14 grams / ½ ounce	3%
Fresh yeast	10 grams / ⅓ ounce	2.1%
Total	**1360 grams / 3 pounds**	**286.1%**

Oil for greasing bowl
Flour for dusting
Ice for steam

Equipment

Scale	2 large cutting boards
Large mixing bowl	*Couche* for two boards
Wooden spoon	Baking stone(s) or tiles
Bowl scraper	Cast-iron or stainless steel roasting pan
Plastic film	*Lame* or razor
Digital thermometer	Peel
Standing electric mixer fitted with the hook	Wire racks
Large bowl or container	

Prepare the *mise en place* for the rye *levain*.

To make the rye *levain*, combine the rye flour and water with the culture in a large mixing bowl, stirring with a wooden spoon to blend. When blended, scrape down the edge of the bowl, cover with plastic film, and set aside to ferment at 70°F (20°C) for 14 to 16 hours.

When ready to make the final dough, prepare the *mise en place*.

Combine the bread flour with the water, rye *levain*, salt, and yeast in the bowl of a standing electric mixer fitted with the hook. Mix on low speed until blended. Increase the mixer speed to medium and mix for 5 to 10 minutes, or until the dough begins to pull away from the sides of the bowl, feels elastic, and gives some resistance when tugged.

Lightly oil a large bowl or container.

Scrape the dough into the prepared bowl. Cover the bowl with plastic film and set aside to ferment for 1 hour.

Lightly flour a clean, flat work surface.

Uncover the dough and divide it into two 680-gram / 24-ounce rounds on the floured surface. Cover with plastic film and bench rest for 15 minutes.

Cover the cutting boards with the *couche* and dust the *couche* with flour.

Uncover the dough and, if necessary, lightly flour the work surface. Gently press on the dough to degas and carefully shape each round into a *bâtard* (see pages 68–69) or into a neat round shape. Place one *bâtard* (or round) on each of the *couche*-covered boards. Cover with plastic film and proof for 1 hour.

About an hour before you are ready to bake the loaves, place the baking stone(s) or tiles into the oven and pre-heat to 470°F (243°C). If using a pan to create steam (see page 70), place it in the oven now.

When ready to bake, uncover the dough and, using a *lame* or a razor, immediately score the loaves as directed on pages 63–65. To make the required steam, add 1 cup of ice to the hot pan in the oven. Using a peel, immediately transfer the loaves to the hot baking stone(s) in the preheated oven.

Bake, with steam, for 15 minutes. Then, reduce the oven temperature to 440°F (227°C) and bake for an additional 25 minutes, or until the crust is deep brown and firm to the touch and the loaves make a hollow sound when tapped on the bottom.

Remove from the oven and transfer to wire racks to cool.

Demonstration

Sourdough Rye Bread with Walnuts

(Adapted from Jeffrey Hamelman's *Bread*)

Makes 2 loaves

Estimated time to complete: 16 hours or up to 18 hours
Improved mix
Desired dough temperature (DDT): 75°F (25°C)

Ingredient	Amount	Baker's Percentage
For the rye *levain*:		
Coarse rye flour	220 grams / 7¾ ounces	100%
Water	187 grams / 6⅔ ounces	85%
Liquid *levain* culture (see pages 75–76)	11 grams / ⅓ ounce	5%
Total	**418 grams / 14¾ ounces**	**190%**
For the final dough:		
Bread flour	377 grams / 13⅓ ounces	71.4%
Fine rye flour	151 grams / 5⅓ ounces	28.6%
Water	340 grams / 12 ounces	64.3%
Rye *levain*	418 grams / 14¾ ounces	79%
Fresh yeast	11 grams / ⅓ ounce	2.14%
Salt	14 grams / ½ ounce	2.6%
Toasted walnuts	189 grams / 6⅔ ounces	35.7%
Total	**1500 grams / 3 pounds 5 ounces**	**283.74%**

Oil for greasing bowl

Flour for dusting

Ice for steam

Equipment

Scale

Large mixing bowl

Wooden spoon

Bowl scraper

Plastic film

Digital thermometer

Standing electric mixer fitted with the hook

Large bowl or container

2 *brotformen*

Peel

Baking stone(s) or tiles

Cast-iron or stainless steel roasting pan

Lame or razor

Wire racks

Prepare the *mise en place* for the rye *levain*.

To make the rye *levain*, combine the rye flour and water with the culture in a large mixing bowl, stirring with a wooden spoon to blend. When blended, scrape down the edge of the bowl, cover with plastic film, and set aside to ferment at 70°F (20°C) for 14 to 16 hours.

When ready to make the final dough, prepare the *mise en place*.

Combine the bread and fine rye flours with the water, rye *levain*, yeast, and salt in the bowl of a standing electric mixer fitted with the hook. Mix on low speed until blended. Increase the mixer speed to medium and mix for about 5 to 10 minutes, or until the dough begins to pull away from the sides of the bowl, feels elastic, and gives some resistance when tugged. Mix in the walnuts on low speed.

Lightly oil a large bowl or container.

Scrape the dough into the prepared bowl. Cover the bowl with plastic film and set aside to ferment for 1 hour.

Lightly flour a clean, flat work surface.

Uncover the dough and divide it into two 750-gram / 26-ounce rounds on the floured surface. Cover with plastic film and bench rest for 15 minutes.

Lightly flour the *brotformen*.

Uncover the dough and, if necessary, lightly flour the work surface. Gently press on the dough to degas and carefully shape each piece into a neat round shape. Place one round into each floured *brotform*. Cover with plastic film and proof for 1 hour.

About an hour before you are ready to bake the loaves, place the baking stone(s) or tiles into the oven and preheat it to 470°F (243°C). If using a pan to create steam (see page 70), place it in the oven now.

Lightly flour a peel. Uncover the dough and flip it onto the floured peel.

Using a *lame* or a razor, immediately score the top of each loaf as directed on pages 63–65. To make the required steam, add 1 cup of ice to the hot pan in the oven. Using the prepared peel, immediately transfer the loaves to the hot baking stone(s) in the preheated oven.

Bake, with steam, for 15 minutes. Then, reduce the oven temperature to 440°F (227°C) and bake for an additional 40 minutes or until the crust is deep brown and crisp and the loaves make a hollow sound when tapped on the bottom.

Remove from the oven and transfer to wire racks to cool.

Demonstration

Whole Wheat and Rye Sourdough Bread

(Adapted from Jeffrey Hamelman's *Bread*)

Makes 2 loaves

Estimated time to complete: 16 hours or up to 18 hours

Improved mix

Desired dough temperature (DDT): 75°F (25°C)

Ingredient	Amount	Baker's Percentage
For the rye *levain*:		
Rye flour	133 grams / 4⅔ ounces	100%
Water	113 grams / 4 ounces	85%
Liquid *levain* culture (see pages 75–76)	7 grams / ¼ ounce	5%
Total	**253 grams / 9 ounces**	**190%**
For the final dough:		
Bread flour	468 grams / 1 pound 1½ ounces	66.7%
Whole wheat flour	233 grams / 8¼ ounces	33.3%
Water	514 grams / 1 pound 2⅛ ounces	73.3%
Rye *levain*	253 grams / 9 ounces	36%
Salt	18 grams / ⅔ ounce	2.67%
Fresh yeast	14 grams / ½ ounce	2%
Total	**1500 grams / 3 pounds 5 ounces**	**213.97%**

Oil for greasing bowl

Flour for dusting

Ice for steam

Equipment

Scale	Large cutting board
Large mixing bowl	*Couche*
Wooden spoon	Baking stone(s) or tiles
Bowl scraper	Cast-iron or stainless steel roasting pan
Plastic film	*Lame* or razor
Digital thermometer	Peel
Standing electric mixer fitted with the hook	Wire racks
Large bowl or container	

Prepare the *mise en place* for the rye *levain*.

To make the rye *levain*, combine the rye flour and water with the culture in a large mixing bowl, stirring with a wooden spoon to blend. When blended, scrape down the edge of the bowl, cover with plastic film, and set aside to ferment at 70°F (20°C) for 14 to 16 hours.

When ready to make the final dough, prepare the *mise en place*.

Combine the bread and whole wheat flours with the water, rye *levain*, salt, and yeast in the bowl of a standing electric mixer fitted with the hook. Mix on low speed until blended. Increase the mixer speed to medium and mix for about 7 minutes, or until the dough begins to pull away from the sides of the bowl, feels elastic, and gives some resistance when tugged.

Lightly oil a large bowl or container.

Scrape the dough into the prepared bowl. Cover the bowl with plastic film and set aside to ferment for 1 hour.

Cover the cutting board with the *couche* and dust the *couche* with flour.

Lightly flour a clean, flat work surface.

Uncover the dough and divide it into two 750-gram / 26-ounce rounds on the floured surface. Cover with plastic film and bench rest for 10 minutes.

Uncover the dough and, if necessary, lightly flour the work surface. Gently press on the dough to degas and carefully shape each piece into a neat round shape. Place one round on one side of the *couche*-covered board, fold the *couche* up to make a double layer of cloth to serve as a divider between the loaves, and place the remaining loaf next to the fold. Cover with plastic film and proof for 1 hour.

About an hour before you are ready to bake the loaves, place the baking stone(s) or tiles into the oven and preheat it to 470°F (243°C). If using a pan to create steam (see page 70), place it in the oven now.

Uncover the dough and, using a *lame* or a razor, immediately score the loaves as directed on pages 63–65. To make the required steam, add 1 cup of ice to the hot pan in the oven. Using a peel, immediately transfer the loaves to the hot baking stone(s) in the preheated oven.

Bake, with steam, for 15 minutes. Then, reduce the oven temperature to 440°F (227°C) and bake for an additional 40 minutes, or until the crust is reddish brown, the sides are firm to the touch, and the loaves make a hollow sound when tapped on the bottom.

Remove from the oven and transfer to wire racks to cool.

Demonstration

Haferbrot

Makes 2 loaves

Estimated time to complete: 6½ hours
Improved mix
Desired dough temperature (DDT): 75°F (25°C)

Ingredient	Amount	Baker's Percentage
For the soaker:		
Toasted rolled oats	250 grams / 8¾ ounces	100%
Cold water	250 grams / 8¾ ounces	100%
Total	**500 grams / 1 pound 1½ ounces**	**200%**
For the final dough:		
Bread flour	416 grams / 14⅔ ounces	100%
Water	229 grams / 8 ounces	55%
Milk powder	12 grams / ½ ounce	3%
Malt syrup	12 grams / ½ ounce	3%
Unsalted butter or lard	12 grams / ½ ounce	3%
Salt	13 grams / ½ ounce	3.2%
Fresh yeast	6 grams / ¼ ounce	1.5%
Soaker	500 grams / 1 pound 1½ ounces	120%
Total	**1200 grams / 2 pounds 10⅓ ounces**	**288.7%**

Oil for greasing bowl
Flour for dusting
Butter for greasing pans
Rolled oats for finishing
Ice for steam

Equipment

Scale	Plastic film
Plastic container with lid	Two 9-inch loaf pans
Wooden spoon	Damp kitchen towel
Standing electric mixer fitted with the hook	12 x 18-inch sheet pan
Large bowl or container	Cast-iron or stainless steel roasting pan
Bowl scraper	Wire racks

Prepare the *mise en place* for the soaker.

To make the soaker, place the oats in a plastic container with a lid. Add the water, stirring with a wooden spoon to blend. Cover and set aside to soak at room temperature for 30 minutes.

When ready to make the final dough, prepare the *mise en place*.

Combine the bread flour with the water, milk powder, and malt syrup in the bowl of a standing electric mixer fitted with the hook. Mix on low speed until blended. Stop the mixer and autolyse for 15 minutes.

Add the butter, salt, and yeast and mix on low for 5 minutes. Increase the mixer speed to medium and mix for about 10 minutes, or until the dough begins to pull away from the sides of the bowl, feels elastic, and gives some resistance when tugged. Mix in the soaker on low.

Lightly oil a large bowl or container.

Scrape the dough into the prepared bowl. Cover the bowl with plastic film and set aside to ferment for 1 hour.

Uncover and fold the dough. Again, cover with plastic film and set aside to ferment for 1 hour.

Lightly flour a clean, flat work surface.

Uncover the dough and divide it into two 600-gram / 21-ounce rounds on the floured surface. Cover with plastic film and bench rest for 15 minutes.

Lightly butter the loaf pans.

Uncover the dough and, if necessary, lightly flour the work surface. Gently press on the dough to degas and carefully shape each round into a rectangle small enough to fit into a loaf pan.

Place the damp kitchen towel on one half of the sheet pan. Place the oats for finishing on the other half. Working with one loaf at a time, roll the dough on the moistened towel, then roll the damp dough over and into the rolled oats. The dampness will help the oats adhere to the dough during baking.

Place one oat-coated piece of dough, seam side down, into each prepared loaf pan.

Cover with plastic film and proof for 1½ to 2 hours.

About an hour before you are ready to bake the loaves, preheat the oven to 450°F (232°C). If using a pan to create steam (page 70), place it in the oven now.

When you are ready to bake the loaves, to make the required steam, add 1 cup of ice to the hot pan in the oven. Uncover the dough and immediately transfer the loaves to the preheated oven.

Bake, with steam, for 40 minutes, or until the crust is golden brown, and the sides are firm to the touch.

Remove from the oven and transfer to wire racks to cool.

Demonstration

Kugelhopf

Makes 1 loaf

Estimated time to complete: 14 hours
Improved mix
Desired dough temperature (DDT): 75°F (25°C)

Ingredient	Amount	Baker's Percentage
For the soaker:		
Dark raisins	80 grams / 2¾ ounces	60%
Dried cherries	53 grams / 2 ounces	40%
Dark rum	29 grams / 1 ounce	22%
Total	**162 grams / 5¾ ounces**	**122%**
For the quick sponge:		
Bread flour	88 grams / 3 ounces	100%
Milk	50 grams / 1¾ ounces	56.5%
Fresh yeast	12 grams / ½ ounce	13.6%
Total	**150 grams / 5¼ ounces**	**170.1%**
For the final dough:		
Bread flour	238 grams / 8⅓ ounces	100%
Quick sponge	150 grams / 5¼ ounces	62.6%
Milk	114 grams / 4 ounces	48%
Cold eggs	49 grams / 1¾ ounces	20.8%
Salt	6 grams / ¼ ounce	2.8%
Sugar	49 grams / 1¾ ounces	20.8%
Cold unsalted butter	82 grams / 3 ounces	34.4%
Soaker	162 grams / 5¾ ounces	68%
Total	**850 grams / 1 pound 14 ounces**	**357.4%**

Oil for greasing bowl
Flour for dusting
Butter for greasing mold

Equipment

Scale	Bowl scraper
Small bowl	Standing electric mixer fitted with the hook
Wooden spoon	Large bowl or container
Plastic film	*Kugelhopf* mold
Digital thermometer	Wire rack
Large mixing bowl	

Prepare the *mise en place* for the soaker.

To make the soaker, combine the raisins and cherries with the rum in a small bowl, stirring with a wooden spoon to blend. Cover with plastic film and set aside to soak at room temperature for at least 8 hours.

When ready to make the final dough, prepare the *mise en place* for both the sponge and the final dough,

taking care that the milk for the sponge is about 75°F (25°C).

To make the sponge, combine the bread flour and milk with the yeast in a large mixing bowl, stirring with a wooden spoon to blend. When blended, scrape down the edge of the bowl, cover with plastic film, and set aside to ferment for 30 minutes at room temperature or 75°F (25°C).

Add the soaker and mix on low speed until blended.

Lightly oil a large bowl or container.

Scrape the dough into the prepared bowl. Cover with plastic film and set aside to ferment for 45 minutes.

Uncover and fold the dough. Again, cover with plastic film and set aside to ferment for 45 minutes.

Lightly flour a clean, flat work surface.

Uncover the dough and form it into a neat round on the floured surface. Cover with plastic film and bench rest for 10 minutes.

Uncover the dough and, if necessary, lightly flour the work surface. Gently press on the dough to degas and carefully shape into a neat round. Cover with plastic film and bench rest for 10 minutes.

Lightly butter the *kugelhopf* mold.

Uncover the dough and, using your fingertips, poke a large hole in the center of the round, making an opening that will fit over the center tube of the mold.

To make the final dough, combine the bread flour with the quick sponge, milk, eggs, and salt in the bowl of a standing electric mixer fitted with the hook. Mix on low speed until blended.

Add about a third of the sugar, increase the mixer speed to medium, and mix until blended. Then add the remaining sugar in two additions and mix, for about 5 minutes, or just until some gluten has developed and the dough has some elasticity.

Decrease the mixer speed to low, add the butter a little at a time, and continue to mix for about 5 minutes, or until the dough has come together and pulls away from the sides of the bowl.

Slip the ring of dough into the prepared pan, fitting the opening over the tube. Cover with plastic film and proof for 2 hours.

About a half hour before you are ready to bake the loaf, preheat the oven to 350°F (177°C).

Uncover the mold and transfer to the preheated oven. Bake for 45 minutes, or until the crust is golden brown and shiny and the center is firm to the touch.

Remove from the oven and transfer to a wire rack to cool.

Demonstration

Musli-Brotchen

Makes 2 dozen rolls

Estimated time to complete: 5 hours

Improved mix

Desired dough temperature (DDT): 75°F (25°C)

Ingredient	Amount	Baker's Percentage
For the soaker:		
Dark raisins	88 grams / 3 ounces	24%
Rolled oats	59 grams / 2 ounces	16%
Chopped dried apples	59 grams / 2 ounces	16%
Chopped dried apricots	59 grams / 2 ounces	16%
Sunflower seeds	59 grams / 2 ounces	16%
Millet	44 grams / 1½ ounces	12%
Water	245 grams / 8⅔ ounces	66.7%
Total	**613 grams / 1 pound 5⅛ ounces**	**166.7%**
For the final dough:		
Bread flour	978 grams / 2 pounds 2½ ounces	100%
Water	367 grams / 13 ounces	37.5%
Milk	98 grams / 3½ ounces	10%
Cold unsalted butter	78 grams / 2¾ ounces	8%
Fresh yeast	58 grams / 2 ounces	6%
Cold egg yolks	49 grams / 1¾ ounces	5%
Sugar	39 grams / 1⅓ ounces	4%
Honey	29 grams / 1 ounce	3%
Malt syrup	19 grams / ⅔ ounce	2%
Salt	23 grams / ¾ ounce	1.4%
Toasted chopped hazelnuts	49 grams / 1¾ ounces	5%
Soaker	613 grams / 1 pound 5⅛ ounces	74.73%
Total	**2400 grams / 5 pounds**	**256.63%**

Oil for greasing bowl

Flour for dusting

1 large egg for the egg wash

Equipment

Scale	Two 12 x 18-inch sheet pans
Plastic container with lid	Parchment paper
Wooden spoon	Small bowl
Standing electric mixer fitted with the hook	Whisk
Large bowl or container	Pastry brush
Bowl scraper	Wire racks
Plastic film	

Prepare the *mise en place* for the soaker.

To make the soaker, combine the raisins, oats, apples, apricots, sunflower seeds, and millet in a plastic container with a lid. Add the water, stirring with a wooden spoon to blend. Cover and set aside to soak at room temperature for 30 minutes.

When ready to make the final dough, prepare the *mise en place*.

Combine the bread flour with the water, milk, butter, yeast, egg yolks, sugar, honey, malt syrup, and salt in the bowl of a standing electric mixer fitted with the hook. Mix on low speed until blended. Increase the mixer speed to medium and continue to mix for about 7 minutes, or until the dough is smooth and the gluten is fully developed.

Add the hazelnuts along with the soaker and mix on low speed until well incorporated.

Lightly oil a large bowl or container.

Scrape the dough into the prepared bowl. Cover with plastic film and set aside to ferment for 45 minutes.

Uncover and fold the dough. Again, cover with plastic film and set aside to ferment for 45 minutes.

Lightly flour a clean, flat work surface.

Uncover the dough and divide it into twenty-four 100-gram / 3½-ounce rounds on the floured surface. Cover with plastic film and bench rest for 10 minutes.

Line the sheet pans with parchment paper.

To make the egg wash, combine the egg with 14 grams / 1 tablespoon water in a small bowl, whisking to blend.

Uncover the dough and, if necessary, lightly flour the work surface. Gently press on the dough to degas and carefully shape each roll into a tight, neat round.

Using a pastry brush, lightly coat the top of each roll with the egg wash. (Do not discard the remaining egg wash.)

Transfer the rolls, seam side down, to the prepared baking sheets. Cover with plastic film and proof for 90 minutes.

About an hour before you are ready to bake the rolls, preheat the oven to 400°F (205°C).

Uncover the dough and again, using a pastry brush, lightly coat the top of each roll with the remaining egg wash.

Transfer the baking sheets to the preheated oven. Bake for 22 minutes, or until the rolls are golden brown and firm to the touch.

Remove from the oven and transfer to wire racks to cool.

Demonstration

Sourdough Bagels

Makes 1 dozen bagels

Estimated time to complete: 16 hours or up to 40 hours

Intensive mix

Desired dough temperature (DDT): 75°F (25°C)

Ingredient	Amount	Baker's Percentage
For the liquid *levain*:		
Bread flour	110 grams / 3¾ ounces	100%
Water	138 grams / 4¾ ounces	125%
Liquid *levain* culture (see pages 75–76)	11 grams / ⅓ ounce	10%
Total	**259 grams / 8¾ ounces**	**235%**
For the final dough:		
High-gluten flour	615 grams / 1 pound 5¾ ounces	100%
Water	235 grams / 8¼ ounces	38%
Liquid *levain*	258 grams / 8¾ ounces	42%
Sugar	40 grams / 1⅓ ounces	6.25%
Malt	30 grams / 1 ounce	5%
Salt	12 grams / ½ ounce	2%
Fresh yeast	10 grams / ⅓ ounce	0.75%
Total	**1200 grams / 2 pounds 9⅓ ounces**	**194%**

Flour for dusting

Vegetable oil for greasing pan

Equipment

Scale	Standing electric mixer fitted with the hook
Large mixing bowl	12 x 18-inch sheet pan
Wooden spoon	Large pot
Bowl scraper	Spatula
Plastic film	Slotted spatula
Digital thermometer	Wire racks

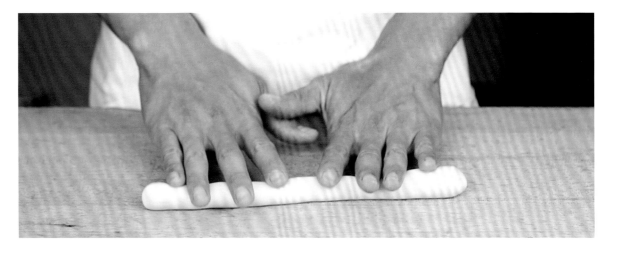

Note

Bagels may be topped with sesame or poppy seeds, coarse salt, cracked pepper, fried garlic or onion bits, or, in fact, almost any savory addition you would enjoy.

Prepare the *mise en place* for the liquid *levain*.

To make the liquid *levain*, combine the bread flour and water with the culture in a large mixing bowl, stirring with a wooden spoon to blend. When blended, scrape down the edge of the bowl, cover with plastic film, and set aside to ferment at 70°F (20°C) for 14 to 16 hours.

When ready to make the final dough, prepare the *mise en place*.

Combine the high-gluten flour with the water, liquid *levain*, sugar, malt, salt, and yeast in the bowl of a standing electric mixer fitted with the hook. Mix on low speed until blended. Increase the mixer speed to medium, and mix for about 8 minutes, or until the dough has come together and the gluten has developed.

Lightly flour a clean, flat work surface.

Scrape the dough onto the floured surface and divide it into twelve 100-gram / 3½-ounce *bâtard*-shaped pieces (see pages 68–69). Cover with plastic film and bench rest for 15 minutes.

Lightly coat a sheet pan with vegetable oil.

Uncover the dough and, if necessary, lightly flour the work surface. Gently press on the dough to degas and

carefully shape each piece of dough into a log about 12 inches (30 centimeters) long. Pinch the ends of each log together to form a bagel-shaped circle. Place the bagels on the prepared sheet pan. Cover with plastic film and proof for 1 hour.

Transfer to the refrigerator and let rest for at least 30 minutes or up to 24 hours.

About an hour before you are ready to bake the bagels, preheat the oven to 450°F (232°C).

Shortly before you are ready to bake, bring a large pot of water to boil over high heat.

Uncover the dough and, using a spatula, carefully transfer the bagels, a few at a time, to the boiling water. Boil for 5 seconds then, working with one at a time and using a slotted spatula, lift the bagels from the water and return them to the greased sheet pan. Continue until all the bagels have been boiled.

If using a topping, sprinkle it on.

Transfer the bagels to the preheated oven. Bake for 20 minutes, or until the crust is shiny and golden.

Remove from the oven and transfer to wire racks to cool.

Demonstration

Leinsamenbrot

Makes 2 loaves

Estimated time to complete: 18½ hours or up to 20½ hours
Short mix
Desired dough temperature (DDT): 80°F (27°C)

Ingredient	Amount	Baker's Percentage
For the soaker:		
Flax seed	78 grams / 2¾ ounces	100%
Water	235 grams / 8⅓ ounces	300%
Total	**313 grams / 11 ounces**	**400%**
For the rye *levain*:		
Coarse rye flour	297 grams / 10½ ounces	100%
Water	252 grams / 9 ounces	85%
Liquid *levain* culture (see pages 75–76)	15 grams / ½ ounce	5%
Total	**564 grams / 1 pound 4 ounces**	**190%**
For the final dough:		
Bread flour	313 grams / 11 ounces	66.7%
Dark rye flour	168 grams / 5½ ounces	33.3%
Soaker	313 grams / 11 ounces	66.7%
Water	125 grams / 4½ ounces	26.6%
Rye *levain*	565 grams / 1 pound 4 ounces	120%
Fresh yeast	12 grams / ½ ounce	2.5%
Salt	14 grams / ½ ounce	3%
Total	**1510 grams / 3 pounds 5 ounces**	**318.8%**

Oil for greasing bowl
Flour for dusting
Ice for steam

Equipment

Scale	Large bowl or container
Plastic container with lid	*2 bannetons*
Wooden spoon	Baking stone(s) or tiles
Large mixing bowl	Peel
Bowl scraper	Cast-iron or stainless steel roasting pan
Plastic film	*Lame* or razor
Digital thermometer	Wire racks
Standing electric mixer fitted with the hook	

Prepare the *mise en place* for the soaker.

To make the soaker, combine the flax seeds and water in a plastic container with a lid, stirring with a wooden spoon to blend. Cover and set aside to soak at room temperature for at least 12 hours.

Prepare the *mise en place* for the rye *levain*.

To make the rye *levain*, combine the rye flour and water with the culture in a large mixing bowl, stirring with a wooden spoon to blend. When blended, scrape down the edge of the bowl, cover with plastic film, and set aside to ferment at 70°F (20°C) for 14 to 16 hours.

When ready to make the final dough, prepare the *mise en place*.

Combine the bread and rye flours with the soaker, water, rye *levain*, yeast, and salt in the bowl of a standing electric mixer fitted with the hook. Mix on low speed for about 12 minutes, or until the dough has an almost claylike consistency and only a little elasticity.

Lightly oil a large bowl or container.

Scrape the dough into the prepared bowl. Cover the bowl with plastic film and set aside to ferment for 30 minutes.

Lightly flour a clean, flat work surface.

Uncover the dough and divide it into two 750-gram /

26-ounce rounds on the floured surface. Cover with plastic film and bench rest for 10 minutes.

Lightly dust each *banneton* with flour.

Uncover the dough and, if necessary, lightly flour the work surface. Gently press on the dough to degas and carefully shape each round into a *bâtard* (see pages 68–69). Place one *bâtard,* seam side up, into each of the prepared *bannetons*. Cover with plastic film and proof for 2 hours.

About an hour before you are ready to bake the loaves, place the baking stone(s) or tiles into the oven and preheat to 490°F (254°C). If using a pan to create steam (see page 70), place it in the oven now.

Lightly flour a peel. Uncover the dough and flip it onto the floured peel.

Using a *lame* or razor, immediately score the top of each loaf as directed on pages 63–65. To make the required steam, add 1 cup of ice to the hot pan in the oven. Using the peel, immediately transfer the loaves to the hot baking stone(s) in the preheated oven.

Bake, with steam, for 20 minutes. Then, reduce the oven temperature to 400°F (205°C) and bake for an additional 35 minutes, or until the crust is deep brown, the sides are firm to the touch, and the loaves make a hollow sound when tapped on the bottom.

Remove from the oven and transfer to wire racks to cool.

Demonstration

Pretzels

Makes 1 dozen pretzels
> Estimated time to complete: 3 hours or up to 24 hours
> Intensive mix
> Desired dough temperature (DDT): 75°F (25°C)

Ingredient	Amount	Baker's Percentage
High-gluten flour	732 grams / 1 pound 10 ounces	100%
Water	373 grams / 13⅛ ounces	51%
Fresh yeast	29 grams / 1 ounce	4%
Lard or unsalted butter	29 grams / 1 ounce	4%
Malt syrup	22 grams / ¾ ounce	3%
Salt	15 grams / ½ ounce	2%
Total	**1200 grams / 2 pounds 10⅓ ounces**	**164%**

Flour for dusting
¼ cup baking soda for boiling
Pretzel salt for sprinkling

Equipment

Scale	Large pot
Standing electric mixer fitted with the hook	Spatula
Plastic film	Slotted spatula
Two 12 x 18-inch sheet pans	Wire racks
Parchment paper	

Prepare the *mise en place*.

Combine the high-gluten flour with the water, yeast, lard, malt syrup, and salt in the bowl of a standing electric mixer fitted with the hook. Mix on low speed until blended. Increase the mixer speed to medium and mix for about 8 minutes, or until the dough has come together and the gluten has developed.

Lightly flour a clean, flat work surface.

Scrape the dough onto the floured surface and divide it into twelve 100-gram / 3½-ounce *bâtard*-shaped pieces (see pages 68–69) on the floured surface. Cover with plastic film and bench rest for 15 minutes.

Line the sheet pans with parchment paper.

Uncover the dough and, if necessary, lightly flour the work surface. Carefully shape each piece into a log approximately 30 inches (76 centimeters) long that

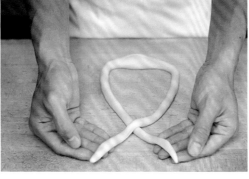
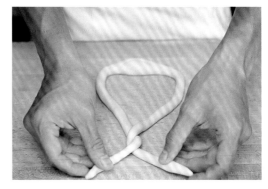

is somewhat fatter in the middle and tapers out to the ends (see photograph above). Turn each log into a pretzel shape by taking the two ends and crossing them twice at the top of a circle of dough (see illustration above). Then pull the ends down and press them into the center of the dough circle, carefully pinching the dough together. Place the pretzels on the prepared baking sheet. Cover with plastic film and proof for 1 hour.

Transfer to the refrigerator and let rest for at least 30 minutes or up to 24 hours.

About an hour before you are ready to bake the pretzels, preheat the oven to 450°F (232°C).

Shortly before you are ready to bake, bring 2 quarts / 1.9 liters water to boil over high heat. Add ¼ cup baking soda.

Uncover the dough and, using a spatula, carefully transfer the pretzels, a few at a time to the boiling water. Boil for 5 seconds then, working with one at a time and using a slotted spatula, lift the pretzels from the water and return them to the sheet pans. Working quickly, generously sprinkle the top of each pretzel with pretzel salt. Continue until all the pretzels have been boiled and salted.

Transfer the pretzels to the preheated oven. Bake for 20 minutes, or until the crust is a deep reddish-brown.

Remove from the oven and transfer to wire racks to cool.

Demonstration

Vinchgauer

Makes 4 loaves

Estimated time to complete: 17 hours or up to 19 hours
Short mix
Desired dough temperature (DDT): 75°F (25°C)

Ingredient	Amount	Baker's Percentage
For the rye *levain*:		
Coarse rye flour	210 grams / 7½ ounces	100%
Water	178 grams / 6⅓ ounces	85%
Liquid *levain* culture (see pages 75–76)	10 grams / ⅓ ounce	5%
Total	**398 grams / 14 ounces**	**190%**
For the final dough:		
Caraway seeds	10 grams / ⅓ ounce	1%
Coriander seeds	3 grams / ⅛ ounce	0.5%
Fennel seeds	3 grams / ⅛ ounce	0.5%
Bread flour	249 grams / 8¾ ounces	41.7%
Fine rye flour	348 grams / 12⅓ ounces	58.3%
Water	398 grams / 14 ounces	66.7%
Liquid *levain*	398 grams / 14 ounces	66.7%
Salt	19 grams / ⅔ ounce	3.12%
Fresh yeast	12 grams / ½ ounce	2%
Total	**1440 grams / 3 pounds 3 ounces**	**240.52%**

Oil for greasing bowl
Flour and coarse rye flour for dusting
Ice for steam

Equipment

Scale	Plastic film
Large mixing bowl	Digital thermometer
Wooden spoon	Small frying pan
Bowl scraper	Spice grinder

Standing electric mixer fitted with the hook
Large bowl or container
2 large cutting boards
Baking stone(s) or tiles

Cast-iron or stainless steel roasting pan
Peel
Wire racks

Prepare the *mise en place* for the liquid *levain*.

To make the liquid *levain*, combine the coarse rye flour and water with the culture in a large mixing bowl, stirring with a wooden spoon to blend. When blended, scrape down the edge of the bowl, cover with plastic film, and set aside to ferment at 70°F (20°C) for 14 to 16 hours.

When ready to make the final dough, prepare the *mise en place*.

Place the caraway, coriander, and fennel seeds in a small frying pan over medium heat. Toast the seeds, stirring frequently with a wooden spoon, for about 4 minutes, or until the seeds are very fragrant and lightly colored. Remove from the heat and allow to cool.

When the seeds are cool, transfer them to a spice grinder and grind to a fine powder. Set aside.

Combine the bread and fine rye flours with the water, liquid *levain*, salt, and yeast in the bowl of a standing electric mixer fitted with the hook. Mix on low speed until blended. Add the ground spices and mix on low for 5 minutes. Increase the mixer speed to medium and mix for about 7 minutes, or until the dough is well blended but has very little gluten development and the dough has some elasticity.

Lightly oil a large bowl or container.

Scrape the dough into the prepared bowl. Cover the bowl with plastic film and set aside to ferment for 30 minutes.

Lightly flour a clean, flat work surface.

Uncover the dough and divide it into four 360-gram / 13-ounce rounds on the floured surface. Cover with plastic film and bench rest for 15 minutes.

Generously dust the cutting boards with coarse rye flour.

Uncover the dough and, if necessary, lightly flour the work surface with coarse rye flour. Gently press on the dough to degas and carefully shape each piece into a tight, neat round, working a bit of the coarse rye flour into the seam. Place the loaves, seam side down, on the prepared boards.

Cover with plastic film and proof for 1 hour.

About an hour before you are ready to bake the loaves, place the baking stone(s) or tiles into the oven and preheat to 470°F (243°C). If using a pan to create steam (see page 70), place it in the oven now.

When you are ready to bake the loaves, to make the required steam, add 1 cup of ice to the hot pan in the oven. Uncover the dough and, using a peel, immediately transfer the loaves, seam side up, to the hot baking stone(s) in the preheated oven.

Bake, with steam, for 18 minutes, or until the crust is a deep reddish brown, the sides are firm to the touch, and the loaves make a hollow sound when tapped on the bottom.

Remove from the oven and transfer to wire racks to cool.

Demonstration

66 Percent Sourdough Rye Bread

(Adapted from Jeffrey Hamelman's *Bread*)

Makes 2 loaves

Estimated time to complete: 16½ hours or up to 18½ hours
Short mix
Desired dough temperature (DDT): 75°F (25°C)

Ingredient	Amount	Baker's Percentage
For the rye *levain*:		
Coarse rye flour	290 grams / 10¼ ounces	100%
Water	246 grams / 8⅔ ounces	85%
Liquid *levain* culture (see pages 75–76)	14 grams / ½ ounce	3%
Total	**550 grams / 19½ ounces**	**188%**
For the final dough:		
Rye flour	270 grams / 9 ounces	56.7%
Bread flour	199 grams / 7 ounces	43.3%
Water	330 grams / 11⅔ ounces	72%
Rye *levain*	550 grams / 1 pound 3½ ounces	120%
Salt	14 grams / ½ ounce	3%
Fresh yeast	7 grams / ¼ ounce	1.67%
Total	**1360 grams / 3 pounds**	**296.67%**

Oil for greasing bowl
Flour and coarse rye flour for dusting
Ice for steam

Equipment

Scale	Large bowl or container
Large mixing bowl	Large cutting board
Wooden spoon	Baking stone(s) or tiles
Bowl scraper	Cast-iron or stainless steel roasting pan
Plastic film	Peel
Digital thermometer	Wire racks
Standing electric mixer fitted with the hook	

Prepare the *mise en place* for the rye *levain*.

To make the rye *levain*, combine the coarse rye flour and water with the culture in a large mixing bowl, stirring with a wooden spoon to blend. When blended, scrape down the edge of the bowl, cover with plastic film, and set aside to ferment at 70°F (20°C) for 14 to 16 hours.

When ready to make the final dough, prepare the *mise en place*.

Combine the rye and bread flours with the water, rye *levain*, salt, and yeast in the bowl of a standing electric mixer fitted with the hook. Mix on low speed until blended. Increase the mixer speed to medium and mix for about 7 minutes, or until the dough is well blended and has some elasticity but very little gluten development.

Lightly oil a large bowl or container.

Scrape the dough into the prepared bowl. Cover the bowl with plastic film and set aside to ferment for 45 minutes.

Lightly flour a clean, flat work surface.

Uncover the dough and divide it into two 680-gram / 24-ounce rounds on the floured surface. Cover with plastic film and bench rest for 15 minutes.

Generously dust the cutting board with coarse rye flour.

Uncover the dough and, if necessary, lightly flour the work surface. Gently press on the dough to degas and carefully shape each piece into a neat round. Place the loaves on the prepared board. Cover with plastic film and proof for 1 hour.

About an hour before you are ready to bake the loaves, place the baking stone(s) or tiles into the oven and preheat it to 470°F (243°C). If using a pan to create steam (see page 70), place the pan in the oven now.

When you are ready to bake the loaves, to make the required steam, add 1 cup of ice to the hot pan in the oven. Uncover the dough and, using a peel, immediately transfer the loaves, seam side up, to the hot baking stone(s) in the preheated oven.

Bake, with steam, for 15 minutes. Then, reduce the oven temperature to 440°F (227°C) and bake for an additional 40 minutes, or until the crust is a deep reddish brown, the sides are firm to the touch, and the loaves make a hollow sound when tapped on the bottom.

Remove from the oven and transfer to wire racks to cool.

Demonstration

Krauterquarkbrot

Makes 2 loaves

Estimated time to complete: 18½ hours or up to 20½ hours

Improved mix

Desired dough temperature (DDT): 75°F (25°C)

Ingredient	Amount	Baker's Percentage
For the rye *levain*:		
Coarse rye flour	107 grams / 3¾ ounces	100%
Water	91 grams / 3¼ ounces	85%
Liquid *levain* culture (see pages 75–76)	5 grams / ¼ ounce	5%
Total	**203 grams / 7¼ ounces**	**190%**
For the final dough:		
Bread flour	380 grams / 13½ ounces	88%
Rye flour	52 grams / 1¾ ounces	12%
Water	277 grams / 9¾ ounces	64%
Rye *levain*	203 grams / 7¼ ounces	47%
Salt	10 grams / ⅓ ounce	2.4%
Fresh yeast	3 grams / ⅛ ounce	0.75%
Quark cheese (see Notes)	56 grams / 2 ounces	13%
Minced fresh herbs (see Notes)	9 grams / ⅓ ounce	2%
Total	**990 grams / 2 pounds 3 ounces**	**229.15%**

Oil for greasing bowl

Flour for dusting

Ice for steam

Equipment

Scale	Large cutting board
Large mixing bowl	*Couche*
Wooden spoon	Baking stone(s) or tiles
Bowl scraper	Cast-iron or stainless steel roasting pan
Plastic film	*Lame* or razor
Digital thermometer	Peel
Standing electric mixer fitted with the hook	Wire racks
Large bowl or container	

Prepare the *mise en place* for the rye *levain*.

To make the rye *levain*, combine the coarse rye flour and water with the culture in a large mixing bowl, stirring with a wooden spoon to blend. When blended, scrape down the edge of the bowl, cover with plastic film, and set aside to ferment at 70°F (20°C) for 14 to 16 hours.

When ready to make the final dough, prepare the *mise en place*.

Combine the bread and rye flours with the water and rye *levain* in the bowl of a standing electric mixer fitted with the hook. Mix on low speed until blended. Stop the mixer and autolyse for 15 minutes.

Add the salt and yeast and mix on low for 5 minutes. Increase the mixer speed to medium and mix for about 7 minutes, or until the dough begins to pull away from the sides of the bowl, feels elastic, and gives some resistance when tugged.

Add the cheese and herbs and mix on low speed just until incorporated.

Lightly oil a large bowl or container.

Scrape the dough into the prepared bowl. Cover the bowl with plastic film and set aside to ferment for 1 hour.

Uncover and fold the dough. Again, cover with plastic film and set aside to ferment for 1 hour.

Lightly flour a clean, flat work surface.

Uncover the dough and gently press on it to degas. Divide the dough into two 495-gram / 17¾-ounce rounds on the floured surface. Cover with plastic film and bench rest for 15 minutes.

Cover a large cutting board with a *couche* and dust the *couche* with flour.

Uncover the dough and, if necessary, lightly flour the work surface. Gently press on the dough to degas and carefully shape each piece into a neat, tight round. Place one round on one side of the *couche*-covered board, fold the *couche* up to make a double layer of cloth to serve as a divider between the loaves, and place the remaining loaf next to the fold. Cover with plastic film and proof for 1 hour.

About an hour before you are ready to bake the loaves, place the baking stone(s) or tiles into the oven and

Notes

Quark cheese, a fresh cheese of European origin, can be found in curd form in specialty food markets.

For the herbs, fresh rosemary needles, thyme, parsley, and chervil may be used.

preheat to 450°F (232°C). If using a pan to create steam (see page 70), place it in the oven now.

Uncover the dough and, using a *lame* or a razor, immediately score the loaves as directed on pages 63–65. To make the required steam, add 1 cup of ice to the hot pan in the oven. Using a peel, immediately transfer the loaves to the hot baking stone(s) in the preheated oven.

Bake, with steam, for 40 minutes, or until the crust is a deep golden brown, the sides are firm to the touch, and the loaves make a hollow sound when tapped on the bottom.

Remove from the oven and transfer to wire racks to cool.

Demonstration

German Fruit Bread

Makes 4 loaves

Estimated time to complete: 20 hours or up to 27 hours
Improved mix
Desired dough temperature (DDT): 82°F (28°C)

Ingredient	Amount	Baker's Percentage
For the soaker:		
Dried figs, quartered	312 grams / 11 ounces	19.84%
Dark raisins	260 grams / 9¼ ounces	16.5%
Prunes, halved	218 grams / 7¾ ounces	13.88%
Dried pears, quartered	154 grams / 5½ ounces	9.78%
Hazelnuts	148 grams / 5¼ ounces	9.39%
Currants	105 grams / 3¾ ounces	6.7%
Pitted dates, halved	82 grams / 2¾ ounces	5.2%
Candied orange peel	54 grams / 1¾ ounces	3.43%
Candied lemon peel	54 grams / 1¾ ounces	3.43%
Water	141 grams / 5 ounces	9%
Dark rum or red wine	42 grams / 1½ ounces	2.64%
Total	**1570 grams / 3 pounds 7 ounces**	**99.79%**
For the rye sour:		
Rye flour	26 grams / ¾ ounce	100%
Water	22 grams / ⅔ ounce	85%
Liquid *levain* culture (see pages 75–76)	1 gram / 1 teaspoon	5%
Total	**49 grams / 1¾ ounces**	**190%**
For the final dough:		
Bread flour	107 grams / 3¾ ounces	50%
Rye flour	107 grams / 3¾ ounces	50%
Rye sour	49 grams / 1¾ ounces	20%
Fresh yeast	11 grams / ⅓ ounce	5%
Salt	7 grams / ¼ ounce	2.9%
Water	159 grams / 5⅔ ounces	75%
Soaker	1570 grams / 3 pounds 7 ounces	740%
Total	**2000 grams / 4 pounds 6⅔ ounces**	**942.9%**

Oil for greasing bowl
Flour for dusting

Equipment

Scale	Standing electric mixer fitted with the hook
Plastic container with lid	Large bowl or container
Wooden spoon	2 large cutting boards
Large mixing bowl	*Couche* for two boards
Bowl scraper	Two sheet pans
Plastic film	Parchment paper
Digital thermometer	Wire racks

Prepare the *mise en place* for the soaker.

To make the soaker, combine the figs, raisins, prunes, pears, hazelnuts, currants, dates, and candied peels in a plastic container with a lid. Add the water and rum, stirring with a wooden spoon to blend. Cover and set aside to soak at room temperature for at least 8 hours or up to 24 hours.

Prepare the *mise en place* for the rye sour.

To make the rye sour, combine the rye flour and water with the rye culture in a large mixing bowl, stirring with a wooden spoon to blend. When blended, scrape down the edge of the bowl, cover with plastic film, and set aside to ferment at 70°F (20°C) for 14 to 16 hours.

When ready to make the final dough, prepare the *mise en place*.

Combine the bread and rye flours with the rye sour, yeast, salt, and water in the bowl of a standing electric mixer fitted with the hook. Mix on low speed until blended. Increase the mixer speed to medium and mix for about 5 to 7 minutes, or until the dough begins to pull away from the sides of the bowl, feels elastic, and gives some resistance when tugged. Stop the mixer and let the dough rest, uncovered, for 30 minutes.

Add the reserved soaker and mix on low speed just until incorporated.

Lightly oil a large bowl or container.

Scrape the dough into the prepared bowl. Cover the bowl with plastic film and set aside to ferment for 30 minutes.

Lightly flour a clean, flat work surface.

Uncover the dough and divide it into four 500-gram / 18-ounce rounds on the floured surface. Cover with plastic film and bench rest for 15 minutes.

Cover the cutting boards with the *couche* and dust the *couche* with flour.

Uncover the dough and, if necessary, lightly flour the work surface. Gently press on the dough to degas and carefully shape each round into a *bâtard* (see pages 68–69). Place one loaf, seam side down, on one side of one of the *couche*-covered boards, fold the *couche* up to make a double layer of cloth to serve as a divider between the loaves, and place a second loaf next to the fold. Repeat the process with the remaining two loaves and the second *couche*-covered board. Cover with plastic film and proof for 15 minutes.

Uncover the dough and, if necessary, lightly flour the work surface. Gently press on the dough to degas. Carefully shape each *bâtard* into a neat oval shape. Return, seam side down, to the *couche*-covered boards, cover with plastic film, and proof for 1 hour.

About an hour before you are ready to bake the loaves, preheat the oven to 400°F (205°C).

Line the sheet pans with parchment paper.

Uncover the loaves and transfer two loaves, seam side down, to each of the prepared sheet pans. Place in the preheated oven and bake for 40 minutes, or until the crust is golden brown and shiny.

Remove from the oven and transfer to wire racks to cool.

Demonstration

Landbrot mit Sauerkraut

Makes 2 loaves

Estimated time to complete: 18½ hours or up to 20½ hours
Improved mix
Desired dough temperature (DDT): 75°F (25°C)

Ingredient	Amount	Baker's Percentage
For the rye *levain*:		
Coarse rye flour	63 grams / 2¼ ounces	100%
Water	53 grams / 2 ounces	85%
Liquid *levain* culture (see pages 75–76)	3 grams / ⅛ ounce	5%
Total	**119 grams / 4⅜ ounces**	**190%**
For the final dough:		
Sauerkraut	227 grams / 8 ounces	42%
Bread flour	421 grams / 15 ounces	78%
Rye flour	59 grams / 2 ounces	11%
Coarse whole wheat flour	59 grams / 2 ounces	11%
Water	346 grams / 12 ounces	64%
Rye *levain*	119 grams / 4⅜ ounces	22%
Salt	14 grams / ½ ounce	2.5%
Fresh yeast	5 grams / ¼ ounce	1%
Total	**1250 grams / 2 pounds 12 ounces**	**231.5%**

Oil for greasing bowl
Flour for dusting
Ice for steam

Equipment

Scale	Large bowl or container
Large mixing bowl	Large cutting board
Wooden spoon	*Couche*
Bowl scraper	Baking stone(s) or tiles
Plastic film	Cast-iron or stainless steel roasting pan
Digital thermometer	*Lame* or razor
Fine-mesh sieve	Peel
Large bowl	Wire rack
Standing electric mixer fitted with the hook	

Prepare the *mise en place* for the rye *levain*.

To make the rye *levain*, combine the coarse rye flour and water with the culture in a large mixing bowl, stirring with a wooden spoon to blend. When blended, scrape down the edge of the bowl, cover with plastic film, and set aside to ferment at 70°F (20°C) for 14 to 16 hours.

When ready to make the final dough, prepare the *mise en place*.

Place the sauerkraut in a fine-mesh sieve and rinse under cold running water. Place the sieve over a large bowl and drain the liquid from the sauerkraut, pushing on it to remove as much liquid as possible. Finally, gather up the sauerkraut in your hands and squeeze out any remaining liquid.

Combine the bread, rye, and coarse whole wheat flours

with the water and rye *levain* in the bowl of a standing electric mixer fitted with the hook. Mix on low speed until blended. Stop the mixer and autolyse for 15 minutes.

Add the salt and yeast and mix on low for 5 minutes. Increase the mixer speed to medium and mix for about 7 minutes, or until the dough begins to pull away from the sides of the bowl, feels elastic, and gives some resistance when tugged.

Add the drained sauerkraut and mix on low speed just until incorporated.

Lightly oil a large bowl or container.

Scrape the dough into the prepared bowl. Cover the bowl with plastic film and set aside to ferment for 1 hour.

Uncover and fold the dough. Again, cover with plastic

film and set aside to ferment for 1 hour.

Lightly flour a clean, flat work surface.

Uncover the dough and divide it into two 625-gram / 22-ounce rounds on the floured surface. Cover with plastic film and bench rest for 15 minutes.

Cover the cutting board with the *couche* and dust the *couche* with flour.

Uncover the dough and, if necessary, lightly flour the work surface. Gently press on the dough to degas and carefully shape each round into a *bâtard* (see pages 68–69). Place one *bâtard* on one side of the *couche*-covered board, fold the *couche* up to make a double layer of cloth to serve as a divider between the loaves, and place the remaining loaf next to the fold. Cover with plastic film and proof for 1 hour.

About an hour before you are ready to bake the loaves, place the baking stone(s) or tiles into the oven and pre-heat to 450°F (232°C). If using a pan to create steam (see page 70), place it in the oven now.

Uncover the dough and, using a *lame* or razor, immediately score the loaves as directed on pages 63–65. To make the required steam, add 1 cup of ice to the hot pan in the oven. Using a peel, immediately transfer the loaves to the hot baking stone(s) in the preheated oven.

Bake, with steam, for 45 minutes, or until the crust is a deep golden brown, the sides are firm to the touch, and the loaves make a hollow sound when tapped on the bottom.

Remove from the oven and transfer to wire racks to cool.

Demonstration

Swedish *Limpa*

Makes 4 loaves

Estimated time to complete: 18 hours or up to 20 hours

Improved mix

Desired dough temperature (DDT): 75°F (25°C)

Ingredient	Amount	Baker's Percentage
For the rye *levain*:		
Coarse rye flour	221 grams / 7¾ ounces	100%
Water	188 grams / 6⅔ ounces	85%
Liquid *levain* culture (see pages 75–76)	11 grams / ⅓ ounce	5%
Total	**420 grams / 14¾ ounces**	**190%**
For the final dough:		
Bread flour	524 grams / 1 pound 2½ ounces	62.5%
Rye flour	314 grams / 11 ounces	37.5%
Water	570 grams / 1 pound 4⅛ ounces	68%
Rye *levain*	420 grams / 14¾ ounces	50%
Salt	23 grams / ¾ ounce	2.8%
Fresh yeast	17 grams / ⅔ ounce	2%
Molasses	101 grams / 3½ ounces	12%
Freshly grated orange zest	19 grams / ⅔ ounce	2.25%
Fennel seeds	6 grams / ¼ ounce	0.75%
Coriander seeds	6 grams / ¼ ounce	0.75%
Total	**2000 grams / 4 pounds 6⅔ ounces**	**238.55%**

Oil for greasing bowl

Flour for dusting

Butter for greasing pans

Ice for steam

Equipment

Scale	Large bowl or container
Large mixing bowl	Large cutting board
Wooden spoon	*Couche*
Bowl scraper	Baking stone(s) or tiles
Plastic film	Cast-iron or stainless steel roasting pan
Digital thermometer	Peel
Standing electric mixer fitted with the hook	Wire racks

Prepare the *mise en place* for the rye *levain*.

To make the rye *levain*, combine the coarse rye flour and water with the culture in a large mixing bowl, stirring with a wooden spoon to blend. When blended, scrape down the edge of the bowl, cover with plastic film, and set aside to ferment at 70°F (20°C) for 14 to 16 hours.

When ready to make the final dough, prepare the *mise en place*.

Combine the bread and rye flours with the water, rye *levain*, salt, and yeast in the bowl of a standing electric mixer fitted with the hook. Mix on low speed until blended. Increase the mixer speed to medium and mix for about 7 minutes, or until the dough begins to pull away from the sides of the bowl, feels elastic, and gives some resistance when tugged.

Decrease the mixer speed to low, add about a third of the molasses, and mix until blended. Then add the remaining molasses in two additions, incorporating well after each addition. When the molasses is fully incorporated, add the orange zest along with the fennel and coriander seeds and mix until blended.

Lightly oil a large bowl or container.

Scrape the dough into the prepared bowl. Cover the bowl with plastic film and set aside to ferment for 1 hour.

Lightly flour a clean, flat work surface.

Uncover the dough and divide it into four 500-gram / 18-ounce rounds on the floured surface. Cover with plastic film and bench rest for 15 minutes.

Cover the cutting board with *couche* and dust the *couche* with flour.

Uncover the dough and, if necessary, lightly flour the work surface. Gently press on the dough to degas and carefully shape each round into a *bâtard* (see pages 68–69). Place a loaf on one side of the *couche*-covered board, fold the *couche* up to make a double layer of cloth to serve as a divider between the loaves, and continue with the remaining loaves. Cover with plastic film and proof for 1 hour.

About an hour before you are ready to bake the loaves, place the baking stone(s) or tiles into the oven and preheat it to 490°F (254°C). If using a pan to create steam (see page 70), place it in the oven now.

When you are ready to bake the loaves, to make the required steam, add 1 cup of ice to the hot pan in the oven. Immediately uncover the loaves and, using a peel, transfer them to the hot baking stone(s) in the preheated oven. Immediately reduce the oven temperature to 400°F (205°C) and bake, with steam, for 1 hour, or until the crust is brown, shiny, and firm to the touch.

Remove from the oven and transfer to wire racks to cool.

Demonstration

Pumpernickel Bread

Makes 2 loaves

Estimated time to complete: 19 hours or up to 21 hours
Improved mix
Desired dough temperature (DDT): 75°F (25°C)

Ingredient	Amount	Baker's Percentage
For the rye *levain*:		
Coarse rye flour	31 grams / 1⅛ ounces	100%
Water	27 grams / 1 ounce	85%
Liquid *levain* culture (see pages 75–76)	2 grams / 1 teaspoon	5%
Total	**60 grams / 2⅛ ounces**	**190%**
For the final dough:		
Bread flour	326 grams / 11½ ounces	60%
Rye flour	217 grams / 7⅔ ounces	40%
Dutch-processed cocoa powder	18 grams / ⅔ ounce	3.3%
Water	239 grams / 8½ ounces	44%
Cold, strong, brewed coffee	108 grams / 4 ounces	20%
Rye *levain*	60 grams / 2⅛ ounces	11%
Salt	13 grams / ½ ounce	2.4%
Fresh yeast	5 grams / ¼ ounce	1%
Molasses	65 grams / 2⅓ ounces	12%
Sugar	24 grams / 1 ounce	4.4%
Lard	92 grams / 3¼ ounces	17%
Unsalted butter	27 grams / 1 ounce	5%
Caraway seeds	6 grams / ¼ ounce	1.1%
Total	**1200 grams / 2 pounds 10⅓ ounces**	**221.2%**

Oil for greasing bowl
Flour for dusting
Butter for greasing pans

Equipment

Scale

Large mixing bowl

Wooden spoon

Bowl scraper

Plastic film

Digital thermometer

Standing electric mixer fitted with the hook

Large bowl or container

Two 9-inch loaf pans

Baking stone(s) or tiles

Wire racks

Prepare the *mise en place* for the rye *levain*.

To make the rye *levain*, combine the coarse rye flour and water with the culture in a large mixing bowl, stirring with a wooden spoon to blend. When blended, scrape down the edge of the bowl, cover with plastic film, and set aside to ferment at 70°F (20°C) for 14 to 16 hours.

When ready to make the final dough, prepare the *mise en place*.

Combine the bread and rye flours and cocoa powder with the water, coffee, rye *levain*, salt, and yeast in the bowl of a standing electric mixer fitted with the hook. Mix on low speed until blended. Increase the mixer speed to medium and mix until the gluten begins to develop and the dough has some elasticity. Add the molasses and sugar and continue to mix for about 7 minutes, or until the dough begins to pull away from the sides of the bowl, feels elastic, and gives some resistance when tugged.

Add the lard, butter, and caraway seeds and mix on low speed, incorporating well.

Lightly oil a large bowl or container.

Scrape the dough into the prepared bowl. Cover the bowl with plastic film and set aside to ferment for 1 hour.

Uncover and fold the dough. Again, cover with plastic film and set aside to ferment for 1 hour.

Lightly flour a clean, flat work surface.

Uncover the dough and divide it into two 600-gram / 21-ounce rounds on the floured surface. Cover with plastic film and bench rest for 15 minutes.

Lightly butter the loaf pans.

Uncover the dough and, if necessary, lightly flour the work surface. Carefully shape each round into a *bâtard* (see pages 68–69). Place one *bâtard*, seam side down, into each of the prepared pans. Cover with plastic film and proof for 1 hour.

About an hour before you are ready to bake the loaves, place the baking stone(s) or tiles into the oven and pre-heat to 450°F (232°C). If using a pan to create steam (see page 70), place it in the oven now.

When you are ready to bake the loaves, to make the re-quired steam, add 1 cup of ice to the hot pan in the oven. Immediately uncover the loaves and transfer them to the hot baking stone(s) in the preheated oven. Immediately lower the oven temperature to 400°F (205°C).

Bake, with steam, for 1 hour, or until the crust is a deep chocolate-brown and firm to the touch and the loaves makes a hollow sound when tapped on the top.

Remove from the oven and transfer to wire racks to cool.

Demonstration

Stollen

Makes 3 loaves

Estimated time to complete: 10½ hours
Improved mix
Desired dough temperature (DDT): 75°F (25°C)

Ingredient	Amount	Baker's Percentage
For the soaker:		
Dark raisins	175 grams / 6 ounces	35.7%
Golden raisins	175 grams / 6 ounces	35.7%
Candied orange peel	70 grams / 2½ ounces	14.3%
Candied lemon peel	70 grams / 2½ ounces	14.3%
Dark rum	70 grams / 2½ ounces	14.3%
Stollen spice mix (see Note)	5 grams / ⅛ ounce	1%
Total	**565 grams / 1 pound 3⅝ ounces**	**115.3%**
For the sponge:		
Milk	87 grams / 3 ounces	62.6%
Fresh yeast	31 grams / 1 ounce	21.9%
All-purpose flour	140 grams / 5 ounces	100%
Total	**258 grams / 9 ounces**	**184.5%**
For the final dough:		
All-purpose flour	280 grams / 10 ounces	100%
Sugar	43 grams / 1½ ounces	15.6%
Milk	70 grams / 2½ ounces	25%
Sponge	258 grams / 9 ounces	92.2%
Salt	4 grams / ⅛ ounce	1.56%
Unsalted butter	140 grams / 5 ounces	50%
Soaker	565 grams / 1 pound 3⅝ ounces	201.43%
Whole almonds	70 grams / 2½ ounces	25%
Slivered almonds	70 grams / 2½ ounces	25%
Total	**1500 grams / 3 pounds 5 ounces**	**535.79%**

Flour for dusting

Melted unsalted butter for finishing

Granulated sugar for finishing

Confectioners' sugar for dusting

Equipment

Scale	Standing electric mixer fitted with the hook
Plastic container with lid	Sheet pan
Wooden spoon	Parchment paper
Large mixing bowl	Thin (broomstick-sized) rolling pin
Bowl scraper	2 plates
Plastic film	Wire racks
Digital thermometer	

Prepare the *mise en place* for the soaker.

To make the soaker, combine the raisins and candied peels with the rum and spices in a plastic container with a lid, stirring with a wooden spoon to blend. Cover and set aside to soak at room temperature for at least 8 hours.

Prepare the *mise en place* for the sponge.

To make the sponge, combine the milk with the yeast in a large mixing bowl, stirring with a wooden spoon to dissolve. When the yeast has dissolved, stir in the flour until well blended. Scrape down the edge of the bowl, cover with plastic film, and set aside to ferment for 30 minutes at 75°F (25°C).

When ready to make the final dough, prepare the *mise en place*.

Combine the flour with the sugar, milk, sponge, and salt in the bowl of a standing electric mixer fitted with the hook. Add half of the butter and mix on low speed until blended. Increase the mixer speed to medium and gradually add the remaining half of the butter, a third at a time. Continue to mix on medium until the butter is fully incorporated and the dough comes together.

Stop the mixer and let the dough rest for 20 minutes. Add the soaker along with both the whole and slivered almonds and mix just until incorporated. Again, let the dough rest for 15 minutes.

Preheat the oven to 425°F (220°C).

Lightly flour a clean, flat work surface.

Divide the dough into three 500-gram / 18-ounce pieces. Shape each piece into a round (see page 68). Place the rounds, seam side down, on the floured work surface. Cover with plastic film and proof for 15 minutes.

Line the sheet pans with parchment paper.

Flatten each round into an oval shape. Using the rolling pin, press lightly into the center to form a definite in-dentation. Flip the dough over and lift the bottom edge up until it just about meets the top edge so there is a neat line running through the center. Place the loaves on the prepared sheet pans seam side up.

Place the pans in the preheated oven and lower the oven temperature to 375°F (191°C). Bake for 35 minutes, or until the crust is golden brown and firm to the touch.

Remove from the oven and transfer to wire racks to cool for 30 minutes.

Place melted butter on one plate and granulated sugar on another. Working with one loaf at a time, dip the top into the butter. Set on a wire rack to allow excess butter to drip off. Then roll the loaves in the granulated sugar and return to the wire racks to finish cooling. When completely cool, lightly dust the entire loaf with confectioners' sugar.

Note

A classic stollen spice mix consists of
3 parts ground cardamom, 1 part ground
nutmeg, and 1 part ground black pepper.

Session 11

Advanced Bread Formulas

This chapter is a catchall for breads that either don't fit neatly into any other category or take additional skill to create. Many of them have been adapted for our use from recipes generated by some of the world's most outstanding artisanal bread bakers. They are an interesting mix of breads that we at The French Culinary Institute teach in one segment.

> *Pain de Mais*
> Harvest Grain Bread
> Oatmeal-Blueberry-Walnut Bread
> Baguette with Wheat Germ
> Buckwheat-Apple-Walnut Bread
> Millet Bread
> Rye and Whole Wheat Crackers
> 90 Percent Whole Wheat Bread with Walnuts
> 30 Percent Whole Wheat *Pâte Fermentée* Baguette
> Molasses Rye Bread
> Rye and Whole Wheat Bread with Seeds
> *Le Pavé d'Autrefois* (Old-Fashioned Slab)
> Spelt Bread
> *Miche*

Demonstration

Pain de Mais

Makes 2 loaves

Estimated time to complete: 16 hours or up to 18 hours
Improved mix
Desired dough temperature (DDT): 75°F (25°C)

Ingredient	Amount	Baker's Percentage
For the poolish:		
Bread flour	65 grams / 2¼ ounces	100%
Water	65 grams / 2¼ ounces	100%
Fresh yeast	0.6 gram / pinch	0.1%
Total	**130 grams / 4½ ounces**	**200.1%**
For the final dough:		
Bread flour	323 grams / 11⅓ ounces	75%
Cornmeal	108 grams / 3¾ ounces	25%
Water	254 grams / 9 ounces	59%
Olive oil	21 grams / ¾ ounce	5%
Salt	10 grams / ⅓ ounce	2.3%
Fresh yeast	4 grams / 1 teaspoon	1%
Poolish	130 grams / 4½ ounces	30%
Total	**850 grams / 1 pound 14 ounces**	**197.3%**

Oil for greasing bowl
Flour for dusting
Ice for steam

Equipment

Scale	Large cutting board
Large mixing bowl	*Couche*
Wooden spoon	Baking stone(s) or tiles
Bowl scraper	Cast-iron or stainless steel roasting pan
Plastic film	*Lame* or razor
Digital thermometer	Peel
Standing electric mixer fitted with the hook	Wire rack
Large bowl or container	

Prepare the *mise en place* for the poolish.

To make the poolish, combine the bread flour and water with the yeast in a large mixing bowl, stirring with a wooden spoon to blend. When blended, scrape down the edge of the bowl, cover with plastic film, and set aside to ferment at 75°F (25°C) for 12 to 14 hours.

When ready to make the final dough, prepare the *mise en place*.

Combine the bread flour and cornmeal with the water and olive oil in the bowl of a standing electric mixer fitted with the hook. Mix on low speed until blended. Stop the mixer and autolyse for 15 minutes.

Add the salt along with the yeast and poolish and mix on low for 5 minutes. Increase the mixer speed to medium and mix for about 8 minutes, or until the dough has come together but remains slightly sticky. Check the gluten development by pulling a window (see page 64).

Lightly oil a large bowl or container.

Scrape the dough into the prepared bowl. Cover the bowl with plastic film and set aside to ferment for 45 minutes.

Uncover and fold the dough. Again, cover with plastic film and set aside to ferment for 45 minutes.

Lightly flour a clean, flat work surface.

Uncover the dough and divide it into two 425-gram / 15-ounce rounds on the floured surface. Cover with plastic film and bench rest for 15 minutes.

Cover the cutting board with the *couche* and dust the *couche* with flour.

Uncover the dough and, if necessary, lightly flour the work surface. Gently press on the dough to degas and carefully shape each round into a *bâtard* (see pages 68–69). Place one *bâtard* on one side of the *couche*-covered board, fold the *couche* to make a double layer of cloth to serve as a divider between the loaves, and place the remaining loaf next to the fold. Cover with plastic film and proof for 1 hour.

While the dough is proofing, place the baking stone(s) or tiles into the oven and preheat to 450°F (232°C). If using a pan to create steam (see page 70), place it in the oven now.

When ready to bake, uncover the dough and, using a *lame* or a razor, immediately score the loaves as directed on pages 63–65. To make the required steam, add 1 cup of ice to the hot pan in the oven. Using a peel, immediately transfer the loaves to the hot baking stone(s) in the preheated oven.

Bake, with steam, for 40 minutes, or until the crust is golden brown, the sides are firm to the touch, and the loaves make a hollow sound when tapped on the bottom.

Remove from the oven and transfer to wire racks to cool.

Demonstration

Harvest Grain Bread

(Adapted from a recipe by Didier Rosada)

Makes 2 loaves

Estimated time to complete: 16 hours
Improved mix
Desired dough temperature (DDT): 75°F (25°C)

Ingredient	Amount	Baker's Percentage
For the soaker:		
Poppy seeds	21 grams / ¾ ounce	20%
Sesame seeds	21 grams / ¾ ounce	20%
Sunflower seeds	21 grams / ¾ ounce	20%
Pumpkin seeds	21 grams / ¾ ounce	20%
Flax seeds	21 grams / ¾ ounce	20%
Water	107 grams / 3¾ ounces	100%
Total	**212 grams / 7½ ounces**	**200%**
For the poolish:		
Bread flour	53 grams / 2 ounces	100%
Water	53 grams / 2 ounces	100%
Liquid *levain* culture (see pages 75–76)	0.05 gram / pinch	0.1%
Total	**106 grams / 4 ounces**	**200.1%**
For the final dough:		
Bread flour	375 grams / 13¼ ounces	70%
Whole wheat flour	160 grams / 5⅔ ounces	30%
Rolled oats	27 grams / 1 ounce	5%
Cornmeal	16 grams / ½ ounce	3%
Brown sugar	16 grams / ½ ounce	3%
Water	347 grams / 12¼ ounces	65%
Poolish	106 grams / 4 ounces	20%
Salt	13 grams / ½ ounce	2.4%
Fresh yeast	8 grams / ¼ ounce	1.5%
Soaker	212 grams / 7½ ounces	40%
Total	**1280 grams / 2 pounds 13 ounces**	**239.9%**

Oil for greasing bowl

Flour for dusting

Butter for greasing pans

Mixed seeds of the same varieties used in soaker for finishing

Ice for steam

Equipment

Scale	Standing electric mixer fitted with the hook
Plastic container with lid	Large bowl or container
Wooden spoon	Two 9-inch loaf pans
Large mixing bowl	Damp kitchen towel
Bowl scraper	12 x 18-inch sheet pan
Plastic film	Cast-iron or stainless steel roasting pan
Digital thermometer	Wire rack

Prepare the *mise en place* for the soaker.

To make the soaker, combine the poppy, sesame, sunflower, pumpkin, and flax seeds in a plastic container with a lid. Add the water, stirring with a wooden spoon to blend. Cover and set aside to soak at room temperature for 12 hours.

Prepare the *mise en place* for the poolish.

To make the poolish, combine the bread flour and water with the culture in a large mixing bowl, stirring with a wooden spoon to blend. When blended, scrape down the edge of the bowl, cover with plastic film, and set aside to ferment at 75°F (25°) for 12 hours.

When ready to make the final dough, prepare the *mise en place*.

Combine the bread and whole wheat flours, oats, cornmeal, and brown sugar with the water and poolish in the bowl of a standing electric mixer fitted with the hook. Mix on low speed until blended. Stop the mixer and autolyse for 15 minutes.

Add the salt and yeast and mix on low for 5 minutes.

Increase the mixer speed to medium and mix for about 7 minutes, until the dough begins to pull away from the sides of the bowl, feels elastic, and gives some resistance when tugged. Mix in the soaker on low speed until blended.

Lightly oil a large bowl or container.

Scrape the dough into the prepared bowl. Cover the bowl with plastic film and set aside to ferment for 1 hour.

Lightly flour a clean, flat work surface.

Uncover the dough and divide it into two 640-gram / 22½-ounce rounds on the floured surface. Cover with plastic film and bench rest for 15 minutes.

Lightly butter the loaf pans.

Uncover the dough and, if necessary, lightly flour the work surface. Gently press on the dough to degas and carefully shape each round into neat loaf shape so it will fit into one of the prepared pans.

Place the damp kitchen towel on one half of the sheet pan. Place the mixed seeds for finishing on the other

half. Working with one loaf at a time, roll the dough on the moistened towel, then roll the damp dough over and into the mixed seeds. The dampness will help the seeds adhere to the dough during baking.

Place one loaf, seam side down, into each of the prepared pans. Cover with plastic film and proof for 1 hour.

About an hour before you are ready to bake the loaves, preheat the oven to 450°F (232°C). If using a pan to create steam (see page 70), place it in the oven now.

When you are ready to bake the loaves, uncover the dough. To make the required steam, add 1 cup of ice to the hot pan in the oven. Immediately transfer the loaves to the preheated oven.

Bake for 35 minutes, or until the crust is a deep golden brown and the sides are firm to the touch.

Remove from the oven and transfer to wire racks to cool.

Demonstration

Oatmeal-Blueberry-Walnut Bread

(Adapted from Jeffrey Hamelman's *Bread*)

Makes 2 loaves

Estimated time to complete: 6 hours or up to 24 hours
Improved mix
Desired dough temperature (DDT): 75°F (25°C)

Ingredient	Amount	Baker's Percentage
Dried blueberries	130 grams / 4½ ounces	16.7%
Whole wheat flour	161 grams / 5⅔ ounces	20.8%
Rolled oats	130 grams / 4½ ounces	16.7%
Water	403 grams / 14¼ ounces	52%
Bread flour	484 grams / 1 pound 1 ounce	62.5%
Milk	136 grams / 4¾ ounces	17.5%
Honey	48 grams / 1¾ ounces	6.25%
Vegetable oil	48 grams / 1¾ ounces	6.25%
Salt	19 grams / ⅔ ounce	2.5%
Fresh yeast	11 grams / ⅓ ounce	1.4%
Toasted walnuts	130 grams / 4½ ounces	16.7%
Total	**1700 grams / 3 pounds 12 ounces**	**219.3%**

Oil for greasing bowl

Flour for dusting

Butter for greasing pans

Rolled oats for finishing

Ice for steam

Equipment

Scale	Plastic film
Small heat-proof bowl	Two 9-inch loaf pans
Large bowl	Damp kitchen towel
Wooden spoon	12 x 18-inch sheet pan
Standing electric mixer fitted with the hook	Cast-iron or stainless steel roasting pan
Large bowl or container	Wire racks
Bowl scraper	

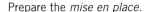

Prepare the *mise en place*.

Place the blueberries in a small heat-proof bowl, cover them with boiling water, and set aside to rehydrate for 1 hour. Drain well and set aside until completely cool.

Combine the whole wheat flour and rolled oats in a large bowl. Add the water, stir with a wooden spoon to combine, and set aside for 30 minutes.

Combine the bread flour with the oat mixture, milk, honey, oil, salt, and yeast in the bowl of a standing electric mixer fitted with the hook. Mix on low speed until blended. Increase the mixer speed to medium and mix for about 7 minutes, or until the dough begins to pull away from the sides of the bowl, feels elastic, and gives some resistance when tugged. Add the rehydrated blueberries along with the walnuts and mix on low speed until incorporated.

Lightly oil a large bowl or container.

Scrape the dough into the prepared bowl. Cover the bowl with plastic film and set aside to ferment for 1 hour.

Uncover and fold the dough. Again, cover with plastic film and set aside to ferment for 1 hour. (Alternatively, the dough may at this point be placed in the refrigerator for up to 18 hours.)

Lightly flour a clean, flat work surface.

Uncover the dough and divide it into two 850-gram / 30-ounce rounds on the floured surface. Cover with plastic film and bench rest for 15 minutes.

Lightly butter the loaf pans.

Uncover the dough and, if necessary, lightly flour the

work surface. Gently press on the dough to degas and carefully shape each round into neat, loaf shape so it will fit into one of the prepared pans.

Place the damp kitchen towel on one half of the sheet pan. Place the rolled oats for finishing on the other half. Working with one loaf at a time, roll the dough on the moistened towel, then roll the damp dough over and into the oats. The dampness will help the oats adhere to the dough during baking. Place the loaves, seam side down, into the prepared pans. Cover with plastic film and proof for 90 minutes.

About an hour before you are ready to bake the loaves,

preheat the oven to 450°F (232°C). If using a pan to create steam (see page 70), place it in the oven now.

When you are ready to bake the loaves, uncover the dough. To make the required steam, add 1 cup of ice to the hot pan in the oven. Immediately, transfer the loaves to the preheated oven.

Bake, with steam, for 15 minutes. Then, reduce the oven temperature to 400°F (205°C) and bake for an additional 30 minutes, or until the crust is deep golden brown and the sides are firm to the touch.

Remove from the oven and transfer to wire racks to cool.

Demonstration

Baguette with Wheat Germ

(Adapted from a recipe by Didier Rosada)

Makes 4 loaves

Estimated time to complete: 15½ hours

Improved mix

Desired dough temperature (DDT): 75°F (25°C)

Ingredient	Amount	Baker's Percentage
For the wheat sponge:		
All-purpose flour	190 grams / 6¾ ounces	80%
Fine whole wheat flour	22 grams / ¾ ounce	20%
Water	140 grams / 5 ounces	66%
Fresh yeast	0.6 gram / pinch	0.3%
Total	**352 grams / 12½ ounces**	**166.3%**
For the final dough:		
Wheat germ	18 grams / ⅔ ounce	3%
All-purpose flour	573 grams / 1 pound 4¼ ounces	97%
Fine whole wheat flour	15 grams / ½ ounce	3%
Water	423 grams / 15 ounces	72%
Salt	15 grams / ½ ounce	2.4%
Yeast	44 grams / 1½ ounces	1%
Wheat sponge	352 grams / 12½ ounces	60%
Total	**1440 grams / 3 pounds 2¾ ounces**	**238.4%**

Oil for greasing bowl

Flour for dusting

Ice for steam

Equipment

Scale	Standing electric mixer fitted with the hook
Large mixing bowl	Large bowl or container
Wooden spoon	Baking stone(s) or tiles
Bowl scraper	Cast-iron or stainless steel roasting pan
Plastic film	4 baguette pans
Digital thermometer	*Lame* or razor
Shallow baking dish	Wire racks

Prepare the *mise en place* for the wheat sponge.

To make the sponge, combine the all-purpose and fine whole wheat flours and water with the yeast in a large mixing bowl, stirring with a wooden spoon to blend. When blended, scrape down the edge of the bowl, cover with plastic film, and set aside to ferment at 75°F (25°C) for 12 hours.

When ready to make the final dough, prepare the *mise en place*.

Preheat the oven to 350°F (177°C).

Place the wheat germ in a shallow baking dish, spreading it out in an even layer. Place in the preheated oven and bake, stirring occasionally, for about 5 minutes, or until lightly colored and fragrant. Remove from the oven and set aside to cool.

Combine the all-purpose and fine whole wheat flours and cooled wheat germ with the water in the bowl of a standing electric mixer fitted with the hook. Mix on low speed until blended. Stop the mixer and autolyse for 15 minutes.

Add the salt and yeast along with the sponge and mix on low for 5 minutes. Increase the mixer speed to medium and mix for about 7 minutes, or until the dough begins to pull away from the sides of the bowl, feels elastic, and gives some resistance when tugged.

Lightly oil a large bowl or container.

Scrape the dough into the prepared bowl. Cover the bowl with plastic film and set aside to ferment for 1 hour.

About an hour before you are ready to bake the loaves, place the baking stone(s) or tiles into the oven and preheat to 470°F (243°C). If using a pan to create steam (see page 70), place it in the oven now.

Lightly dust a clean, flat work surface.

Uncover the dough and divide it into four 360-gram / 13-ounce logs on the floured surface. Cover with plastic film and bench rest for 15 minutes.

Uncover the dough and, if necessary, lightly flour the work surface. Carefully shape each log into a baguette (see page 69) and place each baguette, seam side down, into a baguette pan. Cover with plastic film and proof for 30 minutes.

Uncover the dough and, using a *lame* or a razor, immediately score the loaves as directed on pages 63–65. To make the required steam, add 1 cup of ice to the hot pan in the oven. Immediately transfer the loaves to the hot baking stone(s) in the preheated oven.

Bake, for 25 minutes, or until the crust is reddish brown, the sides are firm to the touch, and the loaves make a hollow sound when tapped on the bottom.

Remove from the oven and transfer to wire racks to cool.

Demonstration

Buckwheat-Apple-Walnut Bread

(Adapted from a recipe by Didier Rosada)

Makes 5 loaves

Estimated time to complete: 18 hours or up to 20 hours
Desired dough temperature (DDT): 75°F (25°C)

Ingredient	Amount	Baker's Percentage
For the buckwheat poolish:		
Bread flour	197 grams / 7 ounces	80%
Buckwheat flour	49 grams / 1¾ ounces	20%
Water	246 grams / 8⅔ ounces	66%
Salt	1 gram / pinch	0.1%
Fresh yeast	1 gram / pinch	0.1%
Total	**494 grams / 17½ ounces**	**166.2%**
For the final dough:		
Dried apples	123 grams / 4⅓ ounces	35%
Dry white wine	454 grams / 16 ounces	129%
Bread flour	352 grams / 12½ ounces	100%
Water	159 grams / 5⅔ ounces	45%
Salt	12 grams / ½ ounce	3.4%
Fresh yeast	38 grams / 1⅓ ounces	2.4%
Buckwheat poolish	494 grams / 17½ ounces	140%
Toasted walnuts	53 grams / 2 ounces	15%
Total	**1685 grams / 3 pounds 11½ ounces**	**469.9%**

Oil for greasing bowl

Flour for dusting

Ice for steam

Equipment

Scale	Large bowl or container
Large mixing bowl	2 large cutting boards
Wooden spoon	*Couche* for two boards
Bowl scraper	Baking stone(s) or tiles
Plastic film	Cast-iron or stainless steel roasting pan
Digital thermometer	*Lame* or razor
Small bowl	Peel
Standing electric mixer fitted with the hook	Wire racks
Fine-mesh sieve	

Prepare the *mise en place* for the buckwheat poolish.

To make the buckwheat poolish, combine the bread and buckwheat flours and water with the salt and yeast in a large mixing bowl, stirring with a wooden spoon to blend. When blended, scrape down the edge of the bowl, cover with plastic film, and set aside to ferment at 70°F (20°C) for 14 to 16 hours.

When ready to make the final dough, prepare the *mise en place*.

Place the apples and white wine in a small bowl and set aside for 30 minutes.

Combine the bread flour with the water in the bowl of a standing electric mixer fitted with the hook. Mix on low speed until blended. Stop the mixer and autolyse for 15 minutes.

Add the salt and yeast along with the poolish and mix on low for 5 minutes. Increase the mixer speed to medium and mix for about 7 minutes, or until the dough begins to pull away from the sides of the bowl, feels elastic, and gives some resistance when tugged.

Drain the apples in a fine-mesh sieve, discarding the liquid. Add the rehydrated apples and walnuts and mix on low speed to incorporate.

Lightly oil a large bowl or container.

Scrape the dough into the prepared bowl. Cover the bowl with plastic film and set aside to ferment for 1 hour.

Lightly dust a clean, flat work surface.

Uncover the dough and divide it into five 335-gram / 12-ounce rounds on the floured surface.

Cover with plastic film and bench rest for 15 minutes.

Cover the cutting boards with the *couche* and dust the *couche* with flour.

Uncover the dough and, if necessary, lightly flour the work surface. Gently press on the dough to degas and carefully shape each piece into a neat, tight round. Place one round, seam side down, on one side of one of the *couche*-covered boards, fold the *couche* up to make a double layer of cloth to serve as a divider between the loaves, and place a second round next to the fold. Repeat the process with the remaining three rounds and the second *couche*-covered board. Cover with plastic film and proof for 1 hour.

About an hour before you are ready to bake the loaves, place the baking stone(s) or tiles into the oven and preheat to 450°F (232°C). If using a pan to create steam (see page 70), place it in the oven now.

Uncover the dough and, using a *lame* or a razor, immediately score the loaves as directed on pages 63–65. To make the required steam, add 1 cup of ice to the hot pan in the oven. Using a peel, immediately transfer the loaves to the hot baking stone(s) in the preheated oven.

Bake for 25 minutes, watching carefully as the crust can brown too quickly. If the crust darkens before

the bread is finished baking, either reduce the oven temperature to 400°F (205°C) or open the oven door slightly. The loaves should be very brown with firm sides and should make a hollow sound when tapped on the bottom.

Remove from the oven and transfer to wire racks to cool.

291

Demonstration

Millet Bread

(Adapted from a recipe by Didier Rosada)

Makes 4 loaves

Estimated time to complete: 18 hours or up to 20 hours
Improved mix
Desired dough temperature (DDT): 75°F (25°C)

Ingredient	Amount	Baker's Percentage
For the *levain*:		
All-purpose flour	28 grams / 1 ounce	100%
Water	21 grams / ¾ ounce	75%
Liquid *levain* culture (see pages 75–76)	3 grams / ⅛ ounce	10%
Total	**52 grams / 1⅞ ounces**	**185%**
For the *pâte fermentée*:		
All-purpose flour	192 grams / 6¾ ounces	100%
Water	125 grams / 4½ ounces	65%
Fresh yeast	4 grams / ⅛ ounce	2%
Salt	4 grams / ⅛ ounce	2%
Total	**325 grams / 11½ ounces**	**169%**
For the soaker:		
Millet seeds	76 grams / 2⅔ ounces	50%
Sesame seeds	30 grams / 1 ounce	20%
Poppy seeds	22 grams / ¾ ounce	15%
Pumpkin seeds	22 grams / ¾ ounce	15%
Water	76 grams / 2⅔ ounces	50%
Total	**226 grams / 8 ounces**	**150%**

For the final dough:

All-purpose flour	325 grams / 11½ ounces	75%
Whole wheat flour	108 grams / 3¾ ounces	25%
Pâte fermentée (see page 111)	325 grams / 11½ ounces	75%
Water	75 grams / 2⅔ ounces	58%
Honey	65 grams / 2⅓ ounces	15%
Levain	52 grams / 1⅞ ounces	12%
Vegetable oil	26 grams / 1 ounce	6%
Salt	13 grams / ½ ounce	3.2%
Fresh yeast	5 grams / ¼ ounce	1.2%
Soaker	226 grams / 8 ounces	52.5%
Total	**1220 grams / 2 pounds 11⅜ ounces**	**322.9%**

Oil for greasing bowl

Flour for dusting

Millet for finishing

Ice for steam

Equipment

Scale	2 large cutting boards
2 large mixing bowls	*Couche* for two boards
Wooden spoon	Damp kitchen towel
Bowl scraper	12 x 18-inch sheet pan
Plastic film	Baking stone(s) or tiles
Digital thermometer	Cast-iron or stainless steel roasting pan
Plastic container with lid	Peel
Standing electric mixer fitted with the hook	Wire racks
Large bowl or container	

Prepare the *mise en place* for the *levain*, *pâte fermentée*, and soaker.

To make the *levain*, combine the flour and water with the culture in a large mixing bowl, stirring with a wooden spoon to blend. When blended, scrape down the edge of the bowl, cover with plastic film, and set aside to ferment at 70°F (20°C) for 12 to 14 hours.

To make the *pâte fermentée*, combine the flour and water with the yeast and salt in a large mixing bowl, stirring with a wooden spoon to blend. The desired dough temperature (DDT) should be 75°F (25°C). When blended, scrape down the edge of the bowl and cover with plastic film. Place the dough in the refrigerator to ferment for 12 hours.

To make the soaker, combine the millet, sesame, poppy, and pumpkin seeds with the water in a plastic container with a lid, stirring with a wooden spoon to blend. Cover and set aside to soak at room temperature for at least 12 hours.

When ready to make the final dough, prepare the *mise en place*.

Combine the all-purpose and whole wheat flours with the *pâte fermentée*, water, honey, *levain*, vegetable oil, salt, and yeast in the bowl of a standing electric mixer fitted with the hook. Mix on low speed until blended. Increase the mixer speed to medium and mix for about 5 minutes, or until the dough begins to pull away from the sides of the bowl, feels elastic, and gives some resistance when tugged. Add the soaker and mix on low speed until incorporated.

Lightly oil a large bowl or container.

Scrape the dough into the prepared bowl. Cover with plastic film and set aside to ferment for 1 hour.

Lightly flour a clean, flat work surface.

Uncover the dough and divide it into four 305-gram / 11-ounce rounds on the floured surface. Cover with plastic film and bench rest for 15 minutes.

Uncover the dough and, if necessary, lightly flour the work surface. Gently press on the dough to degas and carefully shape each round into a neat, tight round. Cover with plastic film and bench rest for 10 minutes.

Cover the cutting boards with the *couche* and dust the *couche* with flour.

Uncover the dough and, using the palm of your hand, flatten each round into a neat disk.

Place the damp kitchen towel on one half of the sheet pan. Place the millet for finishing on the other half. Working with one loaf at a time, lightly press one side of the dough onto the moistened towel, then press the damp dough into the millet. The dampness will help the millet adhere to the dough during baking.

About an hour before you are ready to bake the loaves, place the baking stone(s) or tiles into the oven and preheat to 450°F (232°C). If using a pan to create steam (see page 70), place it in the oven now.

When you are ready to bake the loaves, to make the required steam, add 1 cup of ice to the hot pan in the oven. Using a peel, immediately transfer the loaves to the hot baking stone(s) in the preheated oven.

Bake for 25 minutes, or until the crust is a deep golden brown, the sides are firm to the touch, and the loaves make a hollow sound when tapped on the bottom.

Remove from the oven and transfer to wire racks to cool.

Demonstration

Rye and Whole Wheat Crackers

Makes 4 dozen crackers
    Estimated time to complete: 3 hours
    Short mix
    Desired dough temperature (DDT): 75°F (25°C)

Ingredient	Amount	Baker's Percentage
Coarse rye flour	500 grams / 1 pound 1⅔ ounces	66.7%
Coarse whole wheat flour	250 grams / 8¾ ounces	33.3%
Water	425 grams / 15 ounces	56.7%
Milk	75 grams / 2⅔ ounces	10%
Honey	22 grams / ¾ ounce	3%
Salt	16 grams / ½ ounce	2.2%
Fresh yeast	15 grams / ½ ounce	2%
Ammonium bicarbonate	4 grams / ⅛ ounce	0.53%
Total	1307 grams / 2 pounds 14 ounces	174.43%

Oil for greasing bowl

Seeds, semolina flour, rye or wheat flakes, or coarse salt for topping (see Notes)

Equipment

Scale	Rolling pin
Standing electric mixer fitted with the hook	Small bowl
Large bowl or container	Pastry brush
Bowl scraper	Small biscuit cutter (optional, see Notes) or chef's knife
Plastic film	Spatula
Two 12 x 36-inch sheet pans	Wire racks
Parchment paper	

Prepare the *mise en place*.

Combine the rye and whole wheat flours with the water, milk, honey, salt, yeast, and ammonium bicarbonate in the bowl of a standing electric mixer fitted with the hook. Mix on low speed until blended. Increase the mixer speed to medium and mix for about 8 minutes, or until the dough has come together and pulls away from the side of the bowl but remains slightly sticky.

Lightly oil a large bowl or container.

Scrape the dough into the prepared bowl. Cover the bowl with plastic film and set aside to ferment for 1 hour.

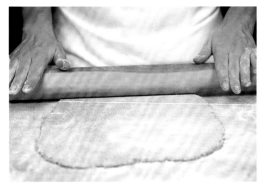  

Notes

You may use almost any seed, flake, or spice to top the crackers.

The crackers may be cut out into any shape, either freehand or with a shaped cutter.

Preheat the oven to 450°F (232°C).

Line the sheet pans with parchment paper.

Lightly flour a clean, flat work surface.

Uncover the dough and, using a rolling pin, roll the dough out to a sheet about ⅛ inch (3 millimeters) thick on the floured surface. Fill a small bowl with water. Using a pastry brush, lightly wet the dough with water. Sprinkle the dough with seeds, semolina flour, rye or wheat flakes, or coarse salt (see Notes for additional topping suggestions). Then, if using a biscuit

cutter, cut the dough out into small circles; if using a chef's knife, cut the dough into squares or rectangles (see Notes).

Using a spatula, transfer the circles to the prepared baking sheets. Cover with plastic film and proof for 1 hour.

Uncover the dough and place the sheet pans in the preheated oven. Bake for 10 minutes, or until brown and crisp.

Remove from the oven and transfer to wire racks to cool.

Demonstration

90 Percent Whole Wheat Bread with Walnuts

Makes 4 loaves
Estimated time to complete: 16 hours
Improved mix
Desired dough temperature (DDT): 75°F (25°C)

Ingredient	Amount	Baker's Percentage
For the *levain*:		
Bread flour	43 grams / 1½ ounces	100%
Water	43 grams / 1½ ounces	100%
Liquid *levain* culture (see pages 75–76)	4 grams / ⅛ ounce	10%
Total	**90 grams / 3⅛ ounces**	**210%**
For the whole wheat sponge:		
Whole wheat flour	243 grams / 8⅔ ounces	100%
Water	163 grams / 5¾ ounces	67%
Salt	1 gram / pinch	0.5%
Fresh yeast	0.2 gram / pinch	0.1%
Total	**407 grams / 14⅓ ounces**	**167.6%**
For the final dough:		
Water	578 grams / 1 pound 4½ ounces	85%
Whole wheat flour	626 grams / 1 pound 6 ounces	92%
Bread flour	55 grams / 2 ounces	8%
Whole wheat sponge	407 grams / 14⅓ ounces	60%
Levain	90 grams / 3⅛ ounces	13.3%
Salt	18 grams / ⅔ ounce	3.2%
Fresh yeast	0.1 gram / pinch	0.02%
Toasted walnuts	146 grams / 5 ounces	21.3%
Total	**1920 grams / 4 pounds 3¾ ounces**	**282.82%**

Oil for greasing bowl

Flour for dusting

Ice for steam

Equipment

Scale	Large bowl or container
Large mixing bowl	Baking stone(s) or tiles
Wooden spoon	Cast-iron or stainless steel roasting pan
Bowl scraper	2 large cutting boards
Plastic film	*Couche* for two boards
Digital thermometer	*Lame* or razor
Standing electric mixer fitted with the hook	Peel
Medium mixing bowl	Wire racks

Prepare the *mise en place* for the *levain* and the whole wheat sponge.

To make the *levain*, combine the bread flour and water with the culture in a large mixing bowl, stirring with a wooden spoon to blend. When blended, scrape down the edge of the bowl, cover with plastic film, and set aside to ferment at 75°F (25°C) for 12 hours.

To make the whole wheat sponge, combine the flour and water with the salt and yeast in the bowl of a standing electric mixer fitted with the hook. Mix on low speed until blended. When blended, scrape the sponge into a medium mixing bowl and cover with plastic film. Set aside to ferment at room temperature for 12 hours.

When ready to make the final dough, prepare the *mise en place*.

Measure out 57 grams / 2 ounces of the water and set aside.

Combine the whole wheat and bread flours with the remaining water, the sponge, *levain*, salt, and yeast in the bowl of a standing electric mixer fitted with the hook. Mix on low speed until blended. Increase the mixer speed to medium and mix until the gluten begins to develop and the dough has some elasticity. Add the reserved water and continue to mix for about 7 minutes, or until dough begins to pull away from the sides of the bowl, feels

elastic, and gives some resistance when tugged. Add the walnuts and mix on low speed to incorporate.

Lightly oil a large bowl or container.

Scrape the dough into the prepared bowl. Cover the bowl with plastic film and set aside to ferment for 1 hour.

Uncover and fold the dough. Again, cover with plastic film and set aside to ferment for 1 hour.

About an hour before you are ready to bake the loaves, place the baking stone(s) or tiles into the oven and pre-heat to 450°F (232°C). If using a pan to create steam (see page 70), place it in the oven now.

Lightly flour a clean, flat work surface.

Uncover the dough and divide it into four 480-gram / 17-ounce rounds on the floured surface. Cover with plastic film and bench rest for 15 minutes.

Cover the cutting boards with the *couche* and dust the *couche* with flour.

Uncover the dough and, if necessary, lightly flour the work surface. Gently press on the dough to degas and carefully shape each round into a *bâtard* (see pages 68–69). Place one *bâtard*, seam side down, on one side of one of the *couche*-covered boards, fold the *couche* up to make a double layer of cloth to serve as a divider between the loaves, and place a second *bâtard* next to the fold. Repeat the process with the remaining two *bâtards* and the second *couche*-covered board. Cover with plastic film and proof for 30 minutes.

Uncover the dough and, using a *lame* or a razor, immediately score the loaves as directed on pages 63–65. To make the required steam, add 1 cup of ice to the hot pan in the oven. Using a peel, immediately transfer the loaves to the hot baking stone(s) in the preheated oven.

Bake, with steam, for 40 minutes, or until the crust is a deep reddish brown, the sides are firm to the touch, and the loaves make a hollow sound when tapped on the bottom.

Remove from the oven and transfer to wire racks to cool.

Demonstration

30 Percent Whole Wheat *Pâte Fermentée* Baguette

Makes 4 loaves

Estimated time to complete: 4½ hours
Improved mix
Desired dough temperature (DDT): 75°F (25°C)

Ingredient	Amount	Baker's Percentage
Bread flour	630 grams / 22¼ ounces	70%
Whole wheat flour	190 grams / 6⅔ ounces	30%
Water	467 grams / 1 pound ½ ounce	74%
Salt	13 grams / ½ ounce	2%
Fresh yeast	5 grams / ⅛ ounce	0.75%
Pâte fermentée (see page 111)	95 grams / 3⅓ ounces	15%
Total	**1400 grams / 3 pounds 1½ ounces**	**191.75%**

Oil for greasing bowl
Flour for dusting
Ice for steam

Equipment

Scale	Baking stone(s) or tiles
Standing electric mixer fitted with the hook	Cast-iron or stainless steel roasting pan
Large bowl or container	4 baguette pans
Bowl scraper	*Lame* or razor
Plastic film	Wire racks

Prepare the *mise en place*. The *pâte fermentée* should be at least 4 hours, but no more than 24 hours old.

Combine the bread and whole wheat flours with the water in the bowl of a standing electric mixer fitted with the hook. Mix on low speed until blended. Stop the mixer and autolyse for 15 minutes.

Add the salt along with the yeast and *pâte fermentée* and mix on low for 5 minutes. Increase the mixer speed to medium and mix for about 8 minutes, or until the dough has come together but remains slightly sticky. Check the gluten development by pulling a window (see page 64).

Lightly oil a large bowl or container.

Scrape the dough into the prepared bowl. Cover the bowl with plastic film and set aside to ferment for 45 minutes.

Uncover and fold the dough. Again, cover with plastic film and set aside to ferment for 75 minutes.

About an hour before you are ready to bake the loaves, place the baking stone(s) or tiles into the oven and preheat to 470°F (243°C). If using a pan to create steam (see page 70), place it in the oven now.

Lightly flour a clean, flat work surface.

Uncover the dough and divide it into four 350-gram / 12½-ounce logs on the floured surface. Cover with plastic film and bench rest for 15 minutes.

Uncover the dough and, if necessary, lightly flour the work surface. Gently press on the dough to degas and carefully shape each log into a baguette (see page 69). Place each baguette, seam side down, into a baguette pan. Cover with plastic film and proof for 30 minutes.

Uncover the dough and, using a *lame* or a razor, immediately score the loaves as directed on pages 63–65. To make the required steam, add 1 cup of ice to the hot pan in the oven. Immediately transfer the loaves to the hot baking stone(s) in the preheated oven.

Bake for 27 minutes, or until the crust is reddish brown, the sides are firm to the touch, and the loaves make a hollow sound when tapped on the bottom.

Remove from the oven and transfer to wire racks to cool.

Demonstration

Molasses Rye Bread

(Adapted from a recipe by Didier Rosada)

Makes 3 loaves

Estimated time to complete: 15½ hours
Improved mix
Desired dough temperature (DDT): 75°F (25°C)

Ingredient	Amount	Baker's Percentage
For the flax seed soaker:		
Flax seeds	54 grams / 2 ounces	100%
Water	107 grams / 3¾ ounces	200%
Total	**161 grams / 5¾ ounces**	**300%**
For the cracked wheat soaker:		
Cracked wheat	161 grams / 5⅔ ounces	100%
Water	161 grams / 5⅔ ounces	100%
Total	**322 grams / 11⅓ ounces**	**200%**
For the *levain*:		
All-purpose flour	89 grams / 3⅛ ounces	100%
Water	89 grams / 3⅛ ounces	100%
Liquid *levain* culture (see pages 75–76)	18 grams / ⅔ ounce	20%
Total	**196 grams / 7 ounces**	**220%**
For the final dough:		
Whole wheat flour	286 grams / 10 ounces	80%
Dark rye flour	72 grams / 2½ ounces	20%
Water	243 grams / 8½ ounces	68%
Molasses	54 grams / 2 ounces	15%
Levain	196 grams / 7 ounces	55%
Salt	12 grams / ½ ounce	3.4%
Fresh yeast	4 grams / ⅛ ounce	1%
Cracked wheat soaker	322 grams / 11⅓ ounces	90%
Flax seed soaker	161 grams / 5¾ ounces	45%
Total	**1350 grams / 2 pounds 15⅔ ounces**	**377.4%**

Oil for greasing bowl
Flour for dusting
Ice for steam

Equipment

Scale	Large bowl or container
2 plastic containers with lids	2 large cutting boards
Wooden spoon	*Couche* for two boards
Large mixing bowl	Baking stone(s) or tiles
Bowl scraper	Cast-iron or stainless steel roasting pan
Plastic film	*Lame* or razor
Digital thermometer	Peel
Standing electric mixer fitted with the hook	Wire racks

Prepare the *mise en place* for the soakers.

To make the flax seed soaker, combine the flax seeds with the water in a plastic container with a lid, stirring with a wooden spoon to blend. Cover and set aside to soak at room temperature for at least 12 hours.

To make the cracked wheat soaker, combine the cracked wheat with the water in a plastic container with a lid, stirring with a wooden spoon to blend. Cover and set aside to soak at room temperature for at least 12 hours.

Prepare the *mise en place* for the *levain*.

To make the *levain*, combine the all-purpose flour and water with the culture in a large mixing bowl, stirring with a wooden spoon to blend. When blended, scrape down the edge of the bowl, cover with plastic film, and set aside to ferment at 75°F (25°C) for 12 hours.

When ready to make the final dough, prepare the *mise en place*.

Combine the whole wheat and dark rye flours with the water, molasses, *levain*, salt, and yeast in the bowl of a standing electric mixer fitted with the hook. Mix on low

speed until blended. Stop the mixer and autolyse for 15 minutes.

Increase the mixer speed to medium and mix for about 3 minutes or until the gluten begins to develop and the dough has some elasticity. Add the cracked wheat and flax seed soakers and continue to mix for about 5 minutes, or until the dough begins to pull away from the sides of the bowl, feels elastic, and gives some resistance when tugged.

Lightly oil a large bowl or container.

Scrape the dough into the prepared bowl. Cover the bowl with plastic film and set aside to ferment for 1 hour.

Lightly flour a clean, flat work surface.

Uncover the dough and divide it into three 450-gram / 16-ounce rounds on the floured surface. Cover with plastic film and bench rest for 15 minutes.

Cover the cutting boards with the *couche* and dust the *couche* with flour.

Uncover the dough and, if necessary, lightly flour the work surface. Gently press on the dough to degas and carefully shape each piece of dough into a neat, tight round. Place one round, seam side down, on one side of one of the *couche*-covered boards, fold the *couche* up to make a double layer of cloth to serve as a divider between the loaves, and place a second round next to the fold. Repeat the process with the remaining two rounds and the second *couche*-covered board. Cover with plastic film and proof for 1 hour.

About an hour before you are ready to bake the loaves, place the baking stone(s) or tiles into the oven and pre-heat to 400°F (205°C). If using a pan to create steam (see page 70), place it in the oven now.

Uncover the dough and, using a *lame* or a razor, imme-diately score the loaves as directed on pages 63–65. To make the required steam, add 1 cup of ice to the hot pan in the oven. Using a peel, immediately transfer the loaves to the hot baking stone(s) in the preheated oven.

Bake, with steam, for 35 minutes, or until the crust is chocolate brown, the sides are firm to the touch, and the loaves make a hollow sound when tapped on the bottom. If the crust darkens before the bread is finished baking, reduce the oven temperature to 380°F (193°C).

Remove from the oven and transfer to wire racks to cool.

Demonstration

Rye and Whole Wheat Bread with Seeds

(Adapted from a recipe by Didier Rosada)

Makes 2 loaves

Estimated time to complete: 16½ hours
Improved mix
Desired dough temperature (DDT): 75°F (25°C)

Ingredient	Amount	Baker's Percentage
For the soaker:		
Flax seeds	22 grams / ¾ ounce	25%
Sesame seeds	22 grams / ¾ ounce	25%
Sunflower seeds	22 grams / ¾ ounce	25%
Rolled oats	22 grams / ¾ ounce	25%
Water	58 grams / 2 ounces	66.7%
Total	**146 grams / 5 ounces**	**166.7%**
For the *levain*:		
Whole wheat flour	99 grams / 3½ ounces	100%
Water	79 grams / 2¾ ounces	80%
Liquid *levain* culture (see pages 75–76)	15 grams / ½ ounce	15%
Total	**193 grams / 6¾ ounces**	**195%**
For the final dough:		
Water	357 grams / 13¼ ounces	74%
Whole wheat flour	386 grams / 13⅔ ounces	80%
Dark rye flour	48 grams / 1¾ ounces	10%
Coarse rye flour	48 grams / 1¾ ounces	10%
Levain	193 grams / 6¾ ounces	40%
Salt	13 grams / ½ ounce	2.7%
Fresh yeast	9 grams / ⅓ ounce	1.8%
Soaker	146 grams / 5 ounces	30%
Total	**1200 grams / 2 pounds 11 ounces**	**248.5%**

Oil for greasing bowl

Flour for dusting

Butter for greasing pans

Ice for steam

Equipment

Scale	Digital thermometer
Plastic container with lid	Standing electric mixer fitted with the hook
Wooden spoon	Large bowl or container
Large mixing bowl	Two 9-inch loaf pans
Bowl scraper	Cast-iron or stainless steel roasting pan
Plastic film	Wire racks

Prepare the *mise en place* for the soaker.

To make the soaker, combine the flax, sesame, and sunflower seeds with the oats in a plastic container with a lid. Add the water, stirring with a wooden spoon to blend. Cover and set aside to soak at room temperature for at least 12 hours.

Prepare the *mise en place* for the *levain*.

To make the *levain*, combine the whole wheat flour and water with the culture in a large mixing bowl, stirring with a wooden spoon to blend. When blended, scrape down the edge of the bowl, cover with plastic film, and set aside to ferment at 75°F (25°C) for 12 hours.

When ready to make the final dough, prepare the *mise en place*.

Measure out 38 grams / 1⅓ ounces of the water and set aside.

Combine the whole wheat and dark rye flours with the coarse rye flour and the remaining water along with the *levain*, salt, and yeast in the bowl of a standing electric mixer fitted with the hook. Mix on low speed until blended. Stop the mixer and autolyse for 15 minutes.

Increase the mixer speed to medium and mix just until the gluten begins to develop and the dough has some elasticity. Add the reserved water and continue to mix for about 5 minutes, or until the dough begins to pull away from the sides of the bowl, feels elastic, and gives some resistance when tugged. Mix in the soaker on low speed.

Lightly oil a large bowl or container.

Scrape the dough into the prepared bowl. Cover the bowl with plastic film and set aside to ferment for 1 hour.

Lightly flour a clean, flat work surface.

Uncover the dough and divide it into two 600-gram / 21½-ounce rounds on the floured surface. Cover with plastic film and bench rest for 15 minutes.

Lightly butter the loaf pans.

Uncover the dough and, if necessary, lightly flour the work surface. Gently press on the dough to degas and carefully shape each round into a loaf shape. Place one loaf into each of the prepared pans. Cover with plastic film and proof for 2 hours.

About an hour before you are ready to bake the loaves, preheat the oven to 450°F (232°C). If using a pan to create steam (see page 70), place it in the oven now.

When ready to bake, to make the required steam, add 1 cup of ice to the hot pan in the oven. Uncover the loaves and transfer the pans to the preheated oven. Immediately lower the heat to 400°F (205°C).

Bake for 45 minutes or until the crust is a deep reddish brown and the sides are firm to the touch. The crumb should be very dry.

Remove from the oven and transfer to wire racks to cool.

Demonstration

Le Pavé d'Autrefois (Old-Fashioned Slab)

Makes 4 loaves

Estimated time to complete: 19 hours or up to 21 hours
Improved mix
Desired dough temperature (DDT): 75°F (25°C)

Ingredient	Amount	Baker's Percentage
For the poolish:		
Bread flour	275 grams / 9¾ ounces	100%
Water	275 grams / 9¾ ounces	100%
Fresh yeast	0.2 gram / pinch	0.1%
Total	**550 grams / 19½ ounces**	**200.1%**
For the final dough:		
Water	333 grams / 11¾ ounces	67%
Bread flour	303 grams / 10⅔ ounces	61.11%
Whole wheat flour	83 grams / 3 ounces	16.67%
Rye flour	55 grams / 2 ounces	11.11%
Buckwheat flour	55 grams / 2 ounces	11.11%
Poolish	550 grams / 1 pound 3½ ounces	111.11%
Salt	16 grams / ½ ounce	3.11%
Fresh yeast	5 grams / ⅛ ounce	1%
Total	**1400 grams / 3 pounds 1½ ounces**	**282.22%**

Oil for greasing bowl
Flour for dusting
Ice for steam

Equipment

Scale	Large bowl or container
Large mixing bowl	2 large cutting boards
Wooden spoon	*Couche* for two boards
Bowl scraper	Baking stone(s) or tiles
Plastic film	Cast-iron or stainless steel roasting pan
Digital thermometer	Peel
Standing electric mixer fitted with the hook	Wire racks

Prepare the *mise en place* for the poolish.

To make the poolish, combine the bread flour and water with the yeast in a large mixing bowl, stirring with a wooden spoon to blend. When blended, scrape down the edge of the bowl, cover with plastic film, and set aside to ferment at 70°F (20°C) for 14 to 16 hours.

When ready to make the final dough, prepare the *mise en place*.

Measure out 72 grams / 2½ ounces of the water and set aside.

Combine the bread, whole wheat, rye, and buckwheat flours with the remaining water, poolish, salt, and yeast in the bowl of a standing electric mixer fitted with the hook. Mix on low speed until blended. Increase the mixer speed to medium and mix just until the gluten begins to develop and the dough has some elasticity. Add the reserved water and continue to mix for about 7 minutes, or until the dough begins to pull away from the sides of the bowl, feels elastic, and gives some resistance when tugged.

Lightly oil a large bowl or container.

Scrape the dough into the prepared bowl. Cover the bowl with plastic film and set aside to ferment for 1 hour.

Uncover and fold the dough. Again, cover with plastic film and set aside to ferment for 1 hour.

Cover the cutting boards with the *couche* and dust the *couche* with flour.

Lightly flour a clean, flat work surface.

Uncover the dough and divide it into four 350-gram / 12½-ounce rectangular pieces on the floured surface (they need not be perfectly shaped). Place one rectangular piece on one side of one of the *couche*-covered boards, fold the *couche* up to make a double layer of cloth to serve as a divider between the loaves, and place a second rectangular piece next to the fold. Repeat the process with the remaining two pieces and the second *couche*-covered board. Cover with plastic film and proof for 1 hour.

About an hour before you are ready to bake the loaves, place the baking stone(s) or tiles into the oven and preheat to 470°F (243°C). If using a pan to create steam (see page 70), place it in the oven now.

When ready to bake, to make the required steam, add 1 cup of ice to the hot pan in the oven. Uncover the loaves and, using a peel, immediately transfer the loaves to the hot baking stone(s) in the preheated oven.

Bake, with steam, for 40 minutes, or until the crust is a deep reddish brown, the sides are firm to the touch, and the loaves make a hollow sound when tapped on the bottom.

Remove from the oven and transfer to wire racks to cool.

Demonstration

Spelt Bread

(Adapted from Michel Suas' *Advanced Bread and Pastry*)

Makes 4 loaves

Estimated time to complete: 19½ hours or up to 21½ hours
Improved mix
Desired dough temperature (DDT): 75°F (25°C)

Ingredient	Amount	Baker's Percentage
For the poolish:		
Whole spelt flour	348 grams / 12¼ ounces	100%
Water	348 grams / 12¼ ounces	100%
Fresh yeast	0.3 gram / pinch	0.1%
Total	**696 grams / 1 pound 8½ ounces**	**200.1%**
For the final dough:		
Whole spelt flour	709 grams / 1 pound 9 ounces	100%
Water	382 grams / 13½ ounces	52.24%
Poolish	696 grams / 1 pound 8½ ounces	98.56%
Salt	19 grams / ⅔ ounce	2.69%
Fresh yeast	4 grams / ⅛ ounce	1%
Total	**1800 grams / 3 pounds 15½ ounces**	**254.49%**

Oil for greasing bowl
Flour for dusting
Ice for steam

Equipment

Scale	Large bowl or container
Large mixing bowl	Baking stone(s) or tiles
Wooden spoon	Cast-iron or stainless steel roasting pan
Bowl scraper	2 large cutting boards
Plastic film	*Couche* for two boards
Digital thermometer	Peel
Standing electric mixer fitted with the hook	Wire racks

Prepare the *mise en place* for the poolish.

To make the poolish, combine the spelt flour and water with the yeast in a large mixing bowl, stirring with a wooden spoon to blend. When blended, scrape down the edge of the bowl, cover with plastic film, and set aside to ferment at 70°F (20°C) for 14 to 16 hours.

When ready to make the final dough, prepare the *mise en place*.

Combine the flour with the water, poolish, salt, and yeast in the bowl of a standing electric mixer fitted with the hook. Mix on low speed until blended. Increase the mixer speed to medium and mix, for about 7 minutes, or until the dough begins to pull away from the sides of the bowl, feels elastic, and gives some resistance when tugged.

Lightly oil a large bowl or container.

Scrape the dough into the prepared bowl. Cover the bowl with plastic film and set aside to ferment for 20 minutes.

Uncover and fold the dough. Again, cover with plastic film and set aside to ferment for 20 minutes.

Uncover and fold the dough. Cover with plastic film and set aside a third time to ferment for 20 minutes.

Uncover and again fold the dough. Cover with plastic film and set aside to ferment for 2 hours.

About an hour before you are ready to bake the loaves, place the baking stone(s) or tiles into the oven and preheat to 450°F (232°C). If using a pan to create steam (see page 70), place it in the oven now.

Cover the cutting boards with the *couche* and dust the *couche* with flour.

Lightly flour a clean, flat work surface.

Uncover the dough and divide it into four 450-gram / 16-ounce rectangular pieces on the floured surface (they need not be perfectly shaped). Place one rectangular piece on one side of one of the *couche*-covered boards, fold the *couche* up to make a double layer of cloth to serve as a divider between the loaves, and place a second rectangular piece next to the fold. Repeat the process with the remaining two pieces and the second *couche*-covered board. Cover with plastic film and proof for 45 minutes.

When ready to bake, to make the required steam, add 1 cup of ice to the hot pan in the oven. Uncover the dough and, using a peel, immediately transfer the loaves to the hot baking stone(s) in the preheated oven.

Bake for 40 minutes, or until the crust is a deep golden brown, the sides are firm to the touch, and the loaves make a hollow sound when tapped on the bottom.

Remove from the oven and transfer to wire racks to cool.

Demonstration

Miche

(Adapted from Jeffrey Hamelman's *Bread*)

Makes 2 loaves

Estimated time to complete: 20 or up to 22 hours
Short mix
Desired dough temperature (DDT): 75°F (25°C)

Ingredient	Amount	Baker's Percentage
For the *levain*:		
Coarse whole wheat flour	124 grams / 4½ ounces	50%
Coarse rye flour	124 grams / 4½ ounces	50%
Water	162 grams / 5¾ ounces	65%
Stiff *levain* culture (54% hydration; see pages 75–76)	50 grams / 1¾ ounces	20%
Total	**460 grams / 1 pound ½ ounce**	**185%**
For the final dough:		
Bread flour	871 grams / 30¾ ounces	87.5%
Fine whole wheat flour	125 grams / 4⅔ ounces	12.5%
Water	871 grams / 30¾ ounces	87.5%
Levain	460 grams / 16½ ounces	46.25%
Salt	23 grams / ¾ ounce	2.25%
Total	**2350 grams / 5 pounds 3⅓ ounces**	**236%**

Oil for greasing bowl
Flour for dusting
Ice for steam

Equipment

Scale	Large bowl or container
Large mixing bowl	2 *bannetons*
Wooden spoon	Baking stone(s) or tiles
Bowl scraper	Cast-iron or stainless steel roasting pan
Plastic film	Peel
Digital thermometer	Wire racks
Standing electric mixer fitted with the hook	

Prepare the *mise en place* for the *levain*.

To make the *levain*, combine the coarse whole wheat and coarse rye flours and water with the stiff *levain* in a large mixing bowl, stirring with a wooden spoon to blend. When blended, scrape down the edge of the bowl, cover with plastic film, and set aside to ferment at 70°F (20°C) for 14 to 16 hours.

When ready to make the final dough, prepare the *mise en place*.

Combine the bread and fine whole wheat flours with the water, *levain*, and salt in the bowl of a standing electric mixer fitted with the hook. Mix on low speed until blended. Increase the mixer speed to medium and mix for about 7 minutes, or until the dough begins to pull away from the sides of the bowl, feels elastic, and gives some resistance when tugged.

Lightly oil a large bowl or container.

Scrape the dough into the prepared bowl. Cover the bowl with plastic film and set aside to ferment for 20 minutes.

Uncover and fold the dough. Again, cover with plastic film and set aside to ferment for 20 minutes.

Uncover and fold the dough. Cover with plastic film and set aside to ferment for 20 minutes.

Uncover and fold the dough. Again, cover with plastic film and set aside a third time to ferment for 90 minutes.

Lightly flour a clean, flat work surface.

Uncover the dough and divide it into two 1175-gram / 2½-pound rounds on the floured surface. Cover with plastic film and bench rest for 15 minutes.

Lightly dust each *banneton* with flour.

Uncover the dough and, if necessary, lightly flour the work surface. Gently press on the dough to degas and carefully shape each piece into a neat, tight round. Place one round, seam side up, into each of the prepared *bannetons*. Cover with plastic film and proof for 2 hours.

About an hour before you are ready to bake the loaves, place the baking stone(s) or tiles into the oven and preheat it to 475°F (246°C). If using a pan to create steam (see page 70), place it in the oven now.

Lightly flour a peel. Working with one loaf at a time, uncover the dough and flip it onto the floured peel.

Using a *lame* or razor, quickly score the loaves as directed on pages 63–65. To make the required steam, add 1 cup of ice to the hot pan in the oven. Using the peel, immediately transfer the loaves to the hot baking stone(s) in the preheated oven.

Bake, with steam, for 30 minutes. Then reduce the oven temperature to 440°F (227°C) and bake for an additional hour, or until the crust is dark reddish brown, the sides are firm to the touch, and the loaves make a hollow sound when tapped on the bottom.

Remove from the oven and transfer to wire racks to cool.

Session 12

Gluten-Free Formulas

For people afflicted with an autoimmune disorder known as celiac disease, the consumption of wheat gluten can be devastating. Celiac disease affects the body's ability to process gluten. When foods containing gluten are ingested by someone with celiac disease, the immune system responds by damaging the small intestine, which prevents the body from absorbing nutrients from food. The possible complications of untreated celiac disease include cancer, osteoporosis, anemia, and seizures.

Some people can tolerate gluten, but not wheat products. For those, it is a good idea to introduce bread or baked goods made with rye, corn, or oats. Spelt is also a good alternative for those sensitive to wheat.

When baking for gluten-intolerant clientele, DO NOT use wheat, triticale, barley, durum, spelt, rye, kamut, semolina, bulgur, or oats. Many breads can be made quite successfully with flours and starches made from grains, legumes, and roots that do not contain gluten. For those with gluten intolerance, it is generally safe to use corn, soy, tapioca, millet, teff, amaranth, nuts, rice, potato, buckwheat, flax, sorghum, and quinoa.

Truly gluten-free products are impossible to produce in a traditional bakery, as the risk of cross-contamination is too great. Any food-processing plant in which wheat or other gluten products are made cannot guarantee that there will be no gluten contamination in a supposedly gluten-free product. No matter what product—bread or other baked good—a baker makes, it is very important that no claim is made about that product that could ultimately compromise a customer's health. If a bakery offers products other than traditional wheat-based breads and baked goods, it should not guarantee that they are gluten free, wheat free, or nut free. It is best to explain what the product actually contains but give a disclaimer about other ingredients used in the bakery with which the product may have come in contact. In the home kitchen, this should not be a problem.

Gluten-Free Lemon Scones
Gluten-Free White Bread
Gluten-Free Banana-Rice Quick Bread
Gluten-Free Buttermilk Biscuits
Gluten-Free Almond Bread

Demonstration

Gluten-Free Lemon Scones

Makes 8 scones

Estimated time to complete: 40 minutes

Ingredient	Amount	Baker's Percentage
Corn flour	155 grams / 5½ ounces	69%
Tapioca flour	70 grams / 2½ ounces	31%
Sugar	45 grams / 1½ ounces	20%
Baking soda	8 grams / ⅓ ounce	3.5%
Cream of tartar	7 grams / ¼ ounce	3.1%
Freshly grated lemon zest	5 grams / ⅛ ounce	2.2%
Xanthan gum	4 grams / ⅛ ounce	1.5%
Salt	2 grams / ½ pinch	0.9%
Whole eggs, at room temperature	50 grams / 1¾ ounces	22%
Unflavored yogurt	215 grams / 7½ ounces	95.5%
Fresh lemon juice	55 grams / 2 ounces	2.4%
Total	**616 grams / 1 pound 5¾ ounces**	**251.1%**

Flour for dusting

Equipment

Scale	Parchment paper
Large mixing bowl	Bowl scraper
Wooden spoon	Bench knife
Medium mixing bowl	8-inch round metal ring
Whisk	Wire rack
12 x 18-inch sheet pan	

Prepare the *mise en place*.

Combine the corn and tapioca flours with the sugar, baking soda, cream of tartar, lemon zest, xanthan gum, and salt in a large mixing bowl, stirring with a wooden spoon to blend.

In a medium mixing bowl, whisk the eggs and yogurt together. Whisk in the lemon juice. Pour the egg mixture into the flour mixture, stirring with a wooden spoon just until moistened.

Preheat the oven to 400°F (205°C).

Line a sheet pan with parchment paper.

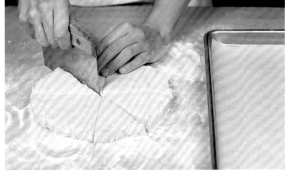

Lightly flour a clean, flat work surface.

Scrape the dough from the mixing bowl onto the floured surface. Using your hands, knead the dough briefly just to bring it together.

Place the 8-inch round metal ring on the floured surface. Pat the dough into the ring. Then remove the ring and cut the round into 8 equal wedges. Transfer the wedges to the prepared sheet pan. Transfer to

preheated oven and bake for about 15 minutes, or until the scones are brown around the edges and on the bottom and springy to the touch.

Remove from the oven and place on a wire rack to cool.

Demonstration

Gluten-Free White Bread

Makes 4 loaves

Estimated time to complete: 2 hours

Ingredient	Amount	Baker's Percentage
Rice flour	250 grams / 8 ounces	69.4%
Fine cornmeal	110 grams / 4 ounces	30.6%
Milk powder	5 grams / ⅛ ounce	1.4%
Sugar	40 grams / 1½ ounces	1.11%
Salt	8 grams / ¼ ounce	0.9%
Xanthan gum	6 grams / ⅛ ounce	1.6%
Water	600 grams / 20 ounces	167%
Whole eggs, at room temperature	150 grams / 5 ounces	41.67%
Fresh yeast	40 grams / 1⅓ ounces	1.11%
Total	**1209 grams / 2 pounds 8⅓ ounces**	**314.79%**

Butter for greasing pans

Equipment

Scale	Four 8-inch loaf pans
Large mixing bowl	Bowl scraper
Wooden spoon	Plastic film
Medium mixing bowl	Wire racks
Whisk	

Prepare the *mise en place*.

Combine the rice flour and cornmeal with the milk powder, sugar, salt, and xanthan gum in a large mixing bowl, stirring with a wooden spoon to blend.

In a medium mixing bowl, whisk the water, eggs, and yeast together. Pour the egg mixture into the flour mixture, stirring with a wooden spoon until thoroughly combined.

Lightly butter the loaf pans.

Scrape an equal portion of the batter into each of the prepared pans. Cover with plastic film and proof for 90 minutes.

About a half hour before you are ready to bake the loaves, preheat the oven to 400°F (205°C).

Transfer the pans to the preheated oven and bake for about 1 hour, or until the loaves are golden brown and springy to the touch.

Remove from the oven and place on wire racks to cool.

Demonstration

Gluten-Free Banana-Rice Quick Bread

Makes 4 loaves

Estimated time to complete: 90 minutes

Ingredient	Amount	Baker's Percentage
Rice flour	316 grams / 11 ounces	94.6%
Potato starch flour	9 grams / ⅓ ounce	2.7%
Garbanzo flour	9 grams / ⅓ ounce	2.7%
Baking powder	9 grams / ⅓ ounce	2.7%
Salt	3 grams / ⅛ ounce	0.9%
Baking soda	3 grams / ½ teaspoon	0.825%
Xanthan gum	1 gram / ½ teaspoon	0.3%
Quick-cooking tapioca	20 grams / ¾ ounce	6%
Whole eggs, at room temperature	100 grams / 3½ ounces	30%
Honey	80 grams / 2¾ ounces	24%
Buttermilk	55 grams / 3 ounces	16.5%
Vegetable oil	26 grams / 1 ounce	7.8%
Mashed ripe bananas (see Note)	99 grams / 3½ ounces	29.7%
Total	**730 grams / 1 pound 10¾ ounces**	218.73%

Butter for greasing pans

Equipment

Scale
Sifter
Large mixing bowl
Wooden spoon
Medium mixing bowl

Whisk
Four 8-inch loaf pans
Bowl scraper
Wire racks

Note

Two bananas will yield about 99 grams /
3½ ounces mashed banana.

Prepare the *mise en place*.

Preheat the oven to 350°F (177°C).

Sift the rice flour, potato starch flour, garbanzo flour, baking powder, salt, baking soda, and xanthan gum into a large mixing bowl. Add the tapioca and stir with a wooden spoon to combine.

In a medium mixing bowl, whisk the eggs, honey, buttermilk, and vegetable oil together until thoroughly combined. Using a wooden spoon, stir in the bananas. Pour the egg mixture into the flour mixture, stirring with a wooden spoon until thoroughly combined.

Lightly butter the loaf pans.

Scrape an equal portion of the batter into each of the prepared pans, filling them about two-thirds full.

Transfer the pans to the preheated oven and bake for about 50 minutes, or until the loaves are golden brown and springy to the touch.

Remove from the oven and place on wire racks to cool.

Demonstration

Gluten-Free Buttermilk Biscuits

Makes 1 dozen biscuits
Estimated time to complete: 40 minutes

Ingredient	Amount	Baker's Percentage
Rice flour	210 grams / 7½ ounces	85.7%
Potato starch	50 grams / 1¾ ounces	20.4%
Tapioca flour	35 grams / 1¼ ounces	14.3%
Baking powder	15 grams / ½ ounce	6.1%
Baking soda	6 grams / ¼ ounce	2.4%
Sugar	5 grams / ¼ ounce	2.04%
Salt	2 grams / ½ teaspoon	0.8%
Xanthan gum	0.6 gram / ¼ teaspoon	0.25%
Whole eggs, at room temperature	100 grams / 3½ ounces	40.8%
Buttermilk	75 grams / 2⅔ ounces	30.6%
Vegetable oil	70 grams / 2½ ounces	28.5%
Total	**570 grams / 1 pound 4¼ ounces**	213.89%

Buttermilk for brushing biscuits

Equipment

Scale	12 x 18-inch sheet pan
Sifter	Parchment paper
Large mixing bowl	¼-cup measure
Wooden spoon	Small bowl
Medium mixing bowl	Pastry brush
Whisk	Wire racks

Prepare the *mise en place*.

Preheat the oven to 400°F (205°C).

Sift the rice flour, potato starch, tapioca flour, baking powder, baking soda, sugar, salt, and xanthan gum into a large mixing bowl.

In a medium mixing bowl, whisk the eggs, buttermilk, and vegetable oil together. Pour the egg mixture into the flour mixture, stirring with a wooden spoon until just combined.

Line a sheet pan with parchment paper.

Using a ¼-cup measure, drop the dough onto the prepared sheet pan, leaving about an inch between biscuits. Using your fingertips, flatten the dough slightly.

Place the buttermilk for brushing the biscuits in a small bowl. Using a pastry brush, lightly coat the top of each biscuit with the buttermilk.

Transfer the sheet pan to the preheated oven and bake for about 12 minutes, or until the biscuits are brown around the edges and on the bottom and springy to the touch.

Remove from the oven and place on wire racks to cool.

Demonstration

Gluten-Free Almond Bread

(Adapted from a recipe by Peter Endriss of Per Se and Bouchon Bakery)

Makes 2 loaves

Estimated time to complete: 3 hours or up to 3½ hours

Ingredient	Amount	Baker's Percentage
Brown rice flour	210 grams / 7½ ounces	42.86%
White rice flour	155 grams / 5½ ounces	31.63%
Almond flour	90 grams / 3¼ ounces	18.36%
Tapioca flour	35 grams / 1¼ ounces	7.15%
Salt	18 grams / ⅔ ounce	3.67%
Xanthan gum	6 grams / ¼ ounce	1.22%
Water	450 grams / 15¾ ounces	9.18%
Whole eggs, at room temperature	100 grams / 3½ ounces	2.04%
Honey	55 grams / 2 ounces	1.12%
Olive oil	25 grams / 1 ounce	5.1%
Fresh lemon juice	5 grams / ⅛ ounce	1.02%
Fresh yeast	18 grams / ¾ ounce	3.67%
Total	**1167 grams / 2 pounds 8¾ ounces**	**127.02%**

Butter for greasing pans

Equipment

Scale	Two 8-inch loaf pans
Large mixing bowl	Bowl scraper
Wooden spoon	Plastic film
Medium mixing bowl	Wire racks
Whisk	

Note

For variations on this recipe, you can add rehydrated dried figs at 12% and cracked black pepper at 0.5%; dried cranberries at 8% and chopped pecans at 8%; boiled potatoes at 20% and fresh minced dill at 0.5%; chopped walnuts at 15% and walnut oil at 5.1% to replace the olive oil. You can also replace the almond flour with cornmeal and add cracked black pepper to taste to the mix.

Prepare the *mise en place*.

Combine the brown rice, white rice, almond, and tapioca flours with the salt and xanthan gum in a large mixing bowl, stirring with a wooden spoon to combine.

In a medium mixing bowl, whisk the water, eggs, honey, olive oil, and lemon juice together. Stir in the yeast until just combined. Pour the egg mixture into the flour mixture, stirring with a wooden spoon until thoroughly combined. There should be no lumps.

Lightly butter the loaf pans.

Scrape an equal portion of the batter into each of the prepared pans, filling them about half full. Cover with plastic film and proof for 2 hours.

About a half hour before you are ready to bake the loaves, preheat the oven to 375°F (191°C).

Transfer the pans to the preheated oven and bake for about 1 hour, or until the loaves are golden brown and springy to the touch.

Remove from the oven and place on wire racks to cool.

Conversion Charts

Conversions of Common Ingredients from Volume to Weight

Ingredient	Weight/Cup in Grams	Weight/Cup in Ounces
Crumbs (bread or cake)	100 grams	3.5 ounces
Currants	150 grams	5.3 grams
Dates (whole, pitted)	170 grams	6 ounces
Eggs (white, whole, or yolk)	225 grams	8 ounces
Figs	200 grams	7 ounces
Flour (A.P., unsifted)	135 grams	4.8 ounces
Flour (A.P., sifted)	115 grams	4 ounces
Flour (bread, unsifted)	140 grams	5 ounces
Flour (bread, sifted)	120 grams	4.3 ounces
Flour (cake, unsifted)	125 grams	4.4 ounces
Flour (cake, sifted)	95 grams	3.4 ounces
Flour (whole wheat, unsifted)	130 grams	4.5 ounces
Fructose	180 grams	6.3 ounces
Fruit juice	250 grams	8.8 ounces
Honey	340 grams	12 ounces
Lard	205 grams	7.3 ounces
Milk	245 grams	8.6 ounces
Milk (evaporated)	250 grams	8.6 ounces
Milk (powdered)	100 grams	3.5 ounces
Milk (sweetened condensed)	305 grams	10.8 ounces
Molasses	340 grams	12 ounces
Nuts (chopped)	130 grams	4.5 ounces
Oats (rolled)	85 grams	3 ounces
Oil	215 grams	7.5 ounces
Peaches (dried)	160 grams	5.6 ounces
Peels (candied)	115 grams	4 ounces
Pineapple (canned, crushed)	250 grams	8.8 ounces
Potato (grated, uncooked)	100 grams	3.5 ounces

Prunes (pitted)	175 grams	6.3 ounces
Raisins	150 grams	5.3 ounces
Rhubarb (cooked)	240 grams	8.5 ounces
Rice (uncooked)	190 grams	6.8 ounces
Shortening	190 grams	6.8 ounces
Sugar (granulated)	200 grams	7 ounces
Sugar (powdered)	100 grams	3.5 ounces
Vinegar	235 grams	8.3 ounces
Water	235 grams	8.3 ounces
Baking powder (double acting)	4.4 grams	0.17 ounce
Baking powder (single acting)	3.4 grams	0.13 ounce
Baking soda	5.3 grams	0.2 ounce
Caraway seed (ground)	3.3 grams	0.13 ounce
Cardamom seed (ground)	2 grams	0.07 ounce
Cinnamon (ground)	2.7 grams	0.1 ounce
Cloves (ground)	2.7 grams	0.1 ounce
Cream of tartar	3.4 grams	0.13 ounce
Extracts	5.4 grams	0.2 ounce
Ginger (ground)	1.9 grams	0.07 ounce
Jam, jelly, or marmalade	6 grams	0.2 ounce
Citrus zest	2.7 grams	0.1 ounce
Mace (ground)	2.3 grams	0.08 ounce
Nutmeg (ground)	2.3 grams	0.08 ounce
Poppy seed (whole)	3.3 grams	0.13 ounce
Salt	5 grams	0.18 ounce

American and Metric Measurements and Conversions

American Volume Measurements

1 gallon	= 4 quarts	= 8 pints	= 16 cups	= 128 fluid ounces	
1 quart		= 2 pints	= 4 cups	= 32 fluid ounces	
1 pint			= 2 cups	= 16 fluid ounces	
1 cup				= 8 fluid ounces	
1 tablespoon				= ½ fluid ounce	= 3 teaspoons

Metric Volume Measurements

1 liter	= 10 deciliters	= 100 centiliters	= 1 mililiters

American Volume to Metric Volume

1 gallon	= 3.78 liters	
1 quart	= 0.946 liter	= 946 milliliters
1 pint	= 0.473 liter	= 473 milliliters
1 cup	= 236.6 milliliters	
1 fluid ounce	= 29.57 milliliters	

fluid ounces x 29.57 = # milliliters per # fluid ounces

Example: to determine the metric equivalent to 12 fluid ounces

12 x 29.57 = 354.8 milliliters in 12 fluid ounces

American Weight Measurements

1 pound = 16 ounces

Metric Weight Measurements

1 kilogram = 1000 grams

Metric Weight to American Weight

1 kilogram	= 2.2 pounds	= 35.2 ounces
1 ounce	= 28.37 grams	

grams / 28.37 = # ounces per # grams

Example: to determine the number of ounces equivalent to 750 grams

750 / 28.37 = 26.44 ounces = 1 pound 10.44 ounces

Temperature Conversions

0° Celsius	= 32° Fahrenheit
37° Celsius	= 98.6° Fahrenheit
100° Celsius	= 212° Fahrenheit

Degrees Fahrenheit to degrees Celsius $[(F°-32) \times 5] / 9 = C°$

Example: 212°F converted to °Celsius

$[(212°F - 32) \times 5] / 9 = [180 \times 5] / 9 = 900 / 9 = 100° C$

Degrees Celsius to degrees Fahrenheit $[(C° \times 9) / 5] + 32 = F°$

Example: 37°C converted to °Fahrenheit

$[(37°C \times 9) / 5] + 32 = [333 / 5] + 32 = 66.6 + 32 = 98.6° F$

Acknowledgments

Many talents are needed to create a cookbook, especially one that is intended to be used not only by home cooks but in the classroom as well. At The French Culinary Institute we have a vast resource of extraordinarily talented people who approach their work with passion and dedication, and many of them have contributed to making this book the valuable resource that it is. I would like to thank all of those who worked so hard to make the book a reality.

At The French Culinary Institue, my gratitude goes to Nils Norén, Kevin Stuessi, Tina Casaceli, Karen Bornarth, Roger Gural, Johnson Yu, Christina Wang, Tara Hill, Melanie Miller, Josh Levine, Gary Apito, Alain Sailhac, and Suzanne Sobel.

To photographer Matthew Septimus, writer Judith Choate, and stylists Pam Morris, Jamie Kimm, and Vivian Lui—an outside group of professionals that we feel are part of our home team—we owe our deepest thanks.

We also gratefully acknowledge the assistance of King Arthur Flour, who provided the props and baking equipment used in the photographs.

And, last but not least, I would like to thank our agent, Kim Witherspoon; our publisher at Stewart, Tabori & Chang, Leslie Stoker; the book's editors, Luisa Weiss, Natalie Kaire, and Kate Norment; and the book's designer, Liam Flanagan.

A heartfelt thanks for all your *pain*.

Dorothy Cann Hamilton

Index